healing oils

healing hands

healing oils, healing hands

discovering the power of prayer, hands on healing and anointing

linda l. smith

RN, MS, HNC, CHTP, CHTI
DIRECTOR, HEALING TOUCH SPIRITUAL MINISTRY PROGRAM

HTSM **Press**
Arvada, Colorado

Healing Oils, Healing Hands—Discovering the Power of Prayer, Hands On Healing and Anointing
A HTSM Press Book/January, 2003
All rights reserved
Copyright © 2003 by Linda L. Smith
Cover design by Ben Wright
Cover Image: Rendition based on Lucas della Robbia's Madonna & Child, c. 1455-60. Enameled terracotta in Orsanmichele, Florence.
Back Cover: Canterbury Cathedral
Interior Design and Production by Pilgrims' Process, Inc.

****

****

****

Library of Congress Cataloging Number:
2002115824
ISBN 0-9677310-2-X
Published by HTSM Press
P.O. Box 741239, Arvada, Colorado 80006
9 8 7 6 5 4 3 2 1
Printed in the United States

Dedication

I dedicate this book to all those who seek to be a blessing to others in healing ministry.

Acknowledgements

Being introduced to the use of therapeutic essential oils has changed not only my healing practice but my life as well. I know there are many who are more knowledgeable than I when it comes to the use of these oils. However my passion for healing ministry drove me to study and research the power that comes from putting together prayer, hands on healing and anointing with these essential oils. I drew upon our scriptural traditions, history and modern science as I developed this book and I looked to those individuals using the oils in their healing practices to inspire me. My vision of a healing ministry expanded once I realized the vibrational frequencies of essential oils enhance prayer, and hands on healing which are both forms of vibrational healing. Finally, I began to see the full picture of healing that Jesus laid down for us over 2,000 years ago when he sent his disciples out to pray, heal and anoint.

I have several people to thank for their support and encouragement along this journey. First of all, to Marilee Tolen who empowered me to start this quest and to Vicki Opfer who continually offered words of encouragement that I could do it. Both of these powerful women possess a passion for the work of healing and I am indebted to both of them for their patience, words of wisdom and knowledge. Dr. David Stewart also encouraged me to stretch and not give up on this writing. Thanks also goes to my faithful assistent Pat Gewecke who by her efficient running of our educational ministry, I was freed to write this book.

My sincere appreciation goes to those individuals who read the manuscript and offered their suggestions—David Stewart, Theresa Kajs, Don Stouffer, Terri Murphy, John Maeder, Marilee Tolen, Karen Boren and Vicki Opfer.

Finally, my thanks go to all those students who have been in my first classes *"Sent to Heal and Anoint,"* offered in the Healing Touch Spiritual Ministry program. Their enthusiasm, openness, and eagerness to learn and expand their healing practices gave me the assurance that I was on the right track.

Table of Contents

INTRODUCTION

Be a Blessing For Others

Several years ago my schedule of teaching, writing and administering the Healing Touch Spiritual Ministry program filled up all my time. There wasn't room for one more thing, or so I thought. That's when my good friend, Marilee Tolen began telling me that I wasn't doing enough—that I needed to take seriously the scriptures on healing in regard to anointing with healing oils. Out of my ignorance, I saw little healing power in the olive oil that was dabbed on the forehead of another during the act of Christian anointing. It was then that she invited me to explore the many hundreds of scripture references concerning aromatic oils that are quite different from olive oil or almond or any other vegetable oil presently used in churches that do anointing. She also convinced me to buy some of these aromatic "essential" oils mentioned in the Bible. Once I got the oils home and smelled them, I was less than impressed. Some of these ancient oils are very earthy in their aroma and didn't particularly appeal to me at that time. But I had invested in them and rather than feel "stuck" with these oils, I began to investigate their healing qualities.

Over the next few months, I purchased some additional quality oils that smell good. Oils like lavender, lemon, and peppermint—fragrances I recognized. I began exploring how these oils work by placing them on the soles of my feet every evening before going to bed. I paid attention to the qualities of these oils and the subtle changes I perceived happening in my own body. The first thing I noticed was that my blood pressure came within normal limits. Having been on medication for the past thirty plus years, this definitely caught my attention. Next I noticed I slept better. I then proceeded to buy more oils and began attending some local classes. I learned which oils to use to help support my immune system when a cold was striking, and which oils relax tight muscles that were causing a headache. There were oils for pain, to ward off infections, for anxiety and sleeplessness, for coughs, skin rashes, and more serious problems as well. The more I investigated the scriptural passages about the oils, the more I realized Marilee was right. These oils heal not only through their chemistry but also heal vibrationally just as the energetic healing and prayer do that we teach in the Healing Touch Spiritual Ministry Program. I wondered, could the ancient Hebrews have been practicing healing with these substances? Where did they learn this knowledge? Did they get it from the Egyptians and their other neighbors? Were aromatic oils their medicine? Is this what they used to treat their children? Was God giving them and us a message that the earth can provide us healing substances for our bodies, minds and spirits?

This led me to delve more deeply into the act of anointing itself. It is a sacred act, signifying that a connection is being made to the Divine. Anointing however is more than placing your thumb dipped in olive oil and pressing it to the forehead of another. The power to heal is not just in the words of the prayers that might be said; there is also healing in the oil itself. There is a rich tradition established in the Scriptures for this kind of anointing. Jesus most probably anointed others although the scriptures don't really tell us that. We do know however, that he taught his disciples how to anoint and then sent them out to heal. I doubt seriously that he told them to just use any cooking oil that was available. Any good Jew at that time knew which oils had healing qualities for they were the common medicines of their day. Oils like frankincense, myrrh, cedarwood and spikenard among so many others. Anointing might include touching with oils, the parts of the body that are ill or having pain. For us today, it might also mean to touch the energy field that extends into the space beyond the physical body.

From the scriptures we know that the act of anointing is a sign of great favor from God. It heralds a time of favor, of blessing and grace. Yes, anointing is a blessing; prayer is a blessing; and, laying our hands upon another in the act of healing is a blessing. To bless another is not just the prerogative of priests and ministers. We each have that ability to be a conduit for God's healing blessings for others. All blessings come from the One Source. When we bless another, we acknowledge our interconnectedness with all of creation. As David Spangler says in his book on *Blessing,* when we bless, we open the door for a holy presence to expand around us, embrace us and become a blessing.[1] To bless is a holy act and learning to bless is akin to learning to manifest holiness in our lives.

[1]David Spangler, *Blessing, The Art and the Practice,* p. 55.

In our healing work in the Healing Touch Spiritual Ministry program, we present hands-on healing from a ministry perspective. Ministry implies being an instrument, a vessel through which God's healing power flows. It is being "other-directed" as we devote our work in God's service to others. Yet those of us who make this work our life's calling realize that we receive blessing as we give it. Blessing is a transfer of spiritual energy. We are but the courier—God is the healer of body, mind and spirit. What we bring to the equation is our loving heart, compassionate mind and open spirit.

This book is ultimately about blessing. It is about anointing with healing oils, about prayer and about healing with our hands. For me, these are forms of blessing that we can extend to others. When we enter into that healing process with someone using our prayer, anointing and touching, we ultimately practice that connectedness between ourselves, the recipient and God. This is a spiritual process in which we share our life, our presence, our knowledge and our heart. We literally open a space for the flow of Spirit. Both giver and receiver are transformed in the experience of blessing.

From the day I committed to learn more about the healing properties of these medicines of the earth, I have been taken in by their power to heal and transform. Rather than the oils being an adjunct to our hands-on healing ministry, I now see them as an integral ingredient that God has given us. When Moses went out into the desert, God gave him a formula of four oils to help sustain the people for the journey. Modern science can now tell us that these particular oils are highly antimicrobial, antiviral and antibacterial. God cared enough about the people to keep them healthy for the journey. Well, God still cares about us and is inspiring many to reawaken to the healing abilities of these medicines of the earth. Using them in our Christian healing ministries then seems only natural.

One note about the layout of this book. I for one have always appreciated it when a writer in referring to a scripture passage, would then quote it so I wouldn't have to search for it in my Bible. Likewise, I like to see the sources that the author is quoting or referring to without having to search in the back of the book. In my first book, *Called into Healing, Reclaiming our Judeo-Christian Legacy of Healing Touch,* I placed both the scriptures and quoted sources in an inside column. I received many compliments on this arrangement and therefore will follow that style of presentation for this book on the healing oils. I hope that it will be a source of inspiration as well as knowledge as you investigate for yourselves the healing power of essential oils for a healing ministry.

Linda L. Smith

CHAPTER 1

ANOINTING —
MAKING SACRED
OUR CONNECTION
TO GOD

Throughout history, people have created ceremonies and rituals to celebrate, bless and heal. The act of anointing was practiced by the ancient Mesopotamians, Egyptians, Syrians, and Persians as well as by the Hebrews. "Anointing" meant they would touch with oil individuals, groups, sacred objects or even their homes to signify a sacred connection to God was being made. It was a way of recognizing the coming together of the physical world and the spiritual world. Oil became a symbol of the healing power of the Divine breaking through into their lives. It was a sign of a unique blessing from God that was at once healing and sustaining. Since oil had such a vital role for our ancestors, let us explore some of the references in both the Old and New Testaments that perhaps can give us some insights into healing for our present today.

Our Judeo-Christian Story

There are hundreds of references to the use of aromatic essential oils and incense in our Judeo-Christian Scriptures. For the nomadic pastoral Israelites, healing oils and fragrances appear to have been ordinary practice for healing and for honoring God. They were so ordinary that the sacred texts do not go into detail but only casually mention them in their stories. Rarely do we find references about how to use them or even which ones to use.

But what was the origin of their knowledge? Where did they get these oils?

The Hebrew people of the Bible lived among other cultures and freely traded with caravans from faraway countries like Egypt, India, China, Sheba, Ethiopia and other distant lands. The area of Palestine was situated at the very crossroads of this trade. Camels carried precious cargos of spices and oils to the far corners of the known world. In some instances, the oils and spices were used as barter for land or even gold. Joseph, the favorite son of Jacob, was sold by his brothers to traveling spice merchants on the trade route to Egypt. They were carrying spices, balm and resins that would bring a handsome price at Pharaoh's court.

In the Jewish scriptural texts there are numerous prescriptions for treating the body and treating the people collectively with healing oils and fragrant incense. The holy texts also instructed the people to purify their homes and sacred places. Clearly there is evidence that they possessed great knowledge about the use of oils for healing. These oils were considered extremely valuable and were used not only for healing but also for honoring God in their religious rituals. What we don't have are the actual formulas or how the essential oils were to be used on the body. These probably remained in the oral traditions and were passed down through generations. Why were they not mentioned in the texts? Probably because they were so commonplace in their culture that everyone knew about oils and how to use them.

At the time of Christ, anointing the body with oils was likewise a common practice for healing. In the story of the Good Samaritan, Jesus extols the Samaritan for his compassionate healing of a stranger. In this parable, the Samaritan poured wine and oil into the man's wounds. Now the wine would have acted as an antiseptic,

Clearly there is evidence that they possessed great knowledge about the use of oils for healing.

"...a caravan of Ishmaelites coming from Gilead, with their camels carrying gum, balm and resin, on their way to carry it down to Egypt." Genesis 37:25

"A Samaritan while traveling came near him, [the wounded man], and when he saw him, he was moved with pity. He went to him and bandaged his wounds, having poured oil and wine on them. Then he put him on his own animal, brought him to an inn, and took care of him. The next day he took out two denarii, gave them to the innkeeper, and said, 'Take care of him; and when I come back, I will repay you whatever more you spend.'" Luke 10:33-35.

cleansing the wounds and the oil used was probably not just any cooking oil but a healing oil that would have been expensive. Jesus' audience would have been very impressed with these actions and with the Samaritan's generosity. Unfortunately in our modern-day retelling of this story, we only remember how significant it was that the Samaritan was a hated second-class citizen looked down upon by their Jewish counterpart. As Jesus relates the story, the Samaritan left the wounded man in the care of the innkeeper and generously offered to pay for any additional care the man might need. The use of the oil and the wine in this story was a mark of how great was this man's compassion towards a total stranger's predicament. Jesus was advising his listeners to be as generous and caring in their healing of one another as this Samaritan.

Oil is soothing to the body and essential oils carry the healing essence of plants. Have you ever used "healing oils" on a wound? Cleared up an infection with a "healing ointment"? What were the ingredients? Could you even read them? Were they made up of petrochemicals or natural oils from healing plants?

Anointing with healing oils appears to be important in Jesus' ministry. The scriptures do not tell us that Jesus actually anointed others himself, but we do know that he taught his disciples how to heal and then sent them out to both heal and anoint all those suffering in body and spirit. As for being anointed himself, Jesus certainly had an appreciation for this kind of healing touch. When Mary of Bethany anointed Jesus shortly before his death, he defended her actions when some of the disciples grumbled about the cost of such an anointing. Her story is told to this very day to honor her for her devotion and healing ministry to Jesus.

Even in those days, essential oils were very costly to produce. A household might only have one or two oils at most and they would have been greatly prized for their fragrance and their healing properties. One might only use a healing oil if sickness really warranted it. In the story of Mary anointing Jesus, this act was done out

"A woman came with an alabaster jar of very costly ointment of nard, and she broke open the jar and poured the ointment on his head. But some were there who said to one another in anger, 'Why was the ointment wasted in this way? For this ointment could have been sold for more than three hundred denarii, and the money given to the poor.' And they scolded her. But Jesus said 'Let her alone; why do you trouble her? She has performed a good service for me...She has done what she could; she has anointed my body beforehand for its burial. Truly I tell you, wherever the good news is proclaimed in the whole world, what she has done will be told in remembrance of her.'" Mark 14: 3-6,8-9

of great honor and devotion to God's anointed one. To break open an alabaster wax jar of costly spikenard and pour the entire contents over Jesus had to be a remarkable gesture of love. No wonder the disciples were so shocked at this woman's public demonstration of extravagance. In today's money, that wax jar was probably worth over $30,000, (her household's fortune) which was enough to feed the entire village for a week! And no wonder Jesus, the Anointed One, blessed her for her act of love and kindness in this anointing.

Have you ever spent all you had as a show of love and appreciation for someone special to you? How was it received?

What do we know about these precious healing oils from the Bible? Let us begin our investigation with the holy anointing oil formula given to Moses.

THE HOLY ANOINTING OILS IN THE OLD TESTAMENT

God gave to Moses a formula for a holy anointing oil shortly after the Israelites began the Exodus trek through the desert. It contained **myrrh, cinnamon, calamus** and **cassia** in an olive oil base. According to *The New Jerome Biblical Commentary*[1] this holy anointing oil was a specific blend for anointing the dwelling, furniture and all those who dwelt in the home. The anointing rendered the home and its occupants holy which meant they were "set apart for God." In a sense, God put his seal upon the people with this special oil blend.

Many believe that Moses used this aromatic blend to protect the Israelites from a plague. Modern science shows that these oils contain either immune-stimulating or antiviral compounds or both. However, we really can't reproduce this holy anointing oil today since we aren't really sure that we know the true botanical origin of myrrh and calamus. The plants we have today that go by these names may not be chemically the same as those during the time of the Exodus.[2]

"This shall be my holy anointing oil throughout your generations." Exod.30:31 (See Exod. 30:22-33 for the entire passage)

[1]Raymond Brown, J. Fitzmyer, and R. Murphy, *The New Jerome Biblical Commentary*, p. 58.

[2]Robert Tisserand, *The Art of Aromatherapy*, p. 23.

"Take a bunch of hyssop, dip it in the blood that is in the basin, and touch the lintel and the two doorposts with the blood in the basin. None of you shall go outside the door of your house until morning." Exodus 12:2

When Moses was trying to win freedom for the Israelites, God instructed him to tell the people to dip a bunch of hyssop in the lamb's blood and strike the lintels of their homes to protect them and their families from a plague. Hyssop is actually a gentle and humble plant. If you are going to "touch" the lintel and have the lamb's blood actually mark the doorway, you would have to strike the doorpost. Hyssop when struck gives off its volatile oil and conceivably could be a protection against plague. Hyssop is anti-microbial and was traditionally used in those times to drive away evil spirits.

Other oils were also esteemed as holy—frankincense, stacte, onycha, galbanum, and spikenard. Many were used in their Jewish religious ceremonies or used by the people to heal and protect their bodies from illness or death. There are many other oils mentioned in the Bible but not necessarily referred to as "holy" oils. These include oils that come from many trees and other plants common in that part of the world. They are scented barks and resins, flowers, roots and seeds. There are references to oils made from sandalwood or aloes, pine, fir, cedarwood, cypress, myrtle, and cistus (Rose of Sharon.) The land given to the Israelites was the land flowing with milk and honey. It was a land rich in wild flowers and trees and plants of every kind. The milk came from the goats, and the honey from the bees that fed on the many fragrant wildflowers growing there.

When the Israelites began the exodus around 1240 B.C. out of Egypt, they took with them resins and gums as well as many precious oils and the knowledge of how to use them. Since the Hebrews had been the Egyptian slaves, many of them were involved in the embalming processes and the production of aromatic oils for healing and perfumes. They took this knowledge with them and would later pass it on to the next generations. Along their way, they traded for more oils from distant lands since the actual distillation of pure grade oils was difficult to achieve and could be accomplished more readily by others like the Egyptians and the Babylonians. In fact, the production of aromatic oils and perfumes was an important business and means of trade.

The ancient Hebrews also used aromatics as part of personal hygiene, as body perfumes and to fragrance their clothes and bed linens. They found that some aromatics helped deter pests. They used others to season their food and wine, and when guests came into their tents or homes, they would anoint the person's head as a sign of welcome. As the Israelites trekked through the desert for forty years, bathing was naturally a luxury. Women used to wear bundles of myrrh and other aromatics in little bags around their necks that hung between their breasts. This acted as a long-lasting and effective deodorant. In the Song of Solomon, there is exotic poetry that speaks of the beauty of these personal fragrances. In fact, there are references to many oils in this beautiful Song of Solomon.

> "While the king was on his couch,
>   my nard gave forth its fragrance.
> My beloved is to me a bag of Myrrh
> That lies between my breasts.
> My beloved is to me a cluster of
>   Henna blossoms
> In the vineyard of En-gedi." The Song of Solomon 1:12-14

The Calling of Kings, Prophets and Priests

To be anointed with a sacred oil was a sign of great favor-of blessing and grace in both the individual and the people's lives. We see this clearly when Moses was directed to anoint Aaron and his sons as a sign that they had been set apart in God's service. They were washed, and specially arraigned with sacred vestments of finest linen that were made with purple, blue and gold threads. And before all the people, they were anointed with God's holy oil, ordained and consecrated as God's chosen priests. They were even warned that if they did not properly dress when going into the tent of meeting or when they came near the altar in the holy place, they would die. Their anointing was a very significant ritual for the whole people of God. This oil was a special blend of myrrh, cinnamon, calamus and cassia.

> "Then you shall bring Aaron and his sons to the entrance of the tent of meeting, and shall wash them with water, and put on Aaron the sacred vestments, and you shall anoint him and consecrate him, so that he may serve me as priest. You shall bring his sons also and put tunics on them, and anoint them as you anointed their father, that they may serve me as priests and their anointing shall admit them to a perpetual priesthood throughout all generations to come." Exodus 40:12-15

Moses was also instructed to take this holy anointing oil and anoint the tabernacle and all the sacred vessels so that they may be holy. Their burnt offerings were likewise anointed before the altar of God. Everything was blessed as a sacred sign of their connection to God.

To be anointed with a sacred oil was a sign of great favor-of blessing and grace.

Aromatic oils were made holy by God and used to designate people and things as sacred. Does anointing play a part in your spiritual life? Are you set apart for God's holy service in life or do you feel this is just a calling for a certain few?

"Samuel took a vial of oil and poured it on his [Saul's] head, and kissed him; he said, 'The Lord has anointed you ruler over his people Israel. You shall reign over the people of the Lord and you will save them from the hand of their enemies all around.'... As he turned away to leave Samuel, God gave him another heart." I Samuel 10:1, 9.

"'Rise and anoint him; for this is the one.' Then Samuel took the horn of oil, and anointed him in the presence of his brothers; and the spirit of the Lord came mightily upon David from that day forward." I Samuel 16:12-13

"Have my son Solomon ride on my own mule, and bring him down to Gihon. There let the priest Zadok and the prophet Nathan anoint him king over Israel; then blow the trumpet, and say 'Long live King Solomon!'" I Kings 1:33-34

"You love righteousness and hate wickedness.
Therefore God, your God, has anointed you
With the oil of gladness beyond your companions;
Your robes are all fragrant with myrrh and aloes and cassia." Psalm 45:7-8

There are other accounts of individuals being set aside for special service to God like the prophets and the kings. When the people cried to God for a king, someone to help them find security, peace and justice, the prophet Samuel anointed Saul and later anointed David as his successor. Samuel told Saul he would save God's people from their enemies and that he would be turned into a different person and indeed, God gave Saul another heart. But when God later rejected Saul as king, Samuel was again told to take his horn of oil and go in search of a new king. When the young David was brought before him, the prophet knew at once that he was God's chosen leader and immediately anointed him before all his brothers. David was greatly loved by God and by the people.

When David was advanced in years, he summoned the prophet Nathan and the priest Zadok to anoint his son Solomon to succeed him. Now there was some politics involved for Solomon was not David's firstborn son. In fact, he was the last. David's second son Adonijah had already claimed the throne. Therefore it was important that Solomon be anointed in a public way so that no one would dispute who was succeeding David.

Solomon went on to reign as a wise leader for many years and set about making peace with Israel's neighbors, fortifying the cities in key areas, developing trade and building the temple and palace in Jerusalem. There is an interesting account of how the Queen of Sheba paid a visit to Solomon's court. She brought frankincense, myrrh and a great amount of spices among many other gifts for the King. Solomon was interested in cedar and other building materials for his great temple and the Queen was eager to trade.

After Solomon there are accounts of many other kings of Israel who were anointed but none compared with David and Solomon. David was a great poet who is attributed as the writer of many of the Psalms. In these poetic stanzas, we find many references to oils and to the use of them in anointing God's chosen ones. Both the psalms and the prophets speak of the "oil of gladness," and "the oil of joy." Whatever oils they were referring to, be they the aroma of myrrh, aloes and cassia or any other number of oils, these aromatics must have lifted the people's spirits and put them in a spiritual place.

What scents and aromas speak to you of an oil of gladness, an oil of joy? What emotions do you think these oils would evoke?

The prophets were considered men of God and likewise were anointed for their duties. They were powerful speakers and often prefaced their oracles with the phrase "thus says the Lord." Clearly, they were people who had intimate relationships with God and through prayer and visions believed they were given messages to proclaim. The prophet and seer Isaiah spoke of himself as anointed to bring good news to the oppressed. Through his anointing God's seal was upon his heart as he spoke many prophecies. The prophets however, were not considered healers. There are a few references acknowledging their medical miracles but that was not their primary role for the chosen people.

Healing in the Promised Land

When the Israelites left Egypt they brought their knowledge of Egyptian medical practices with them. But Jewish theology taught that people should look to God for health and healing and not to man. Even though there were many herbal remedies known during the biblical times, they are not named in Scripture because mentioning the medicinal uses of plants would defy the belief in God's exclusive healing power.

"The spirit of the Lord God is upon me, because the Lord has anointed me; He has sent me to bring good news to the oppressed, to bind up the brokenhearted; to proclaim liberty to the captives, and release to the prisoners; to proclaim the year of the Lord's favor, And the day of vengeance of our God; To comfort all who mourn; to provide for those who mourn in Zion— to give them a garland instead of ashes, the oil of gladness instead of mourning, the mantle of praise instead of a faint spirit." Isaiah 61:1-3

"You have loved righteousness and hated wickedness; therefore God, your God has anointed you with the oil of gladness beyond your companions." Heb.1:9

"Honor physicians for their services, for the Lord created them; for their gift of healing comes from the Most High, and they are rewarded by the king . . . The Lord created medicines out of the earth, and the sensible will not despise them." Sirach 38:1-2, 4.

By Jewish law, the priests became the health officials, holding the people to high standards for hygiene. Laws in the Pentateuch, the first five books of the Bible governed diet and food preparation as well as cleansing of households, fasting, and resting. In Leviticus, the priests were to examine all kinds of skin afflictions and determine whether or not they were leprous. It wasn't until the Hellenistic period (332-152 B.C.) that the Jewish medical profession began to develop. Prior to this period, the role of the physician ranked among the lowest of professions. In the book of Sirach, we have the admonition to honor physicians for their gift of healing comes from God. It instructs the listeners to remember that God created medicines out of the earth and the sensible will not despise them.

The Talmud, written during this period, identified some 70 herbs and other plants as having medicinal properties. Some of these were for cures and others were for prevention. The *Book of Jubilees,* also written in the first century B.C. tells of angels revealing remedies to Noah. These remedies came from trees, plants and roots.[3] Herbs and aromatic oils and tinctures became the medicines whereby the physicians and ordinary citizens healed one another.

Christ—the Anointed One Established a Healing Practice

Anointing continued throughout the Hebrew story and into the early Christian experience. Jesus was referred to as "God's anointed one" carrying out the prophecies of the Old Testament. When Jesus was in his hometown of Nazareth he went to the synagogue where he unrolled the scroll and quoted Isaiah's prophecy regarding the anointing of the one who is to bring good news to the poor. Jesus announced to his stunned audience that this prophecy was fulfilled in their hearing. This clearly identifies Jesus among God's chosen ones who were set apart by their anointing to lead the people through difficult times. It establishes Jesus' kingship in the lineage of David. No wonder the townspeople were enraged and

[3]Vincenzina Krymow, *Healing Plants of the Bible,* p. 17.

"He unrolled the scroll and found the place where it was written: 'The Spirit of the Lord is upon me, because he has anointed me to bring good news to the poor. He has sent me to proclaim release to the captives And recovery of sight to the blind, to let the oppressed go free,to proclaim the year of the Lord's favor.'" Luke 4:17-19

"The message spread throughout Judea, beginning in Galilee after the baptism that John announced: how God anointed Jesus of Nazareth with the Holy Spirit and with power, how he went about doing good and healing all who were oppressed by the devil, for God was with him. We are witnesses to all that he did both in Judea and in Jerusalem. They put him to death by hanging him on a tree; but God raised him on the third day and allowed him to appear not to all the people but to us who were chosen by God as witnesses, and who ate and drank with him after he rose from the dead. He commanded us to preach to the people and to testify that he is the one ordained by God as judge of the living and the dead. All the prophets testify about him that everyone who believes in him receives forgiveness of sins through his name." Acts 10:37-43

wanted to throw him off a cliff! Jesus the carpenter's son was stating unequivocally that he was anointed to save the people.

When Jesus set out on his ministry, he gathered fishermen, tax collectors, farmers and ordinary people to be his trusted followers and to carry on his work to succeeding generations. Daily, the Gospel tells us, he taught them and when he thought they were ready, he established his healing ministry by sending them out in twos to lay-on hands and to anoint all those who were sick. We can only speculate about what Jesus taught his disciples that wasn't written down. Many things were just commonly known and therefore it wasn't necessary to write about them. This we can probably be sure of—Jesus would have made sure that his disciples were well prepared to meet the illnesses and diseases of his day. If he sent them out to lay-on hands and anoint—he would have had to teach them how to use the oils.

"But it is God who establishes us with you in Christ and has anointed us, by putting his seal on us and giving us his Spirit in our hearts as a first installment." 2 Cor. 1: 21-22.

During those initial years after the resurrection, the followers of Jesus referred to him as God's anointed one who had the power of the Spirit upon him. They told the story over and over, how he went about doing good and healing many whom suffered in body and spirit and how he was put to death and rose from the dead. The anointing was important for it linked Jesus not only to the prophecies but also to God himself.

"To one is given through the Spirit the utterance of wisdom, and to another the utterance of knowledge according to the same spirit, to another faith by the same Spirit, to another gifts of healing by the one spirit, to another the working of miracles, to another prophecy, to another the discernment of spirits, to another various kinds of tongues, to another the interpretation of tongues. All these are activated by one and the same Spirit, who allots to each one individually just as the Spirit chooses." I Cor. 12:8-11

As the early church grew it continued the Jewish practice of anointing those who were called to serve the people as deacons, deaconesses and later, the priests. It was a way of acknowledging their uniqueness within the community as set apart for special service. Paul in one of his letters to the people of Corinth, even said that through Christ, we are all anointed into God's service. We have God's seal upon our hearts to prove it.

We are each figuratively anointed by God as a sign of our being chosen for God's service. Have you ever considered creating your own ritual to celebrate your calling in life by anointing your head, hands, and feet with aromatic oils?

Anointing for Healing

"Are any among you sick? They should call for the elders of the church and have them pray over them, anointing them with oil in the name of the Lord. The prayer of faith will save the sick, and the Lord will raise them up; and anyone who has committed sins will be forgiven. Therefore confess your sins to one another, and pray for one another, so that you may be healed." James 5:13-16

[4]James F. White, *Introduction to Christian Worship*, 3rd Edition, p. 270.

Sincere followers of Jesus could heal the sick.

[5]Joseph Martos, *Doors to the Sacred*, p. 329.

"They will lay their hands on the sick, and they will recover." Mark 16:18.

Physical healing continued to be a sign through which people came to believe in Jesus as the Messiah. Paul mentions healing and miracles as spiritual gifts that some individuals had for the community. Christians practiced healing just as Jesus had taught them. In the letter of James to the church at Jerusalem, the practice of prayer, the laying-on of hands and anointing with oil is described as Christian duty. And in Mark, the statement of the power to heal is quite strong. Basically, sincere followers of Jesus could heal the sick. What is most striking about the passage in James is the link of physical healing to forgiveness of sin. The concern here is for full restoration—bodily and spiritually. The purpose of the anointing and prayer is therefore quite clearly physical and spiritual healing.

Healing oils played an important role in the early church. Christians privately used oil, ointments and salves that had been blessed by the bishop or the priests for physical and spiritual healing. After the eucharistic prayer, the oil would be blessed and God was asked to grant that "it may give strength to all that taste of it and health to all who use it."[4] After the liturgy, the oil was taken home by the faithful to be used both externally and internally as a medicine. Christians believed their blessed oil was an especially effective remedy.

The entire Christian community could therefore participate in this anointing of their families and of one another. One writer of this period, Tertullian, mentions that he knew of a Christian who even cured a pagan with this oil.[5]

From the scriptures, it is clear that Jesus expected his work of praying, touching and anointing to be continued. And when his disciples anointed for healing, more than likely they used the most healing oils available to them at that time and not just their olive oil that they used for ordinary purposes. They would have sought out those oils known in their day for their healing properties.

Does your faith community have a ritual involving anointing for healing? Is it performed only by a few selected by the church? Have you ever considered anointing sick members of your own family with healing oils?

Is Anointing for Physical or Spiritual Healing?

By the fifth century, we begin to note in Christian writings some confusion over whether the passage in James is referring to physical healing or only to healing of spiritual sickness. Pope Innocent I (416 A.D.) wrote to assure another fellow bishop that "There is no doubt that the passage speaks about the faithful who are sick and who can be anointed with the oil of chrism that is prepared by the bishop. Not only priests but all Christians may use this oil for anointing, when either they or members of their household have need of it."[6]

The Pope not only thought anointing was for physical healing but he defended the common practice of the laity anointing the sick and declared that consecrated oil was to be used for healing by all Christians.[7] In his letter, the Pope also cautioned that the oil should not be given to those who were doing public penance since it was "a kind of sacrament" and penitents were not allowed to receive the other sacraments. And so we see the Christian church using blessed oil in a more public way in its anointing of penitents as part of their reconciliation process. Anointing in this case was for the forgiveness of sins.

Around 428, Cyril of Alexandria, known for his healing abilities, berated Christians who resorted to pagan magicians when they were sick and advised them to call in the elders of the church instead. Other writings in that century, specifically from Victor of Antioch, quote the passage in James but believed that the healing came as a result of the prayers and not from the oil. To this writer, the oil was considered just a symbol of healing that God does in response to the prayers.

The oil would be blessed and God was asked to grant that "it may give strength to all that taste of it and health to all who use it."

[6]Joseph Martos, *Doors to the Sacred*, p. 329.

[7]Barbara S. Ryan, D Lin and M. Linn, *To Heal as Jesus Healed*, p. 23.

The holy oil of the church was upheld as far more healing than the old ways.

One of the things the church of this period had to deal with was the breakup of the Roman Empire and the spread of Christianity to pagan lands in Europe. In these lands people commonly sought the aid of sorcerers and fortunetellers when they were ill. The holy oil of the church was upheld as far more healing than the old ways of these peoples. Oil was indeed a sacrament of physical and spiritual health at least in some parts of the Empire more than in others. The anointing with oil symbolized the healing power of the Holy Spirit and thus was a holy anointing. It contained the spiritual power that it signified. To confirm this, there were many stories of the healing ability of holy persons who performed miraculous cures brought about by anointing with oil.

Anointing for the Forgiveness of Sins

During the seventh and eighth centuries, stories continued to abound about monks and other saints who physically healed with holy oils. Whether these are exaggerations or not, it is clear that people believed that anointing was a sacred act and a sacrament of healing. Writings of this period show that people asked for oil to cure almost every physical, mental, and spiritual disorder, everything from headaches to lameness to possession and enchantments. But they did not request anointing if they were dying. If they were dying, they requested reconciliation and the Eucharist. But the practice of reconciliation also included anointing. That's because in earlier days, the penitential practice included the anointing of exorcism to drive out the evil spirits from the person. This anointing was exclusively performed by the priests.

People believed that anointing was a sacred act and a sacrament of healing.

Today, people like to tell stories to anyone who will hear them, about their encounters with angels and about miracles and healings. Do you have stories to share? If so, do you tell the world or are you afraid that others might judge you? Or, do you consider them sacred, to be shared carefully?

By the early Middle Ages, the presbyters or elders spoken of in the James passage were synonymous with priests who by then were only men. Bishops now emphasized the importance of priestly anointing and prohibited the practice of lay anointing. People did not want to seek this anointing from the priests because of the harshness of public penitence and social stigma attached to it. In addition, they could only receive this ecclesiastical reconciliation once in their life and if you thought you might fall again, you waited until you thought you were dying to request it. The church rules around this ecclesiastical reconciliation were meant to avoid relapses but had the effect of driving people away from its benefit. After receiving this sacrament they were forbidden to marry, or if married, to have sexual relationships with their spouses. They also couldn't hold office, engage in business or military service.[8] And so it became the practice to only offer anointing just for the seriously ill and was combined with penitence and absolution for sin as preparation for the next life. Interestingly, the prayers used in this anointing ritual were for physical healing and the parts of the body in pain were anointed in the form of a cross. So even though the request at the end of life was for spiritual healing, the ritual involved anointing and prayers for physical healing.

[8]Joseph Martos, *Doors to the Sacred*, p. 289.

From Anointing for Healing to Anointing the Dying

It was in the ninth century that this ritual became known as the Last Rites reserved for the final moments of the soul's journey in this life. Gradually the prayers for physical healing were dropped and the focus of the ritual was on deathbed preparation and absolution for one's sins. Oil was no longer placed on the parts of the body that hurt but only on the senses: the eyes, ears, nostrils, mouth, hands, feet and loins—all parts of the body capable of leading the person into sin. The prayers that were used asked for forgiveness for sin.

It was in this form that the ritual formally became a sacrament of the church. Medieval theologians believed that the anointing part of the ritual cleansed the dying person from the remnants of all his/her sins committed during life. They believed that this was needed for a person to enjoy the glory of heaven and therefore it should not be offered to someone who might recover.[9] Suffering had now taken on a "redemptive" quality. Since martyrdom for the faith was no longer available, people saw illness as redemptive suffering. By the end of this century, the last rites of the Frankish church in Europe included reconciliation, anointing and viaticum (Eucharist.) This practice was eventually adopted by the Roman church as well. *Extrema unctio,* extreme unction was now the final anointing. But who could afford to pay for such a ritual? Certainly not the common man and so this was a sacrament out of the reach of most people.

One theological issue the church grappled with during this time revolved around the origin of the sacraments. The theologians of the early Middle Ages would unanimously agree that they were instituted by the apostles. But by the late Middle Ages, the argument was that Christ instituted all of the sacraments. Thomas Aquinas argued that anointing with oil was a means of spiritual healing to cure the soul of the sickness of sin. The oil was the healing medicine and the prayer asked for it. The sacrament, he said, was always effective in offering God's grace but we had to cooperate with it.

After the Reformation in the 1500s the laying-on of hands and anointing along with its required donations fell into disfavor among most of the reformed groups. The use of blessed oils and many other Christian rituals were discarded.

John Calvin considered anointing as "playacting" and healing as a "temporary gift."[10] Martin Luther thought the James passage was about anointing for healing but the church only spoke about anointing for dying which for him was utter nonsense. It seems the argument continued to revolve around whether anointing was from Christ or from the Church. Luther felt anointing might have some spiritual value for those requesting it. Those who received it in faith could experience peace of soul and forgiveness of sin but the consolation they received came not from the ritual but from God.[11]

[9]Greg Dues, *Catholic Customs and Traditions,* pp. 164-166.

Since martyrdom for the faith was no longer available, people saw illness as redemptive suffering.

[10]James F. White, *Introduction to Christian Worship, 3rd Edition,* p. 272.

[11]Joseph Martos, *Doors to the Sacred,* pp. 339-340.

The Roman Catholic Church continued its practice of blessed oil for this final anointing even though the true meaning of anointing for healing of physical and spiritual health appeared to be lost. The emphasis stayed on forgiveness of sins at the end of one's life. It was actually not until the last 40 years of the twentieth century, a lapse of over 500 years, that a renewed interest in the healing power of anointing with oil began to reshape the Catholic Church's understanding of the anointing of the sick. There has been a return to the early church's use of blessed oil for healing the sick and not waiting until death. Now the emphasis is on healing and strengthening rather than on forgiving sins. The oil is placed on the forehead and hands rather than on the five senses.

This interest in anointing has also touched many Protestant churches who do not have a tradition of anointing the sick. Many are investigating and experimenting with blessed oil for the purpose of healing those sick in body, mind and spirit in their communities. The Episcopal Church has renamed and extensively revised its "Ministration to the Sick." Anointing is now a part of that rite. Lutherans provide "Laying on of Hands and Anointing the Sick" and United Methodists now have both a public and private "Service of Healing" allowing for the laying on of hands, the blessing of oil, and anointing.[12] Presbyterians now have available "A Service for Wholeness for Use with a Congregation" and another "With an Individual."[13] These Christian churches are reconnecting with early Christian roots and in the process, are creating their own healing rituals within their traditions.

Although anointing may feel relatively new for many denominations, all have a history of praying for the sick members of their churches. Ministry to the sick is the responsibility of the whole community and not just the ministers. It is an important part of the love made visible as God acts through the community. Many churches now participate in public healing services. These involve reading the scriptures, offering prayers, the laying-on of hands and sometimes, the anointing with oil. This act of anointing is making a comeback

"Through this holy anointing may the Lord in his love and mercy help you with the grace of the Holy Spirit. May the Lord who frees you from sin save you and raise you up."
Prayer from the Roman Catholic Anointing of the Sick

[12] *United Methodist Book of Worship,* 1992, p. 613-629.

[13] James F. White, *Introduction to Christian Worship,* 3rd Edition, p. 273.

"Lord God, you bring healing to the sick through your son, Jesus Christ, our Lord. May your blessings come upon all who are anointed with this oil, that they may be freed from pain and illness and be made whole. Amen."
Lutheran Church in America and Canada

> *"As you are outwardly anointed with this holy oil, so may our heavenly Father grant you the inward anointing of the Holy Spirit. Of his great mercy, may he forgive you your sins, release you from suffering, and restore you to wholeness and strength. May he deliver you from all evil, preserve you in all goodness, and bring you to everlasting life; through Jesus Christ our Lord. Amen."*
> Prayer from "Ministration to the Sick" in the Episcopal Church's *Common Book of Prayer*

[14]Greg Dues, *Catholic Customs and Traditions*, pp. 148-175.

> *Christians today can expect through anointing that the Spirit of the Lord will be with us.*

and is a sign of hope for many who suffer physically, emotionally and spiritually. Along with the psalmist King David, Christians today can expect through anointing that the Spirit of the Lord will be with us.

Does your faith community have a healing ministry? Do you have community healing services? What about other churches near you. Have you ever attended a healing service in one of them?

Using Anointing in Other Christian Rituals

The use of blessed oil for other spiritual occasions has a long history in Christianity as well. Baptism, confirmation and ordination have been traditional times when many churches have used blessed oil to signify graced moments not only in an individual's life but also the life of the community. It is obvious that some churches are more sacramental because of their emphasis on sacraments. Several denominations recognize special events as sacramental like baptism and Eucharist but let go of the others. Still other Christian communities find no particular benefit in these rituals and prefer to go directly to God without the mediation of rituals of any kind. More will be said about sacraments as ritual later. Understanding the roots of some of these sacraments might give us some insights into how oil played a significant part in the overall sacramental rituals. The word sacrament comes from the word *mysteria* or "mysteries." The Latin writers began using the term *sacramentum* or "sign" to describe the same thing.[14] Fundamentally, it was a time of celebration of how God breaks into our lives. Let us look at three of these sacraments that used oil as part of their ritual.

Baptism

Baptism in the early church was a special occasion that acknowledged the mystery-filled moment of new birth. In those early years, the initiates were called catechumens and would enter into a time of preparation and learning before receiving baptism. These initiates were anointed with special oil called the *oil of catechumens* that was part of their preparation. After the pouring on of water, the newly baptized were anointed with another sweet smelling oil called *chrism,* a mixture of olive oil and balm. In the early church, the deacons and deaconesses would perform this part of the ceremony by anointing the newly baptized, sometimes all over their whole body. The deaconesses would do this for the women and the deacons for the men. The newly baptized would then be dressed in white robes to signify their new position within the church. As time went by, this anointing or signing (marking with a cross) was performed only on the head of the newly baptized. The chrism used was oil previously consecrated by the bishop.

How does your Christian community ritualize baptism? Is oil a part of this ceremony? If so, where is the oil placed on the newly baptized? What kind of oil is used? Does it have a scent?

Confirmation

Confirmation in the faith has an interesting story. In the early church, after baptism, the newly baptized would be immediately led to the bishop who would lay-on hands and give an additional blessing. This was not difficult to do since there was usually a bishop in practically every town. If the initiate had already been anointed, the bishop would add still another anointing. This time the forehead was anointed or signed with perfumed oil often in the form of a cross. Eventually, this second anointing became a distinct ritual from baptism and signified the coming of the Holy Spirit upon the individual. Through this anointing, the Holy Spirit is given to strengthen the individual so they may confess boldly, the name of Christ.

As the church grew the bishop couldn't always be present at all the baptisms. This bestowing of the second anointing was therefore postponed until the bishop visited a particular town or city. The anointing took on its own character and became the bishop's special

Through this anointing, (confirmation) the Holy Spirit is given to strengthen the individual so they may confess boldly, the name of Christ.

"While they were worshiping the Lord and fasting, the Holy Spirit said, 'Set apart for me Barnabas and Saul for the work to which I have called them' Then after fasting and praying they laid their hands on them and sent them off." Acts: 13:2-3.

"And after they had appointed elders for them in each church, with prayer and fasting they entrusted them to the Lord in whom they had come to believe." Acts 14:23

"Do not neglect the gift that is in you, which was given to you through prophecy with the laying on of hands by the council of elders." I Tim 4:14

"Do not ordain anyone hastily, and do not participate in the sins of others; keep yourself pure." I Tim 5:22

"For this reason I remind you to rekindle the gift of God that is within you through the laying on of my hands." 2 Tim I:6

anointing, <u>sealing</u> the person's baptism. This ritual has been called confirmation since the fifth century. In the twentieth century, this sacrament became one of Christian maturity, to be received at a time when the person could freely and maturely make a commitment to their baptism.

Confirmation is only celebrated among a few denominations yet it can be a powerful acknowledgement of choosing one's Christianity. Have you consciously stepped forward and chosen your faith? Sealed it with oil?

Holy Orders

This act (anointing) was a sign of the passing on of power, of blessing and a setting apart of this individual by someone authorized to do so.

"For your love is better than wine,
   your anointing oils are fragrant,
your name is perfume poured out;
   therefore the maidens love you."
Song of Solomon I:2-3

"You anoint my head with oil;
my cup overflows." Psalm 23:5

Ordination to the priesthood also has an interesting and colorful history. In the beginning, the Christian church did not have a formalized priesthood but recognized the Jewish priests since they continued to worship in the Jewish temple. When Christians met in their house-churches to remember the Lord in the breaking of the bread, they selected elders to preside over the Eucharist. Leadership was clearly defined with the elders or *presbyteroi* in charge. The chief elder in each community was called the *episcopus* that in English came to be known as the "bishop." For several hundred years, the elders or presbyters were chosen by the people in their community. The deacons and deaconesses were generally appointed by the bishop as the bishop's assistants. All of these individuals were ritually selected or ordained into their roles by the laying-on of hands and sometimes by anointing. This act was a sign of the passing on of power, of blessing and a setting apart of this individual by someone authorized to do so. There are plenty of references in the New Testament that speak of this selection process for service. As the centuries moved on, there were clearly determined levels of authority and elaborate investiture ceremonies developed. The hands of priests were anointed signifying their sacred duty at the altar of God. Our understanding of the roles of priesthood and servanthood has evolved over time, but one thing is becoming clearer—the priest, elders, presbyters, ministers, deacons, and deaconesses are in service to the whole Christian community.

We are each called to a path of service. Have you celebrated your unique calling in life through ritual or through prayer? Martin Luther reminds us that the milkmaid has as holy a vocation as the nun. We each serve our neighbor and thus are involved in ministry. Have you thought of sealing your path of service with an anointing?

Final Thoughts

Each time a woman puts on perfume, she is anointing herself presumably to smell good. In our culture, we would even say that perfume is used to attract the opposite sex. But in the Scriptures, fragrances were used by the people to make themselves pleasing to God. The Song of Solomon refers to perfume for one's beloved while in the Psalms fragrant oils are poured on the head making one acceptable to God.

These are not just poetic words to inspire us; they speak of a deeper and richer meaning. Anointing with precious fragrant oils connects us to the Divine in a way that other substances do not, even purifying waters. The act of anointing is a sacred act and has formed a sacred tradition that we have nearly lost in our efforts to be purists. Let us examine now, how the rest of the ancient world used aromatic oils for healing and for worship.

"How very good and pleasant it is when kindred live together in unity! It is like the precious oil on the head, running down upon the beard, on the beard of Aaron, running down over the collar of his robes."
Psalm 133:1-2

CHAPTER 2

THE USE OF HEALING OILS— THROUGH THE AGES

The Ancient World of Egypt, India and China

The Israelites were not the first peoples to be aware of the healing properties of plants. By the time the children of Abraham became known as the Hebrew people, the use of incense and aromatic oils were common knowledge among most people of the world. Knowledge of the healing abilities of these substances and how to distill them was traded much like trade secrets between big companies today. The recipes for the oils as well as the blends of oils were fiercely guarded. Many of them were specially prepared for the kings and carried their signature name on them.

How old are the aromatic oils? Do we know who the first peoples were who distilled plant essences for healing?

There is historical evidence dating back at least 4,000 years and it could be even earlier on the use of aromatic plants as incense, perfumes and oils for medical and culinary uses. A terracotta "distiller" which experts believe to be 5000 years old was found in modern-day Pakistan and is now housed in the Taxila Museum. It is believed that this primitive apparatus belonged to ancient civilizations that were more advanced than previously thought.[1] The ancient civilizations in India, China, Greece and Egypt all used essential oils for physical and spiritual health. Clay tablets have been found that reveal in Babylon 57,000 pounds of frankincense was burned every year presumably in their religious rituals. In Assyria, 60 tons of frankincense was used every year in the annual feast of the god Baal. In Israel, at the funeral of Herod, thousands of slaves preceded the king's body, carrying urns of burning frankincense.[2] So, there is evidence that the use of aromatic oils and incense is extremely old in the human family.

[1]Denise Whichello Brown, *Aromatherapy,* p. 3.

[2]Light Miller and Bryan Miller, *Ayurveda and Aromatherapy,* p. 70.

The oldest form of medicine in the world, Ayurveda (Sanskrit for "science of life") dates back five thousand years in India. In the Vedic literature dating around 2,000 B.C. there are lists of over 700 substances including cinnamon, spikenard, ginger, myrrh, patchouly, benzoin, frankincense, jasmine, vetiver and sandalwood. These were more than perfumes-they were used for both liturgical and therapeutic purposes. There are also references to the use of herbs like coriander, fennel, turmeric, pepper, garlic, cumin, clove, lemongrass, and basil.[3] In the Ayurvedic tradition, herbs and aromatics were an important part of the philosophy of healing. An early form of essential oil extraction involved pounding and grinding the fresh or dried herb and subsequent squeezing or expressing of the essential oil.

[3]Marlene Ericksen, *Healing with Aromatherapy,* p. 7.

In China there is an ancient herbal tradition that accompanies the practice of acupuncture that also dates from around 2,000 B.C. They likewise had many aromatics used in religious rituals and in healing like opium and ginger referred to in the *Yellow Emperor's Book of Internal Medicine.*[4] Borneo camphor is still used today in China for ritual purposes.

[4]Julia Lawless, *The Illustrated Encyclopedia of Essential Oils,* p.14.

Our greatest knowledge about oils, their preparation and distillation for healing and perfume comes however, from the Egyptians.

[5]Robert Tisserand, *The Art of Aroma-therapy*, p. 21.

Our greatest knowledge about oils comes from the Egyptians.

Some of their papyrus manuscripts date as far back as 2800 B.C. on the use of herbs and aromatics. One in particular is an account of the writer's journey into Nubia, in which he says "I will cause to be brought into thee fine oils and choice perfumes and the incense of temples whereby every god is gladdened."[5] These ancient healers and perfumers learned to distill the life-blood of plants and, over time, discovered how to use the oils in healing ways. They represent man's first medicine. The priests and priestesses were also the physicians and thus the dispensers of oils for healing all kinds of diseases. Their specific formulations were recorded as recipes for illnesses, for restoring youthfulness, and for preserving the body for the afterlife. Their temples became laboratories for the high priest where they would experiment with various concoctions to achieve their goals. Thus they were the first dispensers of aromatics, the first perfumers, and the first aromatherapists.

Not much has changed in the past 4,000 years. We are still concerned with smelling good, looking good and preserving our youthfulness. What has changed is our present day emphasis on man-made substances rather than nature-made plant essences. Are our present products really an improvement?

Once they discovered the preserving effects of essential oils, the Egyptians perfected the art of embalming by secret formulas that were fiercely guarded. The body was actually soaked in essential oils and after months was wrapped with gauze impregnated with resin, cedarwood oil and myrrh. So strong is the antiseptic power of these essential oils that Egyptian mummies were well preserved for thousands of years. Oils, still viable, have been found in sealed jars in the tombs of ancient Egyptian leaders giving us some indication of the great value placed on these essential oils. For royalty, the embalming process could take six months; for a commoner, it could be accomplished in a few hours.

The Egyptians also used oils for skin and hair care. A fascinating piece of history is their emphasis on smelling good. Being a people near the desert, body odor was probably a concern for them just as it was for the Israelites. The Egyptians solved this problem by molding aromatics into wax cones that they then attached to the top of their heads. During the heat of the day, the wax would melt and run down their hair releasing fragrant smells. The Egyptian language itself had a rich vocabulary regarding smell indicating the importance of odors to their culture. Perfumes and incense were even categorized for morning, evening, meditation, love and war. The Pharaohs and wealthy families all had signature perfumes much like the kings in the Middle Ages had special music composed for them.[6]

[6]Light Miller and Bryan Miller, *Ayurveda and Aromatherapy,* p. 69.

The favorite perfume and incense of the Egyptians was the famous *Kyphi* that was a blend of at least sixteen aromatics. The exact ingredients of *Kyphi* are unknown but researchers believe that it contained calamus, cinnamon, frankincense, henna, juniper and myrrh among many others. *Kyphi* when burned produces a black residue that many wealthy women used to adorn their eyes and is typically seen in Egyptian artwork.[7]

[7]Denise Whichello Brown, *Aromatherapy,* p. 3.

The precious oils of frankincense, myrrh, galbanum, rosemary, hyssop, cassia, cinnamon, and spikenard were used extensively for anointing and healing the sick. In 1817 an ancient Egyptian scroll was found dating back to 1500 B.C. It was a medicinal scroll and mentioned over 800 herbal prescriptions and remedies for many diseases that they successfully treated. Many of these mixtures contained myrrh oil and honey.[8]

[8]D. Gary Young, *An Introduction to Young Living Essential Oils,* Eleventh Edition, p. 15.

Many healing ointments today carry on the traditions of the ancient Egyptians. What in your medicine chest is as powerful as some of these ancient oils?

The World of the Greeks and the Romans

The Greeks learned a great deal from the Egyptians concerning the use of aromatics. Herodotus and Democrates visited Egypt during the fourth century B.C. and declared that the Egyptians were masters of the art of perfumery. The Greeks and the Egyptians both ascribed the efficacy of aromatic medicines to the gods who they believed were the origin of these aromatic plants. There are some writings that show the Greeks were concerned about what parts of the body to apply the aromatic oils. Diogenes would anoint his feet stating that the aroma would then "envelop his whole body and gratefully ascend to his nose."[9] Another Greek writer felt it was important to anoint the breast since it was the seat of the heart, while still others felt that it was the head that needed to be anointed.

[9]Robert Tisserand, *The Art of Aromatherapy,* p. 26.

Hippocrates, considered to be the father of medicine was born in 460 B.C. He said "the way to health is to have an aromatic bath and scented massage every day."[10] He recognized that burning aromatic substances offered protection against contagious diseases and recommended this practice during an epidemic of plague in Athens. The writings of many other physicians refer to the healing ability of aromatic plants, especially that of flowers. In the temples of Aesculapius, the Greek god of healing and the temple of Aphrodite, there were recipes for a number of medicinal oils inscribed on marble tablets. The healing oils were dispensed by the priestesses in the temples for all kinds of ailments. There were celebrated cures that kept these temples of healing very popular places for the Greeks.

[10]Valerie Ann Worwood, *The Complete Book of Essential Oils & Aromatherapy,* p.8.

The first real treatise on what we would in our present day identify as aromatherapy, was written by the Greek Theophrastus (372-285 B.C.) His work titled *Concerning Odors* discusses the effect of fragrance on the mind, observing the connection between taste and smell.[11]

[11]Marlene Ericksen, *Healing with Aromatherapy,* p. 8.

We have all heard the adage "cleanliness is next to godliness." The Egyptians, Babylonians, Greeks and the Romans practiced ritual cleanliness to achieve a higher spirituality. They used fumigation to disperse the oils in their temples and their homes much like our use of diffusion today. Both the Greeks and the Romans used the aromatic oils in their bathhouses scenting their massage oils and bath waters. The Romans were much more lavish in their use of oils and perfumes. They fumigated their temples and political buildings with essential oils and their soldiers are reported to have used aromatic oils on themselves before going into battle to bolster their courage. The Romans used three kinds of perfumes—solid unguents, scented oils and powdered perfumes to fragrance their hair, their bodies and their clothes and beds. The solid unguents included *rhodium,* which was rose scented and *narcissum,* from narcissus flowers. Their most popular scented oils included *susinum,* which was made from honey, calamus, cinnamon, myrrh, and saffron, and *nardinum* composed of calamus, cistus, cardamom, melissa, spikenard, and myrrh. These blends were very expensive and only the most wealthy individuals could afford them.[12]

[12]Robert Tisserand, *The Art of Aromatherapy,* p. 28.

The Greeks probably did not distill their oils but used a process called maceration. This is done by using heavy stones to press the essences of the flower petals into an olive oil base. The Greeks would also have had the resources to pay for aromatic oils and perfumes from their neighbors.

Women, probably more than men in American society, have an appreciation for scented bath waters. Have you ever taken a relaxing warm bath with essential oils? How did it affect you physically, mentally and spiritually?

Our society values scented products for the skin and for our over all enjoyment. How pure are the oils used in your bath products? What about other products like your toothpaste, deodorants and lotions? Can you actually read and understand the ingredients? Do they sound like essential oils or chemicals? Are they labeled "next to nature" and then list petrochemicals?

Rosewater was one of the perfumes and essences brought back to Europe from the east by the Crusaders.

Aromatic Oils Spread Across Europe in the Middle Ages

When the Roman Empire fell, many of the Roman physicians fled to Constantinople taking with them the knowledge of these oils along with their books of Galen, Hippocrates and others. This knowledge was shared with the ancient Arabian peoples who then studied the chemical properties of the oils and refined the art of distillation to produce a higher quality as well as quantity of oil.

The Arabian philosopher and physician Avicenna who lived in the tenth century, wrote over a hundred books. His most renowned book was his *Canon of Medicine* that was used as a standard reference text by many medical schools for 500 years. In it he mentions many essential oils including chamomile, cinnamon, dill and peppermint.[13] His first book however, was on the beneficial effects of the rose. Rosewater was one of the perfumes and essences brought back to Europe from the East by the Crusaders. This rosewater was very popular especially among the women of Europe. Avicenna is credited with creating the refrigerated coil, a breakthrough in the art of distillation that is used to produce pure essential oils.[14] The Arabians were now able to produce much larger quantities of oils to be carried by their caravans from the Far East to medieval Europe. The fame of the Arabian perfumes spread throughout the known world.

If you looked in your closet or wherever you keep lotions and perfumes, how many have "rose" oil in them? Rose is one of the most popular scents in American and European societies.

[13]Denise Whichello Brown, *Aromatherapy*, p. 7.

[14]Julia Lawless, *The Illustrated Encyclopedia of Essential Oils*, p.18

Healing in the Abbeys and Monasteries of Europe

Europeans themselves did not get into the oil production until the 12th century. However, there is evidence that many healers, particularly the monks and nuns in the abbeys and monasteries, cultivated their own aromatic plants and also used many spices, herbs and aromatic oils from the Far East in their healing ministrations. It is good for us to remember that all literary knowledge as well as herbal knowledge rested in the monasteries since it was the monks and nuns who copied the ancient texts. We also know that it was the men and women in these religious orders who practiced various forms of healing. Having visited many European ruins of these abbeys, I have been fascinated by the placement of the herb gardens near their infirmaries and hospices. When weather permitted, the windows of the infirmary would be opened and the fragrance of the herbs would be diffused through the sick room. Sometimes, the ill would be brought out into the garden to sit in the warm sunshine and soak up the healing vibrations of the plants.

Lavender in particular was studied for its medicinal properties along with rosemary, sage, basil, chamomile, melissa and thyme. These plants seemed to do well in the colder Germanic countryside. Some of these abbeys had vast underground storerooms where they kept their herbs and the oils along with the foodstuff, wines and beer. They dispensed medication to the ill in the form of herbal teas, herbal infused oils, medicated beers, medicated wines, brandies, and herbal tinctures.

Hildegard of Bingen, a Benedictine abbess, wrote extensively on the use of herbal remedies, tinctures, salves, ointments and oils as part of her medicine. Her writings were used as a point of reference for abbeys throughout Europe in the 12th century and many centuries to come. Strehlow and Hertzka tell us that Hildegard's abbey at Rupertsberg near Bingen on the Rhine River was a meeting place for all of Europe. Thousands came to seek out her counsel and

All literary knowledge as well as herbal knowledge rested in the monasteries since it was the monks and nuns who copied the ancient texts.

Hildegard of Bingen wrote extensively on theology, prophecy, and medicine. Her book *Liber Compositae Medicinae* (also called *Causae et Curae),* is a handbook on medicine. In it she describes physical illnesses and ways of dealing with those illnesses that can only be appreciated today as holistic medicine. Please see Wighard Strehlow and Gottfried Hertzka, *Hildegard of Bingen's Medicine* for an introduction into this medieval prophetess' healing advice.

[19] Wighard Strehlow and Gottfried Hertzka, *Hildegard of Bingen's Medicine*, p. 45.

One of Hildegard's remedies for liver ailments involved drinking lavender wine. Lavender flowers were boiled in wine or water sweetened with honey. The mixture is drunk lukewarm to alleviate pain in the liver, lungs and the "steam in the chest." "Lavender wine," according to Hildegard, "will provide the person with pure knowledge and a clear understanding." Wighard Strehlow and Gottfried Hertzka, *Hildegard of Bingen's Medicine*, p. 72.

Boiling lavender flowers, either in wine or water, will release the oil held within the flowers which will then float on top of the liquid. Lavender oil is considered a universal oil with sedative, anti-inflammatory and analgesic actions.

[16] As a result of their research on this group of 15th century thieves, Gary Young, ND, and his company produces a blend of oils called "Thieves™" which includes clove, lemon, cinnamon bark, eucalyptus, and rosemary essential oils. This oil was tested at Weber State University in 1997 for its potent antimicrobial properties. It was found to have 99.96 percent kill rate against some airborne bacteria. *Essential Oils Desk Reference*, pp. 123-124.

learn from this great prophetess. Although her work has laid buried for hundreds of years, it is now coming to light perhaps in our day as these two German authors suggest, to assist us in our helplessness with modern diseases like allergies, multiple sclerosis and AIDS. Hildegard's work with herbs, crystals, gemstones and essential oils is now being studied extensively all over Europe. On visiting a recent herb display in Belgium, I was delighted to see frequent references to Hildegard as the authority on herbs and essential oils. Her work is still relevant for our day even after 900 years.

Proper diet was extremely important in Hildegard's medicine. "Herbs," she wrote, "improve proper digestion and assist the body in throwing off accumulated toxins and waste products, furnishing good blood circulation."[15] What healing herbs and aromatic oils are in your culinary cabinet? Do you take seriously that you are what you eat?

Plagues and Thieves Teach Valuable Lessons in Healing

In the Middle Ages, thanks to the caravans from the East and the returning Crusaders, Europeans were exposed to many of the "perfumes of Arabia." It is recorded in history that when Europe was besieged with the plague (Black Death), the spice merchants and perfumers seemed to be immune. When the plague was in full swing, it was discovered that certain thieves could go among the dead and dying in order to rob them and never contracted the plague. When forced to tell how they did it, they confessed that they lathered themselves with a concoction that included clove and rosemary and many other aromatic oils. Their secret was made public and posted for all to see.[16]

Aromatics seemed to be the best antiseptic available to the people at that time against the plague. They used perfumed candles to burn in their sickrooms. Their churches and other public building were fumigated twice a week with sulphur, hops, pepper and frankincense, and aromatic plants were strewn on their streets. Fires made with pine or woods that gave out a pungent smell were set in the streets every twelve hours. It was believed that these measures would help clear the air of the plague. How effective they were, we can only surmise. It is recorded though that the perfumers were virtually immune.

The thieves appear to have been on to something. There must be antimicrobial, antiviral, antibacterial properties in these powerful oils. Could these oils possibly be safe antiseptics for our day as well?

Unfortunately, during the Age of Darkness that swept Europe and the Middle East, many libraries were destroyed and much of the ancient knowledge on the uses of essential oils was lost. Some manuscripts written in old English do survive and give recipes for creating aromatic oil blends that come from the fourteenth, fifteenth, and sixteenth centuries. They used these oils externally for a variety of internal disorders. More than likely they could get these remedies from their local apothecaries. The herbalists and alchemists of the Middle Ages seemed to be concerned with whether a substance was hot or cold, dry or moist. In fact herbs were classified into various categories using these determinations. Hot and dry corresponded to the Chinese yang characteristic, and cold and moist to the yin. A whole science developed over classifying the various degrees of whether a substance was very hot or very cold, very dry or very moist.

In Joseph Miller's *Herbal,* written in 1722, there are a number of essences listed: chamomile, cinnamon, fennel, juniper, bay, pennyroyal, rosemary and thyme. There is also listed four official infused oils: chamomile, dill, myrrh, and rose and one expressed oil, nutmeg. Nearly two hundred years later, William Whitla's *Materia Medica,* published in 1882 listed twenty-two essences that included chamomile, cinnamon, juniper, lavender, lemon, peppermint, rosemary and myrrh.[17]

[17]Robert Tisserand, *The Art of Aromatherapy,* p 40.

Alchemy Gives Way to Chemistry and a New Industry is Born

Scientists found they could produce synthetic drugs more cheaply than they could produce therapeutic grade essential oils.

The use of aromatics was kept alive in Europe primarily through the cosmetic and perfume industry. France in particular took perfume making seriously and became the established center in Europe for production of essential oils and perfumes. They began experimenting with distilling oil from native plants like lavender, sage and rosemary that could then be obtained from their apothecaries. By the 17th century there was a distinction between aromatics and perfumery. The scientists were finally able to identify the chemical constituents and the medicinal properties of the essential oils.

The research of the early herbalists, perfumers, chemists and pharmacists laid the groundwork for producing synthetic counterparts and the growth of our modern drug industry. Alchemy gave way to chemistry and with it the interest in the interrelatedness of matter and spirit and the interdependence of medicine and psychology.[18] Scientists found they could produce synthetic drugs more cheaply than they could produce therapeutic grade essential oils and essences. Logic and deductive reason had won the day. In some instances, these synthetic drugs were more powerful than herbs and aromatic remedies. The older treatments lost their credibility as healing moved into the hands of the "professionals." By the 20th century, the role of essential oils in healing narrowed to that of the perfume, cosmetic and food industries.

Modern drugs grew out of earlier attempts to discover the healing properties of the essential oils—the medicines of the earth. Science thought it could improve upon nature and produce healing substances more cheaply. Many recognize today that drugs such as antibiotics and cortisones can produce problems. Side effects of drugs cause thousands of deaths every year. Does that suggest anything to you?

[18]Julia Lawless, *The Illustrated Encyclopedia of Essential Oils*, p.21.

Medical Aromatherapy Becomes a New Specialty

In the early 1900's a French cosmetic chemist by the name of René-Maurice Gattefossé was burned in an explosion in his laboratory. His entire body was reported aflame. He rolled in the grass to put out the flames but later reported that "both my hands were covered with rapidly developing gas gangrene." To treat his wounds, he used lavender oil which stopped "the gasification of the tissue." Healing, he reported, started the next day.[19] Gattefossé dedicated the rest of his life to the study of essential oils and it is he who coined the term "aromatherapy." Gattefossé knew that his work was pioneering and he would have to be patient to prove the efficacy of fragrant substances. As a chemist, he understood the importance of knowing the chemical makeup of aromatics and as a perfumer, he realized the psychotherapeutic benefits of fragrance itself. In this, he foreshadowed the holistic approach to aromatherapy that is prevalent today.

[19]D. Gary Young, *An Introduction to Young Living Essential Oils,* Eleventh Edition, pp. 16-17.

Gattefossé's research convinced him that many essential oils had even greater antiseptic properties than some of the antiseptic chemicals of his day. Furthermore his research showed that individual components of oils were not as effective as the whole oil. The whole was greater than the sum of the parts. You could not take a particular molecule from an essential oil and expect it to be as therapeutic as the whole oil. His first book, *Aromathérapie,* was published in 1928.

Robert Tisserand has translated and edited Gattefossé's seminal work and it is now available in English as *Gattefossé's Aromatherapy.*

Gattefossé like so many other scientists of his day, used a reductionist approach to aromatherapy. He believed that aromatherapy could be used to treat a symptom or a disease the same way conventional medicine did. He looked for the "active components" responsible for the oils' physiological actions and thus aromatherapy was for him, an integral part of medicine.[20] His belief system was of course closely akin to that of the western medical model of health care. It is no surprise then that he worked closely with doctors, pharmacists and surgeons teaching them what later became a medical

[20]Kurt Schnaubnelt, *Medical Aromatherapy, Healing with Essential Oils,* p. 3.

[21]Dr. Daniel Pénoël and Rose-Marie Pénoël, *Natural Home Health Care Using Essential Oils,* pp. 25-26.

specialty in France. This has set the tone for what Dr. Daniel Pénoël terms the "French model" of aromatherapy.[21]

If aromatherapy is any "different" from the medical model, there must be more to its efficacy than chemistry. Fragrance can have a psychotherapeutic benefit as Gattefossé suspected. Do you also suspect there may be even more to aromatic oils than chemistry and fragrance?

Lesser known, but contributors of great importance, was the work of chemists Otto Wallach and Adolf von Baeyer, both of whom received Nobel Prizes for their work in chemistry. Wallach in the early part of the century was actually able to provide us with a detailed understanding of the various chemical components of essential oils. In those days, chemistry of essential oils received as much attention as the chemistry of drugs. Baeyer pioneered the development of structural formulas of terpene molecules. This was important work for it gave later scientists an understanding of the symmetry of how molecules, specifically how atoms, attach in different positions on a ring system.[22]

[22]Kurt Schnaubnelt, *Medical Aromatherapy, Healing with Essential Oils,* pp. 88-89.

Another French pioneer was Dr. Jean Valnet MD whose career was dedicated to natural medicine and the use of phyto-aromatherapy. He actually used essential oils successfully to treat a number of medical and psychiatric disorders. As a battlefield physician in China during World War II, Valnet ran out of antibiotics. Inspired by Gattefossé's work, he resorted to using therapeutic grade essential oils. He found that they were powerful in preventing infections and he was able to save many lives as a result of the natural healing properties of these oils. Writing in the 1960s, Valnet believed that he was witnessing a world-wide blossoming of a new Hippocratic approach, a collaboration with nature in the work of healing. Aromatic plants and their essences were for him, in the forefront of preventive medicine and not drugs.[23] Gattefossé may have established aromatherapy as a discipline but it was the physician, Valnet who popularized it.

[23]Jean Valnet, *The Practice of Aromatherapy, A Classic Compendium of Plant Medicines and their Healing Properties,* edited by Robert Tisserand, p. 10.

A collaboration with nature in the work of healing! St. Hildegard said as much 900 years before Valnet.

Valnet was one of the great holistic physicians who while acknowledging the existence of bacteria and viruses, did not consider microorganisms to be the primary cause of disease. Instead, he saw microbes as opportunistic invaders taking advantage of the human body that may be malfunctioning. In this view, there is no single cause of disease. Infection does not automatically follow once a microbe enters the body. There are many other factors. A naturally healthy resistance or immunity prevents a microbe from finding a good breeding ground. So in holistic medicine, it is important to treat the patient and not the disease. Valnet found aromatherapy to be an excellent naturopathic and holistic therapy that treats the cause and not the symptoms.

The French were fast becoming the world leaders in this new but very old healing practice. Given the strength of action and the concentration of essential oils, it is no wonder that aromatherapy became a specialized study in medicine for the French. Up until 1990, all phyto-aromatic prescriptions filled by pharmacists were reimbursed by the government health care system. Today that policy is determined by each county within France.

Beauty and Medicine Form a New Model of Aromatherpy

Madame Marguerite Maury, a biochemist who had studied Valnet's work, set up some of the first aromatherapy clinics in Paris, Britain and Switzerland. Not being a physician, she was not comfortable with using essential oils internally as many French physicians were doing under their new medical specialty. The focus of her research was therefore directed towards the rejuvenating properties of essential oils. Aging takes its toll on the physical body and the mind and nature provides aromatic oils that can rejuvenate both.[24] For

[24]Marguerite Maury's *Guide to Aromatherapy, The Secret of Life and Youth,* p. 142.

Maury, this was important news for surgeons, physicians and psychiatrists alike. Her interest in the beauty therapy of the oils goes way beyond the perfume industry's interest in the oils. In the 1950s, she introduced aromatherapy to Britain by teaching her techniques to beauty therapists. She applied essential oils, diluted in a carrier oil, for massage and/or spa treatment. Madame Maury brought together beauty and medicine in her studies on how aromatics work physically, mentally and cosmetically and made a very important contribution to our knowledge of essential oils. Her work essentially set the stage for what we now call the "British Model of Aromatherapy."

Essential oils can improve the elasticity and tone of the skin thus rejuvenating it. Have you noticed lately, the increase in "aromatherapy" products on the market stating that they do just that very thing? Have you read their ingredients? Do they state "pure essential oils?" More than likely, they are filled with petrochemicals that mimic the fragrance of essential oils.

[25]Paul Belaiche, *Traite de Phytotherapie et d'aromatherapie,* cited in Kurt Schnaubelt, *Medical Aromatherapy, Healing with Essential Oils,* p. 5.

[26]Pierre Franchomme, and Daniel Pénoël, *L'aromathérapie éxactement,* cited in Kurt Schnaubelt, *Medical Aromatherapy, Healing with Essential Oils,* pp. 5-6.

[27]Marcel Lavabre, *Aromatherapy Workbook,* p. 7.

The French model with its emphasis on medical aromatherapy has had other significant voices in more recent times. Paul Belaiche published his work in 1979 on the antimicrobial effects of essential oils with their corresponding clinical application.[25] Pierre Franchomme and Daniel Pénoël published their current textbook of medical aromatherapy in 1990.[26] This text classifies the various chemical components of essential oils and is a landmark work (not translated into English as yet). They combine scientific inquiry with a more holistic orientation in their search for understanding how essential oils work. They believe that unaltered essential oils are superior to any synthetic look-alikes. Many regard them as purists in holding to this belief that only unaltered and thus authentic essential oils are therapeutic in nature. They emphasize medicinal and internal use of essential oils. Franchomme was later tapped to be the expert for Estée Lauder in the creation of their lucrative new aromatherapy line, *Origins.*[27] Thus beauty and aromatherapy formed a new partnership. This put Dr. Daniel Pénoël in the role as the definitive French medical authority today on essential oils. Many from around the world have studied with him in France and seek his counsel in all matters pertaining to essential oils.

The most respected writer on aromatherapy from England today is Robert Tisserand. He published his book on *The Art of Aromatherapy* about the same time as the English translation of Valnet's book became available. His approach combines medical aromatherapy and a more esoteric view of essential oils.[28] For him, this was a personal book and thus written for the layperson as well as the physician. When this work was first published in 1976, he spoke favorably on the internal use of medicinal essential oil blends. His later writings reversed this for fear of uninformed laypeople treating themselves.

[28]Robert Tisserand, *The Art of Aromatherapy,* pp. 5-9.

There followed an explosion of popular writings on aromatherapy out of Britain. Massage therapists and laypeople quickly adopted essential oils taking this knowledge out of more conventional medical settings. This certainly has antagonized the medical community and set up turf battles. Essential oils were now to be conservatively diluted with carrier oils for the purposes of massage over the entire body. The British model of aromatherapy had thus become a complementary modality. As a result, there is confusion on how to use the essential oils and a great fear of using them full strength on the body.[29] Their growing lists of contraindications lack scientific or even anecdotal evidence to sustain their fears regarding the use of essential oils.

[29]Marcel Lavabre, *Aromatherapy Workbook,* p. 7.

A third model of aromatherapy comes from the German speaking countries—Germany, Austria and Switzerland. Their emphasis is on the scent or fragrance and they recommend inhaling that fragrance for healing. This does not mean that they do not use essential oils medically as the do the French; their emphasis is simply on the olfactory perception of the oil.

Regulatory Agencies Try to Set the Standards

The Australians and the Americans have developed similar models to the British. Aromatherapy is at best, marginalized and in the hands of laypeople and not the medical community as it is in France. It seems that both in England and in the United States, the goal is not to upset the medical community, and, in the U.S., the FDA. In most western countries, regulatory agencies restrict or prohibit aromatherapy producers from making any medical statements about the use of essential oils. In France, this is not the case.

In the U.S., aromatherapy didn't get a good start until the 1980's. Kurt Schnaubelt, (from Germany) and Marcel Lavabre, (from France) and Victoria Edwards (from England) were prominent in the development of the National Association of Holistic Aromatherapy that advocated aromatherapy as a self-help modality. Their approach is very close to the British model with an emphasis on using the oils diluted for massage. Internal use of essential oils is discouraged, except by the well-educated practitioner.

In a more popular vein, D. Gary Young, a naturopathic physician began his interest in essential oils following a near-fatal logging accident. Introduced to oils, he found that sometimes they relieved his pain and symptoms and sometimes they didn't. Thus began his search into developing pure therapeutic grade essential oils. He studied in France with Dr. Pénoël and in universities in Turkey and Egypt. He came home and developed his own distillers producing some of the highest quality essential oils as confirmed by French laboratories. Dr. Pénoël wrote that the Young Living essential oils are top quality and deserving the term "therapeutic grade." Pénoël went on to say that the Young Living company is destined to "help change the course of medicine."[30] In the last ten years, Gary Young has helped to make essential oils and the knowledge of their use available in a widespread market. In 1998, he was the only American asked to present at the First International Congress on Integrated Medicine held in Grasse, France.[31]

[30]D. Gary Young, *An Introduction to Young Living Essential Oils,* Eleventh Edition, pp. iii-iv.

[31]"Cultivating and Distilling Therapeutic Quality Essential Oils in the United States," Proceedings from the First International Symposium, Grasse, France, March 21-22, 1998, *Integrated Aromatic Medicine,* pp. 139-150.

Today's aromatherapy is very different from the use of aromatic plants throughout history. The influence of science and medicine have overwhelmed the spiritual and esoteric beliefs around the oils. Massage and self-care have helped to bring aromatherapy into the complementary therapies marketplace. Even international companies like Estée Lauder have gotten into the act. Clearly, there is nothing clear about aromatherapy today! According to Dr. Pénoël, the turf battles are raging and the public is often confused about this ancient form of medicine. He pleads with those who are wedded to the many approaches to aromatherapy to remember that our work is about empowerment. We should be focused on enabling each person to manage their own health and well-being. It is imperative that we educate individuals, families and groups in the regular use of essential oils.[32] We are, after all, on this earth to help each other.

[32]Dr. Daniel Pénoël and Rose-Marie Pénoël, *Natural Home Health Care Using Essential Oils,* pp. 25-26.

Let us take a closer look now at the makeup of these essential oils that God gave to us for our health.

CHAPTER 3

THE EARTH'S MEDICINES

"The Lord hath created medicines out of the earth, and the sensible will not despise them."
Ecclesiaticus 38:4 [Book of Sirach]

The oil is the life blood of the plant.

The biblical people used many different healing plants but were careful not to write about them in the scriptures. Since God was the source of health and healing and not man, they did not want to defy the belief in God's exclusive power as healer. But as the writer of Ecclesiaticus states, the sensible should not despise the medicines of the earth. Chapters three and four will look at the healing properties of these marvelous healing medicines given to us by God. Modern-day research on the chemistry and vibrational frequencies may fill in the missing information about these oils for many readers. However, for those looking for ways to apply these healing substances, you may want to skip ahead to chapter five.

What are Essential Oils?

Have you ever walked through a rose garden or rubbed a sprig of rosemary between your fingers and smelled the unique fragrances of these plants? Have you noticed the aroma that comes from peeling an orange or picking fresh mint? What about the smell that comes from brushing your hand through lavender flowers or touching cinnamon sticks? What you have encountered is the essential oils of those plants that are the very life force or essence of the plant. The oil or resin carries nutrients throughout the plant and protects it from any form of stress. The oil has been called the "life blood" of the plant since it protects against infections and other diseases. These oils are tiny droplets produced in glands, sacs, or veins of different plant parts and may be found in any portion of the bush, flower, herb, or tree. It is what gives each plant its characteristic aroma. Some are more volatile than others, meaning they evaporate quickly, infusing the air with their particular fragrance. Just walking under a stand of eucalyptus trees after a rain shower can be quite invigorating as the aroma opens and clears your respiratory passages.

For some plants, the oil may be found in the flower petals like that of rose. Eucalyptus and tea tree oil come from little oil sacs within their leaves. Juniper yields oil from both its berries and twigs and cedarwood and sandalwood oils come from the chopped wood of their trees. This differs from pine and spruce oils which are distilled mainly from their needles. Frankincense and myrrh oils come from the dried resin of those respective trees. The clove tree produces different types of essential oil from its buds, stalks and leaves, and the Scotch pine yields distinct oils from its needles, wood and resin. Three different essential oils come from the orange tree. Neroli oil is obtained from the blossoms, orange oil from the citrus fruit, and petitgrain from the leaves of the tree. The essential oil of a plant is not oily at all but rather is a water-like fluid.

Today when plants are harvested to extract this life force, they are most commonly distilled using specific temperature, pressure and length of time suitable for each one. We call these oils "essential" because without it, the plant could not live. The essential oil from a plant is highly concentrated. For instance, one drop of chamomile essential oil would make about 30 cups of tea. When we steep dried chamomile herb in hot water, we are extracting the essential oil for our relaxing cup of tea. Sometimes the oils are 75-100 times more potent than the dried herb itself.

Do you have a garden or a flowerbox or perhaps pots of herbs or flowers growing in your home? How did you choose the plants? By color or fragrance? Or, was there any other "spiritual attraction" that caused you to pick certain plants for your garden, or windowsill? More than likely you weren't primarily aware of the plant's chemistry or its purity when you chose them.

Ways to Obtain the "Life Blood" of Plants

The plants must first be grown under the right conditions. If plants such as lavender or clary sage are watered with most of our city waters, then they are receiving a dose of chlorine and other chemicals present in the water supply. The plants pick up these chemicals which will alter their chemical makeup and may affect their therapeutic potential. Pollution is another concern. Plants need to properly exchange oxygen and carbon dioxide. If there is a brown cloud hovering over the fields, the chemicals in the atmosphere will eventually settle and the plants will be affected. Soil is yet another concern for pollution. Not just pollution from the air and water but also pollution from fertilizers, herbicides, pesticides and even the diesel exhaust from farm equipment. These pollutions can produce a toxic residue in many oils. Some plants like frankincense and myrrh require a dry arid atmosphere while others like orange and lemon thrive in a tropical climate. Some plants will also have different chemical compositions depending on what part of the world they are grown in. For instance, basil grown in Germany will have a different chemical makeup than basil grown in Egypt. Thyme is another one that will have a different chemical makeup depending on its conditions of growth such as the time of year that it is cut, the altitude, and the amount of light.[1]

[1]Shirley Price and Len Price, *Aromatherapy for Health Professionals*, p. 11.

If we are going to use oils for spiritual healing, would we not want to use pure, essential oils, untainted by chemicals?

Harvesting the plants is also unique for each plant. Plants have been studied for thousands of years to find out when a plant will produce its highest quality and quantity of oil. Some plants like to be picked in the early hours before sun-up while others prefer the cool of the evening to yield their oil. After picking, some plants like to "rest" before distillation and others must go into the distillers immediately to give up their oil. Producing therapeutic grades of essential oils is a botanical science. We must fall in love with the healing powers of plants if we are to unlock their secrets.

Some plants yield a lot of oil and others produce only miniscule amounts. For instance, it takes 500 pounds of sage or rosemary to make a quart of oil but a ton of thyme to produce the same amount. More than 8 million hand-picked jasmine blossoms may produce only 2 pounds of essential oil making it, along with rose the most expensive of all the oils. The amount of plant material and the production time required will of course affect the cost and quality of the oil.[2]

[2]Peter and Kate Damian, *Aromatherapy Scent and Psyche, Using Essential Oils for Physical and Emotional Well-Being*, p. 2.

For gardeners who raise flowers and herbs, "falling in love" with the plants is something they can understand. What this is describing is actually a spiritual awareness of the divine life given to all living things.

Steam distillation seems to be the best method in our present day for extracting the oils from the plants. The plant material is placed in a special chamber. Steam is then forced into the chamber and depending on the particular plant, the steam may be under pressure. As it passes through the plant material, the steam ruptures

We must fall in love with the healing powers of plants if we are to unlock their secrets.

the plant's oil-bearing sacs and cavities and frees the oil which then evaporates into the steam. The steam and vaporized oil is passed out of the chamber and through a coiled tube surrounded by cold water that condenses the steam and oil into a liquid. It is then collected into another chamber. The oil either floats to the top or sinks to the bottom of the water where it can then be drawn off. The water that is left will still have some of the properties of the oil and can be sold as floral waters. Ever since this process was perfected in the Middle Ages, rose and chamomile floral waters have been important for skin care and fragrance.

It is amazing how many of our skin and hair products carry distinctive fragrances reminiscent of the real thing. Could it be wiser to use the "real thing" when possible instead of chemical imitations? Do you think the imitations carry the same spiritual frequency as the real plants do?

All living things are made up of a wide variety of compounds composed of carbon, hydrogen and oxygen.

There are other processes used to extract essential oils as well. One is with the aid of solvents. The problem is that the oil may then be contaminated with the solvent and hence not a true essential oil. This method may yield more oil but it is not always suitable for therapeutic purposes. Some plants will not give up their oil unless a solvent is used. This is the case with jasmine. Oils obtained in this manner are called *concrétes* or *absolutes*. The perfume industry may use this method because it is more economical especially for highly prized oils like rose and neroli. Another method of extracting oils is the cold expression process that uses mechanical means to press the oil from the rind of citrus fruits. Cold-pressed grades of orange, bergamot, mandarin, grapefruit, lemon, and lime oils are obtained in this way. Enfluerage is another process which is very old. It is a method that creates an oil infusion by layering flower petals in fat or olive oil. The fat eventually absorbs the scented molecules from the flowers. Yet another very old method is boiling plant material in a pot with a lid on top which yields an extract or a tincture depending on whether the material was boiled in wine or beer. This was a common method in the Middle Ages.

How Essential Oils Work

To understand how essential oils work, let us take a very brief look at their chemical makeup. All living things, including essential oils, are made up of a wide variety of compounds composed of carbon, hydrogen, and oxygen. These compounds fall basically into two groups. The first group are the <u>hydrocarbons</u> composed of only hydrogen and carbon atoms arranged in chains. These form almost exclusively substances called terpenes (monoterpenes, sesquiterpenes and diterpenes.) They are easy to recognize-all these compounds end in -ene. Monoterpenes are found in most essential oils. Some that are high in monoterpenes include galbanum, angelica, Rose of Sharon, juniper, frankincense, cypress, and hyssop. They are all antiseptic in nature and create an inhospitable environment for microbes. The most important ability of monoterpenes is that they can reprogram miswritten information in the cellular memory. This is very important since improper coding in the DNA results in cells malfunctioning and even producing deadly diseases like cancer.

The sesquiterpenes which are larger molecules, have additional properties of being calming and supporting to the body by helping to reduce inflammation. Some of these may help to reduce pain and spasms as well. Some examples of oils high in sesquiterpenes are sandalwood, cedarwood, myrrh, vetiver, spikenard, patchouly and ginger. Research from universities in Berlin and Vienna show these sesquiterpenes increase oxygenation around the pineal and pituitary glands and cross the blood-brain barrier.[3] They can erase miswritten codes in the DNA. It is believed that sesquiterpenes are particularly effective in dealing with cancer cells that contain misinformation. The oxygen that is delivered to the cell makes it difficult for cancer to reproduce and survive.

[3]Connie and Alan Higley, *Reference Guide for Essential Oils,* p. 7.

The diterpenes are believed to have further properties of being able to aid in getting rid of mucus and some can kill fungus and viruses. Some oils like clary sage that are high in diterpenes appear to balance the body's hormones.

Atoms of carbon, hydrogen and oxygen combine to produce over 3,000 different aromatic molecules.

Limonene has been found to have properties that kill viruses. Ninety percent of the citrus oils have limonene in them. Pinene has strong antiseptic properties and in found in high proportions in the conifer oils—pine, fir, spruce, and juniper.

The second group are the <u>oxygenated compounds</u> and are mainly esters, aldehydes, ketones, alcohols, phenols and oxides. The alcohols provide an inhospitable environment for all kinds of microbes—bacteria, viruses and fungi. They create an uplifting quality and are generally non-toxic and do not cause skin irritations. The phenols are also antiseptic and kill bacteria. In addition, they stimulate the immune system and boost the body's own healing process thereby lifting depression. Phenols however can be toxic to the liver and a skin irritant. Both thyme and oregano are high in phenols. The aldehydes can kill viruses, decrease inflammation, calm the nervous system, dilate blood vessels thereby reducing blood pressure, and can bring down a fever. But aldehydes can cause skin irritation when not used properly. Some examples include lemongrass, lemon verbena and melissa oils. Ketones basically ease digestion and the flow of mucus. Some may help to reduce pain, aid the body in blood coagulation, reduce inflammation and assist the body in getting rid of mucus. Some examples of ketones are jasmine, hyssop, clary sage, tansy, and camphor oils. The esters are generally believed to kill fungi, reduce inflammation and spasms, and both calm and tone the nervous system. Esters can be found in lavender, clary sage, geranium, and Roman chamomile. The effect of the oxides is to aid the respiratory system in reducing mucus. Some examples are found in a wide range of oils such as eucalyptus, hyssop, rosemary, bay laurel and tea tree.[4]

It's amazing—these atoms of carbon, hydrogen and oxygen combine to produce over 3,000 different aromatic molecules each of which belongs to a specific chemical group. Although an essential oil may be made up of molecules from different chemical groups, one or two may predominate. For instance, oil from the fir tree is made up of 95% monoterpenes. It also has camphene and

[4]Shirley Price and Len Price, *Aromatherapy for Health Professionals*, pp. 27-34. See also Julia Lawless, *The Illustrated Encyclopedia of Essential Oils*, pp. 48-49.

limonene (both of these are also terpenes.). Frankincense is 40% monoterpenes and 43% α-pinene and it contains limonese, sesquiterpenes, and borneol as well.[5] Both cinnamon and clove oils on the other hand are mostly made up of esters, phenols and aldehydes. Wintergreen is 90% methyl salicylate, an ester. Sometimes an essential oil will have so many constituents that scientists have not been able to measure or even identify them all. Some of their compounds may even be toxic when isolated but therapeutic when balanced in combination with other constituents to form the plant's lifeblood. Each plant therefore has its own unique chemical constituents that determine its therapeutic effects and its fragrance. It stands to reason that because of climatic conditions, pollution and all the other factors affecting a plant's oil, each distillation will vary in its chemical proportions. This is why it is important to check each batch of oil for its quality and its chemistry. This is done in the chemist lab by a process called gas chromatography which determines the chemical constituents.

[5]*Essential Oils Desk Reference*, p. 49.

Essential oils are not fatty oils. Essential oils come from plant flowers, stems, bark and the leaves of plants. Fatty oils are produced by pressing seeds and nuts such as peanuts, almonds, and soybean nuts, among many others. Fatty oils will feel slippery and leave a telltale grease spot on surfaces. Over time, these oils will go rancid and become worthless. They do not evaporate like essential oils do and they have no antimicrobial properties. Sometimes one of these oils, like olive or almond oil, can be used as a carrier for essential oils.

The complex chemistry of essential oils make them ideal in killing microorganisms like bacteria and viruses. Dr. Kurt Schnaubelt states that essential oils have a 95% success potential against infections. A century of research and evaluation has confirmed that essential oils are effective antimicrobial agents and they don't have the side effects that accompany antibiotics. This is not surprising given the fact that antibiotics have weakened our immune systems producing resistant germs.[6] Even conventional medicine readily admits that we have created a nightmare by overusing antibiotics. Frequent use causes microrganisms to build up a resistance to the antibiotics.

[6]Kurt Schnaubelt, *Advanced Aromatherapy, The Science of Essential Oil Therapy*, p. 101.

Furthermore, a vicious circle is created since antibiotics kill the friendly bacteria in the body as well as leave us open to opportunistic organisms like *Candida albicans.* Their metabolic waste products consequently inhibit the efficient functioning of the immune system. Microbes build up little or no resistance to essential oils. Peter and Kate Damian make the point that this may be due to the fact essential oils are the natural defense mechanism of the plant and their chemical complexity confounds the would-be invaders.[7]

[7]Pete and Kate Damian, *Aromatherapy Scent and Psyche,* p. 13.

Dr. Pierre Franchomme made an interesting presentation at the First International Symposium at Grasse, France in 1998 on the use of essential oils to reset the normal intestinal flora. Whether a disruption in the intestinal tract is due to a change in diet, other bacterial populations, antibiotics, or the ingestion of food contaminants, the normal balance of healthy intestinal flora is upset and there is an overgrowth of unhealthy microbes. Aromatic molecules are quite capable, Franchomme found, of neutralizing pathogenic bacteria thereby acting as antibiotics and fostering the growth of good bacteria that make up 99% of healthy flora.[8] Dr. David Stewart PhD in his book *Healing Oils of the Bible,* refers to these essential oils as "smart medicine." They are imbued with God's intelligence, killing off the bacteria that cause sickness and allowing the good bacteria to continue serving us.[9]

[8]P. Franchomme, "Using Eubiotic and Antibiotic Essential Oils in Resetting the Aerobic and Anaerobic Intestinal Flora: Local and Systemic Effects," pp. 43-50, found in *Integrated Aromatic Medicine, Proceedings from the First International Symposium, Grasse, France, March 21-22, 1998.*

[9]David Stewart, *Healing Oils of the Bible,* p. 20.

In another French study done by Dr. L. Hervieux MD, aromatherapy was found to be very effective in reducing mortality, extending life and providing general relief for HIV-Positive patients. Some of the oils proved to be effective in stopping diarrhea and gastric and intestinal spasms and to stimulate proper functioning of the liver and bile duct. They also decreased mucus in the lungs. They found some oils worked against intestinal parasites, all types of intestinal bacterial infections and fungal infections. HIV patients often experience profound fatigue and essential oils proved to be effective stimulants. Dr. Hervieux concluded that a tritherapy of rosemary, cinnamon bark and eucalyptus radiata can be an effective therapy for AIDS patients, providing them with much appreciated daily relief. The oils can be prescribed in conjunction with traditional therapies.[10]

Schnaubelt also finds that there is a 75% success potential with using essential oils for the psyche, nervous system and hormonal balance. Many of the oils have such an uplifting quality that it is no surprise how they can affect our emotions. However, Schnaubelt finds that aromatherapy is less effective with chronic inflammation and allergies. There is only a 50% success potential here. This is presumably because these conditions develop over many years and often have a hereditary factor involved. Likewise, essential oils only have a limited potential (25%) in affecting metabolic or degenerative condition that have taken years to develop.

It is only within the last couple of hundred years that we started replacing essential oils for healing with chemical synthetics. These synthetics are chemical compounds that can be produced more cheaply and in larger quantities than the pure grade essential oils. The fragrance or the flavor may seem to be the same, but the chemical makeup is quite different.

Even some distributors of essential oils will add other cheaper oils or synthetics to increase their profitability. Essential oils used in the fragrance industry will often remove the terpenes from the oil because of their insolubility in alcohol. The terpenes would make perfume cloudy which would affect its salability. But of course, if you remove the terpenes, you have also destroyed the oil's anti-microbial properties making it ineffective for therapeutic uses. Experts all agree there is a significant difference between therapeutic grade essential oils and the synthetic oils. For instance, a therapeutic grade rose oil may have several thousand components whereas a synthetic rose oil might have just fifty. It is the essential oil's very complexity that provides its many benefits and effects.

Man has tried to improve upon nature but nature still holds many secrets that cannot always be measured through chemistry.

[10]L. Hervieux, MF, "Aromatherapy for HIV-Positive Patients," pp. 61-62, found in *Integrated Aromatic Medicine, Proceedings from the First International Symposium, Grasse, France, March 21-22, 1998.*

As plants of the earth, they are God's gifts for our healing.

What Else can Essential Oils Do For Us?

Essential oils can perform many functions for our bodies, minds and spirits. As plants of the earth, they are God's gifts for our healing and as Dr. Stewart says, they seem to possess a divine intelligence knowing just how to help us. They can support and balance many systems—circulatory, digestive, respiratory, nervous, endocrine and reproductive. When an essential oil fragrance enters the nose, it goes to the lungs and finds its way into the blood stream and every part of the body. Chemical interactions can occur between the oils and our bodies that result in physical changes. There can be hormone and enzyme responses to the chemicals within the oils. Our bodies can become sedated, stimulated or relaxed by the action of certain oils. Pain may be relieved, wounds may heal, inflammation and spasms may cease. In Oxford, England, hospitals are using essential oils known for their sedative or antidepressant qualities to release endorphins and enkephalins (neurochemical analgesics and tranquilizers). Lavender, marjoram, geranium, mandarin, and cardamom have replaced chemical sedatives in these hospitals. These and other oils relax people, lower blood pressure, increase mental acuity, normalize body functions, reduce stress, and even act as aphrodisiacs.[11]

[11]Peter and Kate Damian, *Aromatherapy Scent and Psyche, Using Essential Oils for Physical and Emotional Well-Being,* p. 18.

Some oils will affect more than one system within the body. For instance, peppermint is widely used as an inhalant to open respiratory passages. It is also used to quiet an upset digestive tract. When used on muscle spasms, it tends to release those as well. Some oils can relieve allergy symptoms, others help metabolize nutrients for our bodies, or boost our natural immune systems to fight off diseases. Essential oils can help relieve all kinds of skin conditions, help us to breathe, relax tight muscles and bring pain relief. There are oils that clear our sinuses, help us to relax and sleep better, and relieve headaches, muscle and joint pain. Some act as natural insect repellants like cedarwood and myrrh, many others are natural antiseptics and act as fighters against infection. Essential oils in general, make the environment particularly hostile for microbes like bacteria, viruses, parasites and fungi, yet are safe for us. This is what the essential oil has done for plants and is capable of doing for us.

Essential Oils Can Also Affect Our Minds

Our sense of smell is estimated to be 10,000 times more acute than our other senses and sensitive to some 10,000 chemical compounds. Once registered, scent travels faster to the brain than either sight or sound. The fragrance of an oil travels by way of the olfactory nerve pathways directly to the limbic system in the central portion of the brain where emotions are stored. This area known as the amygdala, plays a major role in storing and releasing emotional trauma. The only way to stimulate this gland is with fragrance or through the sense of smell. Olfactory responses to odors induce the brain to stimulate the release of hormones and neurochemicals that in turn alter the body's physiology and behavior. Smell then, links directly to emotional states and behaviors stored since childhood. For instance, the smell of cinnamon toast takes me nostalgically back to my childhood when my mother would fix this delectably fragrant food on cold winter mornings, and the smell of sweet pea reminds me of playing in my grandmother's backyard where sweet pea grew on the fence. My grandmother also had a wonderfully fragrant cedar chest. When I smell cedar, I am reminded of that chest and of my beloved grandmother. All of these were pleasant childhood memories for me. For some individuals however, certain odors may bring back unpleasant memories. Essential oils enable us to access stored or forgotten memories and thus be able to deal with them. Stored emotions can make us ill but nature's medicines can help us release these emotions wherever they are stored in the body or energy field. Thus all aromas have a potential emotional impact that can reach deep into the psyche, and both relax the mind and uplift the spirit.

The word "emotions" literally means "energy in motion." Emotion is the experience of energy moving through our bodies. This emotional energy actually works at higher speed than thought. Thought and images can take seconds to minutes to evoke a memory while an aroma can evoke a memory in milliseconds.

In France, there is a growing movement for treating the mind and body using a therapy known as olfactotherapy®. This is a therapeutic approach to reawaken the sense of smell and to increase awareness of the odors around us. Gilles Fournil, the founder of this work, is using it to treat dependencies such as alcohol, tobacco, and overeating and certain phobias, stress and panic disorders. Olfactotherapy® is part of the quest for well-being. Fournil states that "if I re-educate my senses, my relationship with the world changes and I gain better understanding of myself." He speaks of awakening life energy and self-healing with fragrances as the catalyst.[12]

[12]Gilles Fournil, "Olfactothérapie®," found in *Integrated Aromatic Medicine, Proceedings from the First International Symposium held in Grasse, France, March, 1998*, pp. 37-42.

There have been a number of intriguing experiments conducted regarding the use of essential oil scents in the past ten years. Experiments have shown that oils like peppermint and lily of the valley increased subjects' performance accuracy by 15 to 25 percent. And office workers enhanced their efficiency and reduced stress when pleasing fragrances were pumped through the air-conditioning system. Stores use fragrances to encourage buying and churches use incense to place worshipers in a spiritual frame of mind. Using scents to affect human behavior is very old indeed and more widespread than we realize. Only essential oils have mood altering properties and as we all know, when we are in a pleasant mood, we are more likely to be open to shopping, eating and even working.

Ancient cultures including the Greeks, Egyptians, and Romans extensively used particular scents in various rituals including religious, marital and sexual rituals. Even today we burn incense or scented candles to set a mood or to relax. The perfume industry constantly markets to us about smelling good in order to attract the opposite sex. Fragrance is considered an important factor in the emotion of love and romance. Rose, neroli (orange blossom) and jasmine are scents commonly associated with lovemaking. On the other hand, scents like juniper are associated with the feeling of strength and confidence.

Research shows that aromatic compounds can combat depression. Citrus oils like bergamot, orange and lemon have been studied for their uplifting effects which in effect decrease the depressive symptoms. These oils were inhaled through diffusion. Lavender has likewise been shown to reduce anxiety, increase mental accuracy and improve mental performance. Lavender both improves depressed mood while exerting a relaxing affect on the brain.

Our research regarding the affects of fragrances upon human physiology and psychology is still in its infancy. Synthetic scents may sometimes temporarily deceive the body but as we have learned in using pharmaceuticals, the results are not always positive or without side effects. We would do well to remember this when we choose to diffuse an oil in our homes or work places. There is a difference between therapeutic grade essential oils and their synthetic counterparts.

Essential Oils Can Affect the Body Through the Skin

Our skin is our waterproof barrier designed to prevent water loss and keep foreign substances out. Essential oils are unique in that they can pass through the epidermal barrier and enter the bloodstream without causing injury or triggering inflammation or water loss. They can do this because of their small molecular structure and weight that allows them to penetrate the skin readily. Essential oils are not water soluble but oil soluble that gives them ready entrance through the epidermis. Essential oils are safe and nontoxic with many of them considered GRAS (Generally Regarded As Safe) by the FDA. One study conducted by scientists at the Institute of Pharmaceutical Chemistry at the University of Vienna tested the ability of Lavender to enter the blood stream when applied on the skin. Lavender was placed in a carrier oil (peanut oil) and massaged on the stomach for ten minutes. Blood samples were drawn at 0, 5,10, 15, 20, 30, 45, 60, 75, and 90 minutes following application of the oil. Noticeable quantities of the chemical constituents of Lavender appeared in the blood after only five minutes and reached a peak at 20 minutes. This experiment as reported in teaching materials produced by Young Living Essential Oils[13] showed that topically applied essential oils dissolved into an appropriate vegetable carrier oil can effectively penetrate into the tissues and bloodstream.

[13]Young Living Level II Training Materials

Essential Oils Also Have the Ability to Act as Antioxidants

Essential oils can assist the removal of potentially harmful chemicals (free-radicals) produced in the body during cellular and tissue metabolism. These free-radicals are also formed when the body tries to remove petrochemicals and heavy metals from tissues. Free radical damage is an on-going problem that only increases with age. In fact, much of the aging process is due to the accumulation of free-radicals. Scientists at Tufts University have developed a way of measuring the ability of foods and oils to destroy free radicals thus slowing the aging process and preventing certain diseases like cancers. The scale is called the ORAC = Oxygen Radical Absorption Capacity. The higher the ORAC score, the more capable a substance is in destroying free radicals.

Antioxidant (ORAC) Scores For Selected Essential Oils	
Sandalwood	1,655
Juniper	2,517
Rosemary	3,309
Rose of Sharon (cistus)	38,624
Cinnamon Bark	103,448
Thyme	159,590
Clove	10,786,875

If we look at selected essential oils from the Biblical times we will see that many of the ancient oils measure quite high on the ORAC scale. Many of the Bible stories report a longevity among the people that borders on myth for our understanding today. Yet, we do know that many of the patriarchs lived to ripe old ages and sustained fairly healthy lives. Could it be that essential oils played a role in their full measure of years? All of the oils listed above were indeed available during Biblical times and the ancient Hebrews traded and bartered for them.

When essential oils are added to foods they can improve absorption, assimilation and utilization of the nutrients. Since the oils can better penetrate the walls of the cells, they can carry nutrients into the cells. This includes vitamins, minerals, enzymes, fats, proteins and carbohydrates. Essential oils are lipid soluble and can penetrate cell membranes bringing an increase of 21% oxygen to the cells within 20 minutes of application. This allows cells to function normally. Cells can release their chemical toxins in an oxygen rich environment thus improving overall health. As we know, sesquiterpenes increase oxygen availability particularly in the limbic system of the brain around the pineal and pituitary glands. This can lead to an increase of antibodies, endorphins and neurotransmitters. Essential oils also carry into the cells, ozone and negative ions which inhibit bacterial growth, anti-oxidants and hormones—all necessary for proper cell functioning.

The ancient peoples understood the healing properties of essential oils. In our modern-day, we look to science to "prove" whether a substance actually works through its chemical interactions or whether we just "think" it does. Could our ancestors have understood that plants also have a spiritual quality about them that allowed for their healing ability?

The Quality of Essential Oils

If an essential oil is going to be applied to the body or inhaled, then it needs to be of the highest quality to achieve the desired healing effects. Therapeutic grades of oil require proper distillation processes as well as attention to growing, harvesting, packaging and distribution. It would be helpful to know the source of your essential oils. Does the company have standards for production, harvesting, and distillation? Do the producers independently verify the frequency of each batch of oils they produce? Are they therapeutic grade? What are their quality control standards? These processes are expensive and will naturally be reflected in the cost of the oils. For instance, frankincense produced in Somalia sells between $30,000 to $35,000 per ton. Distillation is a lengthy process, requiring 12 hours. In the U.S. you can probably go to any health food store and purchase an inexpensive frankincense for $25 an ounce but it may not hold the high frequency needed for healing. Rose is another example of a very expensive oil to produce. It takes 5,000 pounds of rose petals to produce one pound of oil making it one of the most expensive oils to produce. Yet at the health food store you can buy a $2.98 bottle of rose oil and the bottle may even say that it is a "pure essential oil." The old adage of "you get what you pay for" applies here. More than likely these less expensive forms of frankincense and rose oil have been cut with alcohol or other synthetic chemicals. There may be only one or two drops of the real essential oil in it. They may still smell like the original oil, but they do not have the same healing properties. Worse still, these adulterated forms may cause rashes or other skin irritations. Some believe that all essential oils need to be diluted before being applied to the skin. In fact, very few do. However, if you are using an essential oil that has been adulterated with synthetic chemicals, you can expect skin problems and will need to dilute.

The perfume industry has been producing fragrances for centuries that mimic the natural aroma of essential oils. Sometimes they

Therapeutic grade essential oils represent a natural approach to healing.

extract certain molecules from an essential oil and at other times they produce synthetic chemicals that have a similar fragrance but molecularly are quite different from the original oil. When synthetic chemicals are added, the essential oil quality becomes weaker and weaker.

For pure grade essential oils to be used therapeutically it is absolutely necessary that you know the source of the oils. Check the reputation of the company and ask for their quality control standards. The French are the world leaders in producing therapeutic grade essential oils. They have honed this art to a science. It is from the French that many essential oil distillers are taking their lessons. For instance, temperature, pressure and time are all factors in the production of high quality oils. If the pressure or temperature is too high it could cause harshness in the oil or even affect the quality. But it could also produce the same amount of oil in a fraction of the normal time and thus be sold at a less expensive price. The problem is that the oil produced no longer has the same therapeutic quality. Another reason to know the source of your oils.

There are international standards for therapeutic-grade essential oils. ISO (International Standards Organization) and AFNOR (Association French Normalization Organization Regulation) standards are generally the two referred to most often. The AFNOR standards state the percentages of certain chemical constituents that must be present for an essential oil to be considered therapeutic grade. In order to gain the AFNOR stamp of approval, the oils must be sent to France for testing. At present, there are no American standards for therapeutic grade essential oils. Check to see if your essential oils are marked with either of these standard symbols.[14]

[14]Gary Young, *Introduction to Young Living Essential Oils,* Eleventh Edition, pp.10-11

One way to see if an essential oil works is by trying it. The next time you are at the health food store, check out several brands of a particular oil. Do they have the ISO or AFNOR symbols on the bottles? If so, you can probably trust the quality.

What are Some Uses of Essential Oils for Today?

- First aid for cuts, scrapes, injuries
- Assist in relaxation
- Cold and flu prevention
- Pain management
- Depression management
- Support immune function
- Natural antibiotic, antihistamine
- For a more restful sleep
- Pet care
- Natural cleansing products
- Enhance nutritional supplements
- Enhance personal care products
- Get rid of unwanted odors

From this list, you can see some of the reasons why many people consider using essential oils to maintain their health. The oils represent a natural approach to healing. Many of our synthetic drugs today carry potentially serious side effects. We spend billions of dollars every year to counteract these unwanted complications. Because of their chemical structure, essential oils are metabolized in the cells like other nutrients and, unlike many synthetic drugs they don't accumulate in the body since they evaporate so quickly. Essential oils are a safe and natural alternative for healing the body.

Like most Americans, we have probably tried over-the-counter medications at some time or another for colds and flu, or perhaps even taken an aid for sleep or for any number of other problems that interrupted our life styles. Did you ever suffer side effects from these drugs that sent you looking for more "natural" remedies for your symptoms?

How Do You Use Essential Oils?

There are various ways we can apply essential oils for therapeutic benefit and for pleasure. The following methods are commonly used and considered safe. They involve inhalation, and skin absorption through massage, ointments, compresses and baths. The various schools of thought, namely the German, British and French models, emphasize either inhalation, dilution for body massage, directly (neat) on the body or taken internally. As we have seen, the French school which seems to have the most experience with using essential oils therapeutically, liberally use pure essential oils, getting them into the body in whatever way works. If the oil is not "pure" but one that has been cut with solvents or other substances, there may be skin reactions unless they are first diluted. Care must be taken to know the source of the oils and the processes whereby the oils were obtained.

Oils are nature's natural medicines and need to be respected for their potent healing properties. Whether they are inhaled, ingested or rubbed on the body, we must be knowledgeable and use them in a proper way to obtain their full benefits—physical and spiritual. Sometimes the old advice of a little goes a long way needs to be heeded.

Inhalation through diffusion. A diffusor is a device that breaks up the oil into tiny particles and distributes them into the air in the most effective way. This can serve to destroy pathogens in the air as well as raise the oxygen level thus increasing the energy level in the room. The tiny airborne particles stimulate the nerve receptors of the olfactory bulb and transmit the messages of the oil's frequency to the brain. Nebulizers can act to diffuse essential oils into a room and do not require heating the water first. There are numerous other ways to fragrance a room in addition to a diffusor. Simply placing a few drops of pure essential oil in a small saucer of water near a warm radiator or placing the oil in an essential oil burner will disperse the oil into the room.

Steam Inhalation. Essential oils can also be used with steam to clear the lungs and sinus passages of congestion. Gabriel Mojay in *Aromatherapy for Healing the Spirit* recommends adding 2-3 drops of an essential oil to a pint of boiling water. Then drape a towel over your head and breathe in the steam for a few minutes.[15]

[15]Gabriel Mojay, *Aromatherapy for Healing the Spirit,* p. 17.

Applied directly to the skin. Applying oils directly to the skin can act to restore, rejuvenate and nourish the skin. Some oils may be applied directly to the part of the body that is injured or that needs support. Oils may also be applied to specific energy points. It is well known in reflexology that there are energy points on the feet that correspond with other parts of the body—the organs and body structures like the spine. Oils may be applied to the soles of the feet to bring balance and healing to those parts of the body in need of support. Essential oils may be added to massage oils to enhance the physiological benefits of massage itself. Mojay recommends a mixture of 7-10 drops to one ounce of carrier oil. The essential oils promote the flow of blood and lymph and help to soothe tension and increase vital energy. Oils may sometimes be applied to the energy centers like the root, sacral, solar plexus, heart, throat, brow or crown to open and balance those centers. In addition, oils may be applied to the healer's hands then run through the energy field to break up congestion and bring balance to the aura.

Some may want to create their own aromatic ointments. Mojay recommends adding 5-20 drops of an essential oil to a 2 oz. jar of cream or gel base. Twenty drops would yield a 2% mixture. Compresses are another excellent way of applying essential oils to a specific area. Warm compresses are particularly beneficial for chronic backache, rheumatic pain and osteoarthritis. Either the oils can be placed first on the body and then the warm compresses laid on top of the body or the oils can be added to the warm water before soaking the compress. Cold compresses can be used in a similar fashion for headaches, and acute sprains and bruises.

Some of the stronger oils like thyme and oregano may need to be diluted with a carrier oil such as almond oil or even a good vegetable oil. Always check for sensitivity to the oils before applying them. If burning or redness is experienced, use a carrier oil to dilute it. The actions of some oils will be amplified when they are layered or blended together. Their joint actions achieve a more complete healing.

Personal Cleansing. One of the more pleasurable ways to benefit from essential oils is by bathing. Essential oils can be added to bath water along with a bath gel base to act as a dispersing agent for the oils. This is a most relaxing way to soothe muscular aches and pains. Aromatic oils can also be used in personal care items like shampoos, toothpaste, and body soaps.

Dietary Supplement. Some oils are generally regarded as safe (GRAS) by the FDA and may be taken internally as a dietary supplement. Always check recommended uses and suggested number of drops before ingesting any essential oils. Some oils will not be pleasant tasting and are best placed inside a gel cap before swallowing. I recommend to those who want to take an oil internally, to start with 1-3 drops in a gel cap and then increase to the recommended number of drops as tolerated.

Cooking. Many of the oils are excellent flavorings for food like peppermint, lemon, cinnamon, clove, dill, oregano, basil, thyme, bay leaf, and many others. It is the essential oils in these plants that impart the characteristic flavor and bouquet to our dishes. Even the nutritional value of food can be enhanced through proper use of essential oils in cooking. Always check the GRAS list for approved oils for internal use. Only 1-2 drops is necessary and is best added after the food is cooked.

The Essential Oil Cookbook by Menkit Prince presents a very balanced approach to using pure essential oils along with great recipes.

Cleaning. Some oils, particularly lemon, are wonderful in the washing machine, dishwasher or dishwater. They can also be used as a household cleaner and disinfectant for floors and furnishings.

Some essential oils create an environment that is unfriendly to germs and bacteria.

How and Where to Purchase Essential Oils

Now that you are aware of the basics about essential oils, the next step is to find quality therapeutic grade essential oils. Its not as easy as one would think. The last place to find quality oils is in supermarkets or even health food stores. When you pick up a frankincense for $12, you can rest assured it is not a quality oil. The best way to find therapeutic grade oils is by checking out the Internet. Here again, you have to be discriminating. There are hundreds of references to web sites willing to sell "therapeutic" grade essential oils but when you examine their materials, they never mention whether their oils are tested for quality. There are two companies I have found to not only be reputable but to offer top quality oils. These are listed in the appendix.

Another measure of the quality of the oils is the education that the company is willing to invest in for the sake of its customers. Do they offer educational classes or provide educational materials? Do they do ongoing research into the healing abilities of the oils? I found that by talking to knowledgeable individuals about the oils, I could identify ethical companies that practiced integrity in production, distillation, packaging and marketing.

I recommend once you have selected a company, that you order a few basic oils and get to know them before ordering a whole host of different oils. Focus on your intention for the oils. Do you want oils for physical, emotional, mental or spiritual clearing and healing? Are you looking for oils for a first aide kit for those unexpected emergencies like cuts and scrapes or oils for colds and flu? There are several oils I recommend to have on hand that are affordable and generally non-toxic and non-irritating: lavender, peppermint, lemon, cedarwood, frankincense, tea tree, and eucalyptus.

You may also want to have a few prepared blends such as Peace and Calming™, Valor™, Joy™, and Thieves™.

Some Common Sense Precautions

When using therapeutic-grade essential oils it is helpful to remember that these oils are highly concentrated and need to be used properly to prevent harm. We need to be knowledgeable about their individual healing abilities and proper usage. Some have very helpful therapeutic properties such as anti-inflammatory, anti-spasmodic, analgesic, anti-bacterial, anti-viral, and anti-microbial. Some of these oils however can be irritating to the skin or nasal passages, or they are phototoxic. Some essential oils should not be used during pregnancy since they can stimulate contractions or relax muscles.

There are some general cautions that we should bear in mind when using pure therapeutic-grade essential oils. First, we need to read the label thoroughly. How is this oil recommended for our use? Is it safe to be inhaled, placed directly on the body or is it advised that this oil be diluted first in a carrier oil? If the oil produces redness on the skin or a burning irritation, then rub the area with a vegetable oil—never water. Essential oils should never be placed directly in the eyes and ears. If you accidentally get an essential oil in your eye, soothe it with a drop of vegetable oil. Flushing it with water will not help. Be aware that the citrus oils may cause skin problems with exposure to the sun. It's always best to not use citrus oils when planning to be out in the sun. Always keep the lid closely tightly and out of the reach of children. For pregnant women, consult your healthcare practitioner first before using therapeutic-grade essential oils.

There are some general cautions that we should bear in mind when using pure therapeutic-grade essential oils.

What makes an essential oil a healing substance is not just its fragrance or its chemical properties. There is more. Let us turn our attention now to something much more subtle—the electromagnetic properties and vibrational energies of these amazing healing aromatic oils.

CHAPTER 4

VIBRATIONAL REMEDIES

In my healing practice I have noticed when I use essential oils with my clients, their energy fields come quickly into balance before I even do any hands-on work. The oils alone appear to affect the field's subtle vibration. The field would become clearer, fuller, brighter, more even and less dense. The energy centers (chakras) would also open and balance. This happened whether I diffused the oil, used a spray mist of oils (floral waters) in the room, anointed the client's skin or simply put oils on my hands and then moved them through the person's energy biofield. The subtle energy of the person had definitely shifted into a state of balance that made the hands-on therapy I would do so much easier, more effective and longer lasting. Using essential oils then, adds to the energetic healing. This made me want to inquire more deeply about these essential oils and how they worked. Do they heal because of their chemistry alone or is it through their electromagnetic properties and subtle vibrational frequencies?

From my work as an energy practitioner, I understood the subtle energy shifts that occur with hands-on healing so I was fascinated at the prospect of energetic remedies that would work together with prayer and hands-on healing to effect long lasting changes toward wholeness. This chapter will explore the relatively new concept of healing with vibrational remedies.

A New Field of Vibrational Medicine

Vibration underlies every aspect of nature. At an atomic level, vibrating electrons emit energy in the form of electromagnetic waves ranging from radio frequencies in the megahertz band to visible light and beyond. In our bodies, the atoms, molecules, cells, tissues, and organs each have their own vibrational signatures that originate at subatomic levels. The living body also has much slower rhythms that we know as breath, heartbeat, the slow six-second cycles of the cranial-sacral waves that traverse up and down our spines, and the very slow (two-times a minute) contractions of our spleen, as well as the natural vibrations of our other organs. There is an orderliness in all of this that creates an organization that is meaningful. At every level in our bodies, there is evidence of an intrinsic electromagetism of life. The whole body oscillates. Add to this equation therapeutic intention and touch by a healer, and it reveals whole new dimensions in healing yet to be studied. Richard Gerber in his landmark book on *Vibrational Medicine* opened our eyes to a new field of study. Gerber states that we are more than function and structure and chemistry. We have electromagnetic energy fields and subtle energy fields.[1] In his book on *Vibrational Medicine for the 21st Century,* he gives us a vibrational-medicine model. Based on Einsteinian and quantum physics, it views the body as a dynamic energy system. Mind and spirit are true sources of consciousness, and emotions and spirit can influence illness via energetic and neurohormonal connections among body, mind, and spirit. Treatment in this model is with different forms and frequencies of energy to rebalance the body/mind/ spirit complex.[2] This is no longer pseudoscience as many would have us believe. On the contrary, scientists like Jim Oschman, are providing the scientific basis for energy medicine. Living organisms comprise dynamic energy systems and field phenomena and modern science is helping us to understand this. Vibrational therapies are not magic or superstition, Oschman writes, they are based on biology, chemistry and physics.[3]

"All of creation is clothed with your majesty, mirroring your Love throughout the cosmos." Psalm 97

Nan Merrill, *Psalms for Praying,* p. 200.

[1] Richard Gerber, *Vibrational Medicine,* p. 67.

[2] Richard Gerber, *Vibrational Medicine for the 21st Century,* p. 3.

[3] James Oschman, *Energy Medicine, the Scientific Basis,* p. 121.

Our work in healing is to find those combinations that enable the person to move towards a state of harmony and balance—to one of harmonic resonance.

"You forgive our iniquities,
   You heal our disease,
You save us from the snares of fear,
   You crown us with steadfast love
   and mercy,
You satisfy our every need and renew
   our spirit like the eagle's."
   Psalm 103

Nan Merrill, *Psalms for Praying*, p. 210.

[4]Valerie V. Hunt, *Infinite Mind, Science of the Human Vibrations of Consciousness*, p. 66.

Our bodies are made up of such intricate frequencies, we are truly a marvel created by God! In your meditation, try using your breath to bring yourself into harmonic resonance. What are you aware of in your body, your mind and in your spirit?

If healing occurs through changes in the electromagnetic field as the scientists now believe, how can we recognize it when it occurs?

The Healing Process

Healing is the activation of the body's energies toward a dynamic state of equilibrium and balance. We are constantly healing in life towards this state of harmonic health. This whole process is life long and reminds me of how divine we really are as God's creation. Just as health is observed as a dynamic energy field that is flowing, coherent and strong, illness and disease manifest as weak, incoherent disturbances in the field that must be reversed before healing can take place.

All things have a natural or resonant frequency meaning they possess their own vibrational signature that is carried in the structure of their fields. A field's frequency pattern at any given time is a resonating structure that determines the energy it will absorb or be affected by. Dr. Valerie Hunt found that interaction between fields occurs when there are generally compatible harmonic frequencies.[4] The healer's role then is to provide a stimulus and sufficient energy for the person's spiritual being to heal if it chooses. And Oschman states, no matter which healing technique we might employ, there are intricate energetic interactions occurring between individuals even if there is no physical contact. This is true whether we use prayer at a distance, or use hands-on healing, essential oils or any number of other healing remedies including homeopathy, flower essences or magnet therapy. When this electromagnetic interaction occurs, 'resonance' is present. The field of the one receiving the healing will change and often match that of the healer. Both Hunt and Oschmann have observed this phenomenon in their study of healers. Oschmann calls this therapeutic entrainment.[5]

Our work in healing is to find those combinations that enable the person to move towards a state of harmony and balance—to one of harmonic resonance.[6] When disease and illness are present, they may manifest as chemical imbalances but underlying this is an electromagnetic imbalance that has altered the molecules, cells, tissues and organs. Healing means providing the correct or healthy frequency to bring the cells back to a state of coherence, to a state of equilibrium. The healer does this through their intent to present a positive, enlightened presence. They draw upon the Divine Presence, filling their whole being with Light. Their own fields thus become strong, vibrant, coherent and radiant. The healer provides a model of vibrant life, which encourages the ill field to change and become healthy.

The Subtle Energy of Essential Oils

Plants transform the sun's energy through photosynthesis into food energy that humans and animals thrive upon. The essential oils within the plants are a concentrated form of this energy. When we eat plants and herbs that are healthy for us we take in their concentrated energy and, like the plants, we grow and flourish. The energy of each plant carries its own unique vibration or electromagnetic frequency that keeps it in harmony with nature. So when we eat these plants and herbs we take in their energy (vibration) and it affects our own vibratory level. And, we don't even have to consume plants in order to be affected by their subtle energy. Have you ever noticed that just being near certain plants is enough to change your outlook or emotions? Buying flowers at the market, or walking in a rose garden, or through a field of poppies or sunflowers can lighten our spirits as we come into harmony with the energy of the plants. A pine grove, an arboretum, a park, or your own backyard flower garden or flowerbox can even spark memories of times when plants have

[5]James Oschman, *Energy Medicine, the Scientific Basis*, pp. 107-109.

[6]Coming into "Harmonic resonance" is defined as when the applied frequency and the host frequency reach certain relationships relative to each other, the host amplitude can increase dramatically.

"From the depths of our soul
    You call us to love,
    To grow toward harmony
        And wholeness." Psalm 76

Nan Merrill, *Psalms for Praying*, p. 153.

When we raise a person's vibration it results in restoring health to the body, clarity to the mind and attunement to the spirit.

lifted your spirits and put you in another place. The energy of the plants has succeeded in affecting your energy biofield—your aura and energy centers (chakras), and brought you into harmony within yourself and with your environment. This is the effect of the subtle energy within plants. The frequency of the oil was a good match for your physical, emotional, and spiritual needs.

Bruce Tainio of Tainio Technology in Cheny, Washington, developed equipment to measure the bio-frequency of humans and foods. The body was found to have a normal vibrational range (electrical frequency) between 62 and 68 megahertz (MHz). When an individual's frequency is within that range, they are said to be in a state of health. Energy disturbances in the field will actually precede the appearance of disease and illness in the body. Tanio's research showed that when the human frequency range drops below the norm of 62 MHz, abnormal processes have the opportunity to develop. Below 58 MHz, cold and flu symptoms can develop. *Candida* species (yeast microbes) develop when the body's frequency is around 55 MHz and Epstein Barr syndromes at 52 MHz. Cancers develop when the body's frequency falls to around 42 MHz.[7] Much more research needs to be done in this exciting area of study but it does open up the possibility of healing with vibrational medicines and/or treatments. The important point to draw from Tanio's work is that there is a measured decrease in the electromagnetic frequency during states of illness and an increase during states of wellness and balance.

One of the best ways Gerber tells us that we can change dysfunctional patterns in our energy bodies is to administer therapeutic doses of what he calls "frequency-specific subtle energy in the form of vibrational medicines."[8] This aids the body to resonate in the needed mode in order to return to a state of health or wellness. Oschman calls this "energetic pharmacology" and is referring to natural substances from the plant kingdom to distinguish it from chemical pharmacology.[9]

[7]Connie and Alan Higley, *Reference Guide for Essential Oils*, p.4.

[8]Richard Gerber, *Vibrational Medicine*, p. 85.

[9]James Oschman, *Energy Medicine, the Scientific Basis*, p. 139.

Have you ever felt "out of sorts" or "just not yourself" and later devel-oped a cold or the flu or maybe a headache? Could it be that your "frequency" or vibration had shifted and the cold, flu or headache was just the manifesta-tion of that shift?

Each essential oil has its own unique frequency. They range from 52 to 320 megahertz, the frequency of rose oil. By applying an essential oil with a particular frequency to the human body, the oil's higher frequency will raise the vibratory quality of that individual. When several oils are blended together, each having a different MHz frequency, a frequency will emerge that may be higher or lower than the various components. Thus, the plant's therapeutic properties create special vibrational remedies capable of healing or rebalancing the body/mind/spirit. Dr. Terry Friedmann MD, a holistic physician and past president of the American Holistic Medical Association tells us that when we raise a person's vibration it results in 'restor-ing health to the body, clarity to the mind and attunement to the spirit."[10] This is the "coming into resonance" needed for healing and it is exactly our same goal in prayer and in hands-on healing work. The more we are able to create resonance with another person—the more we will be able to facilitate healing into wholeness.

[10] Terry Shepherd Friedmann, *Freedom Through Health*, p. 62.

There is a theory that it is the vibration of a particular aroma molecule that actually gives it its smell. Dr. Luca Turin at the University College in London has been working on the vibration rate of aromatic oils, which is a feature of their chemistry. He believes that the smell of an essential oil is due to its vibration and not to its mo-lecular shape which until recently was the explanation for the smell mechanism (the shape of the aroma molecule "locks" into an olfac-tory receptor, which sends a message to the brain).[11] According to Turin, it will take many years to build up a database of the frequen-cies of essential oils.

[11] Valerie Ann Worwood, *The Fragrant Heavens*, p. 130.

The more we are able to create resonance with another person—the more we are able to facilitate healing into wholeness.

This could help us understand why certain aromas are pleasing to us one time and not another. It could be that the frequency of the oil is either not the same (the oil is of a lesser quality) or we are not resonating with the oil at that present moment due to our own lowered frequency level. In other words, this oil may not be what my body/mind/spirit needs in order to come into balance at this moment in time.

Just as many things can affect our field's vibratory quality, the subtle energy of the essential oils can also be affected by how the plant was grown, and the oil distilled, packaged and distributed. It is most important to know the integrity of the company that is distributing the essential oils. Do you trust that the oils are pure and not cut with solvents, and other extenders? Are the company's motives clear or are they muddied with a desire for money? Do their marketing tactics put down the competition in an effort to promote their own products? If a company can only get your business by decrying the competition, what does it say about their ethics? These vibrations can actually affect the subtle quality of the oils. In addition, the oil's frequency can be affected by who is handling the oil. If the person holding the oil is harboring negative thoughts, this could affect the frequency of the oil as well. This means the subtle energy of the oil can be affected by one's intentionality. If my intention is positive to clear someone's energy field, the oil I select will assist in the clearing. But what if I don't have an oil known for clearing congestion from the field? Will other oils work? Strangely, the answer is yes. I can with intention clear a person's field with whatever oil I have. That is the power of the energy of intention. We need to remember that when we work with essential oils, our intention can be a powerful influence on the healing qualities of the oils upon the subtle energy field.

The frequency rates for essential oils may be the most important factor in using oils with hands-on healing.

The frequency rates for essential oils may be the most important factor in using oils with hands-on healing. When working with the energy field and the energy centers, our goal is to bring the subtle energy body into balance. What does the client need at this juncture in his/her healing process? Is it harmony and balance, clarity, relief of pain, integration, energy, relaxation, restfulness or sleep, spiritual/inner awareness, emotional release, peacefulness/ calmness, strength, connection to God or sense of Higher Self? Choosing the right essential oil and the right hands-on treatments that will help facilitate achieving your mutual goals with your client is important. Equally important is the power of intention and the ability to listen to one's spiritual guidance.

Surprisingly, this is not new information about frequencies and healing. Our ancestors may have had these insights thousands of years ago. Have you noticed that modern holistic practitioners are now "discovering" this ancient knowledge? There is hope!

Essential Oils and Prayer

The measured frequencies of essential oils can be affected by our thoughts and by our prayers. Bruce Tainio in his experiments found that negative thoughts lower the frequencies of the oils by as much as 12 MHz and that positive thoughts raise them by 10 MHz. Prayer raises the vibration even higher by 15 MHz.[12] Many have had these insights about intentions and prayer and realized that prayers can change energy and enhance the effectiveness of healing work. Dr. David Stewart even emphasizes that essential oils magnify intent.[13] The oils will respond to your thoughts, he says, and go where you have directed their healing vibrations. This is all the more reason why we should bring ourselves to our healing work with a clean heart, filled with compassion and unconditional love.

Essential oils are also well suited for aiding meditation and prayer. The peoples of the world have used fragrances to promote feelings of closeness with God for thousands of years. Incense was used to bless sacrifices and to bless altars. The peoples of ancient Egypt, Arabia, Greece, Babylonia, and Asia may have used frankincense and myrrh. In India and China, it may have been cinnamon,

[12]Connie and Alan Higley, *Reference Guide for Essential Oils,* p. 4-5.

[13]David Stewart, *Healing Oils of the Bible,* p. 92.

"The Lord said to Moses: Take sweet spices, stacte, and onycha, and galbanum, sweet spices with pure frankincense and make an incense blended as by the perfumer, seasoned with salt, pure and holy; and you shall beat some of it into powder, and put part of it before the covenant in the tent of meeting where I shall meet with you; it shall be for you most holy. When you make incense according to this composition, you shall not make it for yourselves; it shall be regarded by you as holy to the Lord."
Exodus 30:34-36

"Let my prayer be counted as incense before you,
And the lifting up of my hands as an evening sacrifice." Psalm 141:2

"Another angel with a golden censer came and stood at the altar; he was given a great quantity of incense to offer with the prayers of all the saints on the golden altar that is before the throne. And the smoke of the incense, with the prayers of the saints, rose before God from the hand of the angel."
Rev. 8:3-4

aloes, and cassia. We know that the Jewish people used frankincense, stacte, onycha and galbanum to create a pure and holy incense. Native Americans traditionally have used sweetgrass and sage. Buddhists burn various kinds of incense from China and India during their prayers. As the holy smoke rises, the prayers of the nations are universally offered to the Creator, the Source of all that is.

Christians have been using the aromas of oils and incense since those very early days of the church. Mary set an example for us when she poured the fragrant spikenard over Jesus' head, allowing the oil to flow down his body and fill the room with its aroma. As the early Christians told this story over and over to one another, spikenard became a sacred fragrance that could put them in touch with memories of Jesus. The fragrance and the memory were connected and spikenard became a holy oil for them. The early church also carried on the traditions that were common in the Jewish world that used incense and the aromas of certain oils to come into the presence of the Divine. They carried on the pure and holy incense tradition given to Moses. Throughout our Christian history to this very day, incense, containing frankincense is used in many churches to honor the Divine and to bring those present into a spiritual place of connection to God.

In Catholic churches around the world, the priest or bishop on special occasions will incense the altar, the vessels, the Scriptures, then they will incense the other priests who are present and incense the people, going around the church and through all the aisles. A few years ago, I attended services at the Domo Cathedral of Milan, Italy on Pentecost, a high holy day of the church. There was so much smoke rising with the dozen or so swinging incensors that you could hardly see the high altar. In essence, what this did was to change not only the energy within the space of the church, but also the energy of those present. It cleared our subtle energy fields allowing for a greater spiritual connection with God. I remember sitting in that great Cathedral listening to the spoken word in Italian that I did not understand. But I felt lifted up to the heavens as I breathed in the familiar incense that since my childhood has been a reminder of all things holy.

Native Americans have a similar tradition. When going into a sweat lodge or going on a vision quest, the medicine man or leader will burn sage or sweetgrass and "smudge" not only the lodge but also the aura of the person as a cleansing and preparation for the spiritual work with the Great Spirit, the Creator. The sage and sweetgrass then, become a holy incense given to the people by the Great Spirit for healing.

Our Energetic (Vibrational) Self

We are more than physical bodies—we have higher spiritual (vibrational) bodies as well.

We are more than physical bodies—we have higher spiritual (vibrational) bodies as well. They are known by scientists as the "biofield" and collectively, they extend about an arm's length from the body in all directions. This energy field or auric field as it is also called, can be viewed as having several layers or "bodies" within it. For our purposes here, let us consider the energy field as having four layers.[14] The first is the **etheric field** that is a layer closest to the body and extends 2-4 inches out. It is considered a double of the physical body and provides a unique form of energetic information to the cells of the body that help to guide human growth and development. In other words, the field exists first and the body grows into it. Gerber calls it an "invisible scaffolding" upon which grows the new individual in the womb.[15] It is in the etheric field where pain and discomfort are experienced first then later reflected in the physical body as pain or discomfort. Most people if they try, can see this field as a soft glow around the body that is either pale gray or light blue in color.

The second layer is the **emotional field** and is the one where we most likely store our emotions.[16] This field is not as structured as the etheric field and may appear as soft clouds of color for those who can see colors around people. These can be multiple different colors

[14]Many writers refer to the auric field as having seven layers. As I am describing the field here, the fourth layer, the astral or spiritual layer encompasses 4 through 7.

[15]Richard Gerber, *Vibrational Medicine for the 21st Century,* p. 24.

[16]Scientists also speak of the emotional memory stored within our very cells. Each layer of the field is not just beyond the body, but also encompasses the body. That means the emotional body is not just in the space beyond the body but is also throughout the physical body and the cells as well.

depending on whether the person you are looking at is experiencing a heightened emotion. This field particularly reflects the lower emotions such as anger, sadness and desire. For instance, anger may produce the frequency of red and we then see red in the field, envy may look like a dirty green, depression or sadness may appear as a dull grayish-blue. All the different emotions we experience will exhibit the many colors and hues of the rainbow. The emotional layer extends further from the body then does the etheric layer and may be up to 8-20 inches out from the physical borders. If you see colors in the field, start noting whether those colors are related to the emotions the person before you is exhibiting.

The third layer of the field is referred to as the **mental field** and vibrates faster than the etheric and emotional layers. The energy of this field is involved in thought, creativity, invention and inspiration. It presents as a bright lemon yellow around people who are thinking or abstracting, using their logic, concentrating or studying or speaking. It appears as a halo 12-24 inches out from the body and will mostly be around the head but could also be seen around the whole body. Since so many of us "live in our heads," those who have the ability to see fields tell us that our America culture tends to produce a lot of yellow. Like the other two fields discussed, the mental field is invisibly connected to the physical body. This suggests that certain mental problems may actually have their origin at this higher energy level.

The fourth layer, sometimes called the **spiritual body,** is composed of even higher spiritual layers. Many have identified this high spiritual part of us, as where the soul resides. This is the level at which our "higher self" operates. Each of us has a wise inner knowing that always knows what is going on in our life even if we are not conscious of it. This higher self sees the big picture and often communicates to our conscious self through dreams. The spiritual body could be multiple colors as well but may have a predominance of rose or violet or appear as a soft white glow up to three feet from the body. The higher emotions like compassion may show up as a

"Yes, You are the Light of my life;
You shine through my darkness.
Yes, with You I can do all things;
And my spirit soars like an eagle.
Your ways lead to wholeness, O Loving
    Presence;
Your Word in me is life,
How tenderly You live in my Heart!"
Psalm 18

Nan Merrill, *Psalms for Praying*, p. 28.

soft pink in the field, elation may be a bright yellow, and joy may be many different vibrant colors or even a pure white. These layers may be visualized when the person you are viewing is in a spiritual place or who may be meditating.

Besides having an energy field, we also have energy centers which are whirling wheels of energy that emanate from an energy power current that lies somewhere along the spinal column. The ancient Sanskrit word for these energy centers is *chakras*. To individuals who are clairvoyant and see these energy centers, they appear as whirling wheels of color and light.

Besides having an energy field, we also have energy centers which are whirling wheels of energy.

The power current extends from the top of the head where the crown center exists to the base or root center found in the floor of the perineum. There are five more centers that emanate from this power current and whirl outward from the front of the body and from the back as well. Each of these seven centers provides energy for a part of the body and each are connected with hormonal glands that keep the body in perfect working order. The flow of subtle energy through these energy centers is strongly affected by our personalities and our emotions as well as our spiritual development.

The **root center** provides energy for the legs, kidneys, lower bowel and the adrenal glands. The emotional and spiritual issues are about being rooted and grounded in life; it is about one's basic life force that holds us here on this earth. It has to do with our survival and personal safety. This is a very slow vibrating center and for those who have the ability to see, its vibrational frequency produces the color of red, like that of the earth. The earth spinning in space creates a vibration-frequency that we connect to with every step we take upon it. Since the earth is the gift of God to each of us, we literally are connecting to God each time we put down our foot.

The **sacral center** is found in the lower belly and governs the genital system, bowel and the lower back. This energy is about relationships with people, money and things. It is known as our emotional center and our center of creativity. The energy here keeps us in communion-relationship with God and others and helps us to express the divine creativity in our lives. This center has a slightly higher vibration on the color scale producing orange.

The next center is the **solar plexus** found over the stomach area. It supplies energy for the stomach, liver, gallbladder, spleen, pancreas, upper intestines and the middle of the back. The emotional and spiritual issues are about personal power, ego and self-esteem. Issues are related to whether we feel "empowered" or "powerless" at home and at work. When we stand in our power, this center helps us to express our courage and fortitude in serving God. We have enough self-esteem to choose rightly as we walk humbly with our God. The frequency at this center produces yellow on the color spectrum.

The fourth center is at the center of our being and is very important since this is where the emotional and spiritual issues surrounding love and nurturance most strongly affect us. The amount of life-energy flowing through the **heart center** is influenced by our ability to feel love toward ourselves and others. This center produces the vibration observed as green but can sometimes appear as rose as we deepen our spiritual heart connection to God. How much we feel "lovable" can actually affect the flow of nurturing life energy to our heart and lungs. This center also supplies energy for the thymus gland important for the immune system, the shoulders, arms, breasts, the circulatory system in general, and the upper back. The heart is called the "transformer" in that it transforms the energy from the three lower (physical) centers and from the three higher (spiritual) energy centers. It does this at the heart level for our highest good.

The fifth center is at **the throat** area and spins to the vibration of sky blue. The energy here supplies the throat, neck, thyroid and parathyroid glands. The emotional and spiritual issues are about

"O Holy One, You see the
           intentions of my heart;
      As I surrender to your love,
           I grow in peace and gratitude.
For to lose my life is to find life;
      O keep me steadfast in love for You,
           Life of my Life! Psalm 18

Nan Merrill, *Psalms for Praying*, pp. 27-28.

self-expression and communication. It is about speaking one's truth and having the right will to express our concerns and opinions and creative ideas. When we swallow our truth and refuse to stand up for what we believe, this center becomes clogged and muddy and eventually will manifest as physical problems in the throat area.

The sixth center is **the brow** and is situated in the forehead, also called the third-eye area. It supplies energy for the eyes, ears, nose, the brain, and the pituitary gland (the master gland of the body.) The vibration is now very high and produces the color of deep indigo or the night sky color. This center is about intuition (inner knowing or inner seeing), wisdom and vision. The clear vision of this center helps us to see where we are headed and what we are doing with our lives. It is also about clarity of thought and how well we are able to express our thinking. As we make it a habit of connecting to Spirit on our spiritual journey, this center becomes stronger and more vibrant in color.

The uppermost center is the **crown center** at the top of the head. Its spin is so fast that it produces the color of violet white on the color spectrum. The energy at this center supplies the brain and the pineal gland and provides energy for the skeletal, muscular and skin systems. This is our highest center of connection to God so it is about our spirituality and spiritual path in life. Here resides our sense of purpose and meaning in life. Many do not come to explore the issues at the seventh energy center until their later years or when they are facing a life-threatening illness.

Do you see colors around people or perhaps even see these energy centers? Many people do see auras as pale light emanating from around the body like steam rising from a hot pavement. I have only run across two people in all my teaching who actually see energy centers. They describe it as a gift they didn't ask for but simply have.

From a vibrational perspective, these seven centers are more than regulators of physiological functioning in the body's endocrine glands. They are considered emotional and spiritual energy processors.

With a little practice, most people can see at least the first layer of the field. Try taking your eyes slightly out of focus as you look for auras. A dim room is helpful since auras are not visible in bright light.

From a vibrational perspective, these seven centers are more than regulators of physiological functioning in the body's endocrine glands. They are considered emotional and spiritual energy processors. Each center processes different emotional events and traumas throughout our lifetime. We even tend to store specific emotional memories in these centers. This may explain why certain emotions affect one part of the body more than others. When we have a chronic problem associated with a particular energy center there may be a block or constriction of the flow of this life-giving energy which can even result in physical dis-ease. One of the most important causes of blockage in the energy centers is chronic emotional stress and emotional energy imbalance. Just as toxins in our environment can cause physical illness, emotional traumas can poison our bodies and our spirits. Chronic anger, bitterness, hopelessness, loneliness, depression and hatred may lead to physical and emotional illnesses because these negative emotions create imbalances in the energy centers and cut off the flow of life-giving energy.

Often, we are not consciously aware of the emotional or spiritual issues since they lay buried in our fields or even in our bodies. Vibrationally, if the emotion or spiritual issue gets released, the physical manifestation of that problem will also be resolved and the person will move back to a place of wholeness. In the Christian tradition, we have referred to this type of healing as receiving the grace of God. Indeed, the energy centers are like "graced places" within our being where we receive (or block) God's grace or gifts to us. As we let go of our emotional and spiritual pain that is blocking our communion with God, we are healed.

Learning to Assess the Energy Field

With this brief understanding of our energy (vibrational) self, we can use our hands to scan someone's field to see if the energy is open and balanced or whether there are any blocks or uneven places in the biofield. Basically, we are looking for any differences as we run our palms above the body. Beginning above the head, slowly bring your hands through the field about 2 inches away from the body. Scan the entire field, paying particular attention to the area over each of the energy centers. It is best to always keep your hands moving in order to assess for subtle differences. At first, you may only pick up temperature differences—heat or cold in some places. With practice, you will begin to pick up more subtle changes in the field like density, pain, blocks, magnetic pulls and protective energy. Where do you feel these differences? Do they correspond with the client's description or with their physical problems? If you pick up a difference like heat over a joint, it could be from a recent problem or an old one that manifests in times of stress or fatigue. The person may not have mentioned anything about that joint because it didn't seem all that important at the time. Our inquiry may jog their memory or we may get a blank stare. Getting confirmation one way or another is helpful in knowing how to proceed next.

One helpful tool I have found in my assessment is to use a pendulum that is any small object that will hang on the end of a string.[17] There is nothing magical about using a pendulum. It works very similarly to muscle testing.[18] The swing of the pendulum is affected by the energy currents and will give a visual demonstration of the energy flow of the chakras. With enough practice, you will be able to pick up the natural spin of the energy over these energy centers. When the centers are open and flowing the pendulum will swing clockwise and be about the same size in diameter for each energy center. When the energy is misaligned or perhaps even standing still the pendulum will go in other directions or not move at all. Eventually, with practice, you will be able to feel the energy with your palm

[17]Using a pendulum to assess the energy centers is quite easy. You do not have to have a "special" pendulum, even a small weight on the end of a string will do. The length of the string needs to be about 6 inches. Hold the string so that the pendulum weight is about 3 inches from the body over each energy center. The energy from the person's chakra will be reflected in the swing of the pendulum. Try to clear your mind so that it won't interfere with the natural swing produced by the energy centers. With practice, this will become easy.

[18]You can use muscle testing to determine which essential oil is helpful for this person at this time. Muscle testing is from applied kinesiology. You can test the muscle strength of the person's arm when a single food, herb, medication or essential oil is placed either in their field or in their hand. If their arm resists your downward pressure, the field interaction is positive and the substance is not harmful to the person. If the muscles become weakened and the arm cannot resist pressure, the field interaction is poor and the substance should be avoided.

without using a pendulum. With this added information, you can make further inquiries to the client, looking not only for physical problems in the present and past, but also about emotions, relationships, worries, or troubling memories. If you have a counseling background you will find this to be a natural area of inquiry. If not, our role is not to pry into someone's present or past but simply to be a healing presence in the moment.

"Arise, O Divine Love!
    Confront all within me
    That is not whole!

Deliver me from deadly Fears and doubts,
    Shine your Light into My darkness.
May my heart receive the Bounty of your
    Love." Psalm 17

Nan Merrill, *Psalms for Praying*, pp. 24-25.

Now, with all your gathered information, listen inside for spiritual guidance asking for direction and clarity in this present healing moment. The client has given you clues in their descriptions of what they see as their problems; and, their field and energy centers have given you additional clues on what is not in balance energetically. Ask the Holy Spirit to intuitively direct you in knowing what hands-on therapies and/or essential oils will be most helpful in this person's healing process. God is the healer, yet we as a healing presence must be knowledgeable and useful as God's instrument of healing. We first need a wealth of information stored in our psyche from which that inspirational knowledge can evolve.

Assessment skills like hand scanning and using a pendulum or muscle testing take practice. Begin with yourself and with family and friends and take some time to practice. Before you know it, your skill will start to develop and you will be amazed at the ease with which you can approach hands-on healing. Remember, if this work is valuable to you, it will take skill.

Using Essential Oils To Clear the Energy Field

Different plant substances like essential oils and flower essences can help people achieve emotional equilibrium by rebalancing the subtle life-energy patterns of the field and the energy centers. Perhaps someday in the future, it will be common for physicians and psychologists to use essential oils, homeopathy and flower essences as vibrational remedies to rebalance the emotional and spiritual patterns that contribute to physical and mental illnesses. Many of the lay public are not waiting for western health practitioners to incorporate these energetic remedies. They are educating themselves and using natural remedies from the earth to balance their own energies.

To begin working with a client, I like to set the "Sacred Space" first. There are a number of oils and blends of oils that are helpful in setting the sacred space for healing. Lavender, cedarwood, hyssop or juniper are wonderful single oils that can be misted or diffused in the room to clear the energy. Pine, rosemary and lemon are also good as general cleansers. To bring in positive energy to the healing space, you can use bergamot and orange to promote joy and optimism; lavender will promote calmness and balance; cedarwood will strengthen the connection with the Divine; and rose will promote love and compassion. To set up an energy boundary to protect the healing space from negativity, you can use fennel, rosemary, juniper, or lemon. There is a wonderful blend of oils that I have found to protect the healing space called *White Angelica*™. It is an oil of protection that clears the field and prepares it for deeper work. It strengthens the field as well as expands it creating a feeling of wholeness. When I sense negative energy, *White Angelica*™ tends to neutralize it. I will often use this oil on myself to strengthen and protect my own field as I begin my work with others.

You can also experiment with blending some of the single oils.[19] Add no more than 10-15 drops of the oils in 4 oz. of spring water in a misting bottle. You can mist the room, your hands as well as the client. Make sure you have a sheet covering the client so that the oil does not stain their clothing. Some oils like cedarwood or blends that have an almond or olive oil base will leave a residue.

Next, I ask for guidance on whether I need to use an essential oil for anointing. Again, I can use my pendulum, holding it over the various bottles of oils I have and simply asking if this person needs a particular oil in the way of anointing. I have learned that when the pendulum moves in a clockwise fashion for me, it is a positive indicator. If I get a yes on an oil, I like to look it up in my references before

---

"The Beloved dwells in the holy Temple,
   The sacred place within our hearts,
   Loving and testing each one of us.
Divine Love offers both the the good and
   the unloving opportunities to grow, to
   become whole,
   enduring with Love those who choose the
   way of darkness." Psalm 11

Nan Merrill, *Psalms for Praying*, p. 16.

[19]Please see chapter 9 for a further discussion on blending essential oils.

"You prepare a table before me
   in the presence of all my fears;
   you bless me with oil, my cup overflows.
Surely goodness and mercy will follow me
   all the days of my life;
and I shall dwell in the heart of the Beloved
   Forever." Psalm 23

Nan Merrill, *Psalms for Praying*, p. 40.

I place a drop in my palm and then anoint the brow of the client. In this work, I am constantly learning about the power of the oils to work. Essential oils can affect the state of mind for both client and practitioner. For example, frankincense can slow and deepen the breath, and create a sense of calm. Sandalwood can promote inner unity with mind, body, and spirit. Lemon can uplift and clarify the mind. The varied effects of many of the oils are described in later chapters.

As I begin my hands-on work, I like to use the blend *Valor*™ to balance the electrical energies in the body and enhance physical strength. Using it on the soles of the client's feet is a nice way of "resetting someone's internal clock" as I begin my work with their physical body. This particular oil blend is a wonderful choice when the person I am working with is trapped in fear or conflict. When I find physical pain manifesting in the etheric field over some particular area like an ankle or wrist, I first need to relieve that discomfort before I do anything else. I may use *PanAway*™ directly on the part of the body that hurts. This blend was particularly formulated to help heal injuries where ligaments are inflamed.

For the emotional body, I love the blend known as *Joy*™. This oil includes rose oil, the oil that has the highest known frequency. I use it for emotional traumas and painful memories and heartaches. *Joy*™ is a wonderful blend of ancient and modern oils giving a beautiful fragrance that has been known to lift spirits and decrease depression, anxiety and grief in many.[20] Sandalwood is a single oil that helps when the person is overly emotional or trapped in dependency issues or has faith concerns. Simply placing this oil on the palms of my hands as I run them through the field to clear it will assist in bringing an awareness to deal with these issues. *Harmony*™ is another blend that contains sixteen essential oils, one of which is frankincense. This oil is specifically blended for balancing the energy centers of the body. I find that it also balances and opens the energy field as well. *Harmony*™ is particularly helpful when someone feels trapped in their situation or feels ignored in life.

"Let all the fragmented parts of my being gather around You, help me to face them one by one.
Love's healing presence will mend all that has been broken, and I shall be made whole." Psalm 7

Nan Merrill, *Psalms for Praying*, p. 9.

[20]Carolyn L. Mein, DC, *Releasing Emotional Patterns with Essential Oils*, p. 29.

For the mental body, *Clarity*™ and *Peace and Calming*™ are two blends that help with mental clarity and when the brain is overactive. *Clarity*™ helps to dispel feelings of repression and guilt and *Peace and Calming*™ helps relieve indecisiveness, moodiness and the fear of being a victim. Peppermint is a great single oil to relieve fears of dependence and failure and lavender oil is helpful for feelings of abandonment. A very inexpensive oil, lemon, relieves feelings of sadness and frustration. With all of these oils except the peppermint, I might anoint the brow and the temples as well as use the oils on my palms as I clear the entire field. Peppermint is too strong to use around the face but can be used on the back of the neck and placed in the palms of your hands and the vapors breathed.

For the spiritual body, frankincense and rose oils are high spiritual oils that lift and elevate the mind, increasing spiritual focus. One additional blend for the spiritual body that I recommend is called *Mystical Rose.* This oil was specially blended for the healer Ron Roth to create a sacred space for healing. It contains pure essential oils of rose, sandalwood, amber, musk and patchouly in a base of olive, aloe vera and castor oils. It has a most beautiful fragrance that Roth associates with the fragrance of mystics when they are deeply connected to God in prayer. I use this oil especially for my clients who may be experiencing grief and deep heartaches.

When faced with a specific problem like sinus congestion, sore muscles, earaches, or more serious problems like migraine headaches, bronchitis, or even cancer or serious chronic diseases, don't be afraid to stop and look up the specific oils recommended for these problems. This is a wonderful way to educate yourself and when the field does change and the problem either resolves itself or shifts significantly, you will remember the next time a similar situation presents itself, which oil(s) you used with success.

As we let go of our emotional and spiritual pain that is blocking our communion with God, we are healed.

Healing Fragrances

There is no doubt—fragrances can be healing. They can bring back pleasant as well as unpleasant memories. In either case, those memories and emotions can be healed. Fragrances can bring us into a higher place where we can heal our spiritual brokenness and be at peace with God. What sets us apart as human beings are our emotions. These God-given fragrances can help bring clarity and balance to our emotional selves.

Finding the right fragrance is really not all that hard. Begin with the oils that you have. As you inhale their aroma, see where it takes you. What emotions rise up into your awareness? Are they pleasant or unpleasant? Do particular memories come up? Are they joyful or sad? Where in your body do you feel the emotion? At your brow (head), in your chest (heart) or at the pit of your stomach (gut)?

Many essential oils have a particular affinity with specific energy centers. They may support and promote a healthy vibrational pattern for those energy centers. In this way, they work in concert with the hands-on healing techniques to bring balance and harmony to that area. To do this, I may mist the area above the energy center or place the oil directly on the palms of my hands and hold them in the space above the energy center or I may even anoint the body at the specific energy center. For heart, solar plexus and sacral centers, I place the oil in the hand of the client and ask them to place it on their own body. One thing I have learned is that the fragrance of the oil needs to be a pleasant one for the client. Allow them to smell the oil before you place it on the body or run it through the field. Some oils may not be pleasant for a particular client and they will experience a negative reaction. Simply choose another oil.

Here are some individual oils and oil blends that I have found helpful in opening and balancing the energy centers, our emotional processors. For the—

Crown Center: Rose, frankincense, myrrh, and *Mystical Rose*™ help strengthen spirituality and promote a sense of spiritual connection; angelica connects us with angelic guidance; cedarwood and galbanum strengthen a connection to the Divine; lavender helps integrate spirituality into everyday life; rosemary helps us to remember our spiritual path and dedication; sandalwood promotes deep meditation; spikenard increases love for God; and thyme restores spiritual fortitude.

Brow Center: Rosemary and peppermint for mental alertness; juniper, lemon, pine, aloes/sandalwood for tranquil and calming effects; calamus blended with frankincense quiets and clarifies the mind; *Clarity*™ and *Peace and Calming*™ for clarity of thought; cedarwood for release of stress and to clear and strengthen the mind; myrrh for inner stillness and peace; sandalwood to help calm mental chatter; and *Mystical Rose* for spiritual path connection and for grief.

Throat Center: Chamomile helps express truth calmly and without anger; fennel promotes uninhibited communication; cypress, rosemary, basil, peppermint, cedarwood, myrtle and hyssop for clarity in self-expression; *Thieves*™, a blend that wards off infections; myrrh aids communication when there is lack of self-confidence; and frankincense for courage to speak one's truth.

Heart Center: Rose promotes love especially when the heart center is wounded with grief; bergamot opens the heart and allows love to radiate, also especially good for grief; melissa relieves emotional blocks from grief; geranium increases capacity to listen with the heart; lavender calms and stabilizes the emotions of the heart; spikenard promotes hope; pine and fir open the chest to receive love; frankincense connects the heart with spiritual realities; *White Angelica*™ for loneliness and disharmony, and *Mystical Rose*™ for heartache.

"Cleanse my heart in innocence
  that I might childlike be,
Singing songs of thanksgiving and
  proclaiming the Beloved's way."
Psalm 26

Nan Merrill, *Psalms for Praying*, p. 45.

Solar Plexus: Juniper protects against negative influences and restores confidence; cedarwood and pine strengthen self-confidence and will; chamomile encourages calm acceptance of limitations; rosemary protects from external influences and boosts self-confidence; hyssop encourages clarity in direction; *Harmony*™ opens and balances the center; fennel encourages confidence and assertiveness; and frankincense promotes courage and fortitude.

Sacral Center: Sandalwood helps connect sensuality with spirituality; cedarwood promotes emotional releases; cypress relieves inner turmoil; clary sage is emotionally uplifting; geranium nourishes feminine creativity; rose connects sexuality with the heart center; patchouly helps awaken creativity; *Di-Tone*™ is a blend helpful for opening the second center and calming the lower GI tract; and frankincense for its tranquilizing yet clarifying effects.

Root Center: Onycha *(Styrax benzoin)* helps ground and comfort; myrrh strengthens, energizes and supports; cedarwood connects with the earth; sandalwood promotes inner unity of body, mind and spirit; thyme acts as a tonic for exhaustion; myrtle to encourage feelings of forgiveness, acceptance and empowerment; hyssop to strengthen personal boundaries; cypress for cohesion and stability; frankincense to encourage feelings of centering, stability and protection; and *Valor*™ (placed on the soles of the feet) for strength and grounding.

Final Thoughts

Hands-on healing techniques and the oils are both facilitators of God's healing that takes place within the person's own energy being.

All living substances have a unique vibrational signature. As facilitators of vibrational healing, we have a responsibility to be knowledgeable in the art of prayer, hands-on energetic healing, and the vibrational frequencies of these powerful healing plants of the earth. Any of this work—prayer, hands-on and anointing with healing oils can stir up emotions trapped in the field. These emotions and feelings may have been stored for a very long time in both the field and in the body and may have played a part in the development of illness. Depression may be stored anger or sadness. There may be anxiety, stress, tension, fear, abuse, insecurity and feelings of being overwhelmed in life that impact a person's present time. These healing techniques may stir up, agitate or boost the subtle energy. Neither energy healing nor the essential oils directly change the energy field. What they do is stimulate the human energy field allowing it to reorganize and balance itself. The hands-on healing techniques and the oils are both facilitators of God's healing that takes place within the person's own energy being.

Choices. We have many choices about our own personal healing. We can choose to be absent in the decision-making, letting the medical community make those decisions for us, or we can be an active participant, choosing an integrative approach that includes prayer, hands-on (energetic) healing and healing substances like essential oils along with traditional western healthcare. Choices!

CHAPTER 5

USING OUR HANDS TO HEAL

Healing Touch Spiritual Ministry, like other forms of energetic healing, has its origin in the laying-on of hands that can be found in all spiritual paths. It is based on a philosophy of caring and compassion and is oriented towards service to humanity. It is healing not for its own sake but for the sake of others. In our Judeo-Christian path, there are many ways to use one's hands with the intention of healing that are based in the Scriptures and in Christian tradition.

The healing techniques described in this chapter are inspired from many of these Christian traditions. For the past two thousands years, we have, as the people of God, used rituals, symbols, objects, and practices at various stages of our history to assist us in making manifest God's healing in our lives. For our forebears they were a means of mediation with the Divine Mystery. In some cases it wasn't the official church but lay people who practiced these rituals, many of which simply flowed from our Jewish roots. The early Christians placed symbols like crosses on their tombs and on the walls of their house-churches and later on the catacomb walls. They continued the Jewish practice of blessing lights in the evening and eating sacred meals together. They used bread, wine, purifying waters, oil, and the laying-on of hands in their gatherings. These rituals were aimed at making visible, the divine mystery of God—where God touches our lives. Some of these rituals were aimed at restoring health and wholeness to both individuals and the community. The laying-on of hands and anointing with oil are examples of this great healing tradition.

As centuries passed, superstition crept into many of our Christian practices and uneducated priests often promoted practices that were far from the Church's sound traditions and far from the early Christian experience. The Reformation challenged these practices, and in an effort to reform the church, sometimes threw out the good along with the bad. Since then, most Christians have been suspect of rituals, symbols, objects and practices as any form of mediation with God. Yet, these practices, when grounded in the Scriptures or in sacred tradition, help us as a people to be in contact with the Divine in life.

In this chapter, we will explore some healing ways that are based on sound spiritual practices, paying particular attention to the flow of energy within our body/mind/spirit as we connect to the movement of Spirit in our lives. As you become more adept at bringing together prayer, hands-on healing and anointing, you will find that other Christian practices may speak to you in ways of healing. Be attentive to how the Holy Spirit leads you in this work. All of the techniques described come from my own healing practice. There may be similar variations of these techniques that you have come across in your work. This only serves to remind me of how the Holy Spirit works in diverse ways to inspire many in this healing work of ours.

Healing of the Heart

The scriptures themselves consider the heart the center of our being. There are hundreds of references in the Bible to the heart. It is through the heart that we communicate to God, both our brokenness and emotional turmoil, as well as our joy and ecstasy. It is through our hearts that God knows us better than we know our-

"Are any among you suffering? They should pray. Are any cheerful? They should sing songs of praise. Are any among you sick? They should call for the elders of the church and have them pray over them, anointing them with oil in the name of the Lord. The prayer of faith will save the sick, and the Lord will raise them up; and anyone who has committed sins will be forgiven. Therefore confess your sins to one another, and pray for one another, so that you may be healed." James 5:13-I

"'For the hearts of those who call to Me,
For those who cry out for wholeness,
I shall now make Myself known,'
    says the Beloved;
'I shall make Myself known in their hearts.'"
Psalm 12

Nan Merrill, *Psalms for Praying*, pp. 17-18.

[1]Doc Lew Childre, *Cut-Thru*, p. 70.

"Your ways lead to wholeness,
    O Loving Presence;
    your Word in me is life;
How tenderly You live in my
    heart!"
Psalm 18

Nan Merrill, *Psalms for Praying*, p. 28.

[2]Paul Pearsall, *The Heart's Code*, p. 4.

selves. The scriptures also tell us that the Spirit of God resides in our hearts. When we are not "centered" we say we are not coming from our hearts. Or when we are not fully committed to something, we say our heart is not in it.

The heart is more than a physical pump located in the chest; the heart is where we find our soul—the deepest part of us. As the fetus develops, the heart is there pumping before the brain and nervous system even starts to develop. It has its own rhythm and does not rely upon the brain to give it direction. The heart in fact generates electrical energy or heart waves as measured by electrocardiogram (ECG). The heart's electromagnetic field reaches to all the cells in the body and has even been measured several feet from the body.

The frequencies within this field change as our thoughts and emotions change with emotions causing the most immediate and measurable changes in the electrical system of the heart.[1]

The heart is naturally intuitive. The meaning of life is found in the deeper heart. We "speak from the heart," "know things in our hearts," "feel touched at our hearts," and "find it in our hearts to do good." There is a natural empathy that flows from the heart. It is at this center that emotional and spiritual issues surrounding beauty, love and nurturance are most strongly felt. Here we feel love within and around us; here we can find the kinder places within us. Paul Pearsall in his book, *The Heart's Code,* states that he has little doubt that the heart is a major energy center of the body and a conveyor of a code that represents the soul. His research suggests that the heart thinks, and cells remember.[2] The heart has an emotional intelligence. The more we are able to listen with our hearts, the more balanced and coherent our emotions become. It follows that the more balanced and coherent our emotions, the less likely we will experience sickness and disease.

The heart is also where we feel heartache and grief. "Our hearts can be broken," "our heartstrings pulled out," "our hearts ripped from our chest." The pain that I speak of is more than emotional, it can also manifests as physical and spiritual pain. Our pain can be as deep as the ocean; it can be filled with fear and despicable suffering. Our pain can even manifest as broken physical hearts in the way of heart disease, heart attacks and failed hearts.

What can we do to help heal hurting hearts in our world today? The soul of the Healing Touch program is heart work. As practitioners, we aim to have an open heart as we practice deep compassion, forgiveness, gentleness and acceptance in our healing work. We reach out and touch hurting hearts not with an expectation that the healing will look a certain way, but with trust that God will answer our prayer for healing. In scientific language, we energetically synchronize our hearts to the heart of another who is hurting. We extend the qualities of love that are nurturing, connecting and integrating. As we lift the hurting person to God in our prayer, hands-on healing and anointing, our healing work becomes sacred work. We enter into that divine work of being couriers for God's healing grace.

There are two healing techniques described here that may be helpful for those who have hurting hearts. There may be many variations of these methods, all of which have as their goal, the relief of suffering, the solace of grief and heartache, and the healing of brokenness.

"Relieve the blocks in my heart that keep
   me separated from You;
see all the darkness within me;
   fill it with your healing light.
Look at my pain and all my fears;
   They shut out love and Life."
Psalm 25

Nan Merrill, *Psalms for Praying*, p. 44.

Heart Balancing

The first healing technique to be described is called Heart Balancing. Energetically, this is a balancing of the energy of all the major energy centers to the heart. It serves to boost and equalize the energies flowing throughout the whole energy system. It is particu-

"May my heart be as your Heart;
May my mind be as your Mind—
As your steadfast love guide me,
As I live in faithfulness to You."
Psalm 26

Nan Merrill, *Psalms for Praying*, p. 45.

If essential oils are desired for this healing technique, first assess for the appropriate oil. Some suggestions include:

Rose, geranium, Harmony, Joy, or Mystical Rose to enhance feelings of love and harmony.

Geranium specifically helps the person reconnect to their feelings.

Harmony is ideal in opening and balancing all of the energy centers.

Spikenard calms the heart and gives a profound sense of peace.

Sandalwood has tranquil effects on troubled souls.

Myrrh is for deep tranquility and inner stillness.

Lavender calms and stabilizes both mind and heart and is helpful for abandonment issues.

Once you have determined which oils are appropriate, ask the Holy Spirit to direct you on how the oils are to be used-on the body, in the field or diffused in the room.

larly helpful for people suffering from heartache, grief and loss, and heart issues like abandonment, anger, unworthiness, and abuse.

To do energetic healing work, we must learn to heal from the heart, meaning we must connect to our Divine Source first. We are not acting alone in this work; neither do we claim the results. Acting as God's instruments, we pray for this person's greatest good and allow God to be God. It begins with the client lying comfortably on their back on a healing table or a raised bed. It can also be modified to accommodate someone sitting in a chair. Each position is held from 1 to 3 minutes depending on the flow of energy. It does not matter whether the practitioner stands on the right or on the left of the recipient for this healing technique. In the following description, suggestions are made for appropriate essential oils that can be used with this hands-on technique but others may be used as well.

> *Prayer*
> "*Create in me a clean heart, O Gracious One,*
> *And put a new and right spirit within me.*
> *Enfold me in the arms of love, and*
> *Fill me with your Holy Spirit.*
> *Restore in me the joy of your saving grace,*
> *and encourage me with a new Spirit.*"
> *Psalm 51*
> Nan Merrill, *Psalms For Praying*, p. 100.

Begin by centering and connecting to the divine presence and set your intention for the work. It is important for the healer to be in a place of unconditional love and compassion for the person before them. You will want to balance and open each energy center first. This can be done by holding one hand above and one below each energy center of the body. When balancing the energy at the root and crown centers you will only need to hold one hand above. Begin with the root then progress up through the centers—sacral, solar plexus, heart, throat, brow and crown. Hold each position for 3-5 minutes or however long it takes to feel a strong movement of energy in both of your hands.

Next, hold your upper hand on the heart center in the front of the body and your lower hand over the root. Hold this position for approximately 1-3 minutes. Keeping your upper hand on the heart, move your lower hand to the sacral center and then to the solar plexus, holding each place again for 1-3 minutes. Then move your lower hand underneath your upper hand and move your upper hand to the throat center, followed by the brow and the crown centers.

To finish, bring your upper hand back to the heart for a double hand boost to the heart and hold it as long as you feel guided.

Sacred Heart Blessing

Another healing technique that works at the heart level is called the Sacred Heart Blessing. In those first centuries of the Church, the early Christian Fathers reflected on the pierced body of Christ, pouring out both water and blood like flowing fountains. For them, the Church was born from the opened side of Jesus, and like the heart of Jesus, the Church pours out grace like a fountain. By the Middle Ages we had had over a thousand years of reflecting on the wounded heart of Jesus. Devotion had developed to the human Jesus and to his "Sacred Heart." Medieval art, hymns, prayers and treatises portray the suffering of the crucified Jesus and often his dying out of love for us. This honoring of the love of Jesus symbolized by his heart became a widespread popular tradition in the church first among the great religious orders of that day then by the laity as well. Many Christian mystics had visions and mystical experiences of the love of God's heart for humanity. Pictures of Jesus from that period represent the heart of Jesus with radiating light or fire surrounding it. In the 1600s, a French Visitation nun, Sister Margaret Mary Alacogque, had visions of the sacred heart of Jesus that eventually gave shape to the official devotional practices of the Sacred Heart in the Catholic Church. She, like many other women mystics of the earlier

"'Be still and know that I am Love.
  I am exalted among the nations,
  I am exalted in the earth!'
The One who knows all hearts is with us;
The Beloved is our refuge and our strength."
Psalm 46

Nan Merrill, *Psalms for Praying*, p. 91.

Middle Ages, experienced an exchange of hearts with Jesus. The reformation did not completely throw out a devotion to the heart of Jesus. On the contrary, many reformers insisted that the true meeting point between God and humankind was in the "heart," that is, in the will and affections. Notable was the influence of the music of Charles Wesley, one of the founders of Methodism. His prodigious body of hymns can still be heard sung by many denominations today. Listen to the words of one of Wesley's classics: "O for a Heart to Praise My God."

O for a heart to praise my God,
A heart from sin set free,
A heart that always feels thy blood
So freely shed for me.

A heart resigned, submissive, meek,
My great Redeemer's throne,
Where only Christ is heard to speak,
Where Jesus reigns alone.

Oh! For a lowly, contrite heart,
Believing true and clean;
Which neither life nor death can part
From him that dwells within.

A heart in everything renewed,
And full of love divine
Perfect and right, and pure, and good,
A copy, Lord of thine.

Thy gracious nature, Lord, impart;
Come quickly from above,
Write thy new name upon my heart,
Thy new best name of love![3]

[3]Quoted in *Sacred Heart, Gateway to God* by Wendy Wright, p. 67-68.

As with any ritual or tradition, there have been excesses in the devotion to the Sacred Heart. This image, however, can be helpful for us in our healing ministry as we envision an awareness of God's heart filled with love and compassion as revealed to us through the heart of Jesus Christ. Listen to the words of a more contemporary writer and mystic, Dag Hammarskjöld as he calls upon the heart of God.

> Give us
> A pure heart
> That we may see thee,
> A humble heart,
> That we may hear thee,
> A heart of love
> That we may serve thee,
> A heart of faith
> That we may live thee.[4]

[4]Dag Hammarskjöld, *Markings*, p. 214.

To have a heart inhabited by God's heart means we must love others—even those who are difficult to love. Spiritual writer Wendy Wright states that we must "practice an energetically engaged love that mucks in the messiness of things."[5] Loving others, even our enemies, is what the heart of God is all about. Love of neighbor, according to theologian Karl Rahner, is a contemporary form of Sacred Heart devotion. It is not pious sentimentality; it is gentle strength. The Gospel states that God's heart is gentle and humble. Jesus invited his hearers to take his yoke upon their shoulders. "Come to me . . . and learn from me; for I am gentle and humble in heart, and you will find rest for your souls" he says. Matt. 11:28-29. Gentleness wishes no harm to the other but wishes only good. This is not weakness; on the contrary, it takes great strength to extend this kind of love even to the most difficult in life. Pierre Teilhard de Chardin, a twentieth-century theologian and a scientist, reflected on the Sacred Heart as cosmic fire. In Christ's heart, love for God and love for the world are reconciled.

[5]Wendy Wright, *Sacred Heart, Gateway to God*, p. 79.

"O Loving Presence, I cherish
  your dwelling place, my heart;
  O, that I might radiate Love
    Divine;
Keep me always in your
    presence,
Ever-ready to praise your Name.
Make me holy, complete in You,
Write my name among the
    saints."
Psalm 26

Nan Merrill, *Psalms for Praying*, p. 45.

⁰Quoted in *Sacred Heart, Gateway to God* by Wendy Wright, p. 110.

The great secret, the great mystery,
is this: there is a heart of the world . . .
and this heart is the heart of Christ.
Pierre Teilhard de Chardin[6]

The tradition of the Sacred Heart devotion gives us rich and insightful dimensions of Christian spirituality and theology. This particular healing technique takes its inspiration from this honoring of the heart of God for us, the people of God. When we think about the radiating love of God's heart, we cannot help but praise and give thanks for God's love in our lives. The Sacred Heart Blessing is useful particularly when the recipient is suffering from grief, heartache, loss of a loved one, or is having trouble staying in their heart center or connecting their head and heart. Although the steps in this technique appear simple, it can have profound effects and is considered an advanced healing technique. As you progress in your development as a facilitator of healing for others, you will begin to see the depth of this simple healing. Try to visualize the radiating love that comes from the Heart of God as you place your hands on the person before you. The key is being in resonance with the loving compassionate heart of God. It is done with the recipient lying on their back on the massage table or a raised bed.

"The Beloved is gracious to us
   and blesses us;
the Radiant One shines upon us.
O, that Love's Way be followed
   in all the earth,
Love's saving power among all the nations."
Psalm 67

Nan Merrill, *Psalms for Praying*, p. 128.

Scripture
"Blessed are the pure in heart,
For they shall see God."
Matt. 5:8

Prayer
Loving heart of God, bless this healing work.
Radiate the light of your love
upon this person and
Mend their every broken place.

Begin by sitting in a chair at the head of the table for this technique. Center and connect with the Spirit, setting your intention for the work. Now place your left hand on the recipient's heart center. As you do this, your left arm will extend down the side of the head. With your right hand, place your palm on the right side of the recipient's head. Your fingertips will extend down over the ears. Then gently move the head, pressing it against your left arm. You will be holding this position for approximately 5-10 minutes.

Now you are ready to begin this Sacred Heart Blessing. Focus your attention on your own heart center and with the aid of the Holy Spirit go to a place of unconditional love in your own heart for this person whom you are holding in your arms. Connect with the Sacred Heart of Jesus, remembering the great love that he holds for each of us. Your prayer is one of blessing this person with wholeness, balance and harmony. See the person receiving whatever healing they need in this moment. See their brokenness mended with the oil of gladness, the oil of joy.

As you continue to hold your hands in this position, if it seems appropriate, you can pray aloud: "The living love of Jesus now fills you. This warm light fills, calms and heals your heart and mind. Be at peace."

With this healing technique, you may notice how the energy balances between the brain and the heart. Emotional releases may occur and there may be tears. Reassure the recipient and simply be a compassionate listening companion. This is not an opportunity to fix anyone or give advice. Simply be a healing presence as Christ would be.

If essential oils are desired for this healing work, first assess which oil is appropriate. Some suggestions include:

Rose, Joy, geranium, myrrh, or Mystical Rose can be used for issues around grief and loss.

Bergamot, lavender, frank-incense, or cedarwood for calmness, depression, and stress related conditions.

Sandalwood is particularly known for its tranquil and calming effects on troubled souls.

Cypress is helpful for times of inner turmoil and transition.

Galbanum mixed with frankincense is helpful for a sense of surrendering to God.

Hyssop is helpful for melancholy and pessimism.

Basil is known to open the heart and bring harmony to the mind.

For this technique you may wish to anoint the client's brow and the heart before beginning. Simply put a drop of oil in the client's palm and ask them to place it on their own heart. Or, you may simply have the oil on your own palms as you rest your hands on their body.

Sign of the Cross Blessing

The Sign of the Cross came into use as a religious gesture of blessing during the Middle Ages. However, its use can be dated all the way back to the second century. Christians would trace with one finger, a cross on the forehead, mouth and breast. This simple gesture was introduced into the Christian liturgy during the 4th century with the tracing of the cross on the forehead of candidates for baptism. It was also used as a gesture of blessing over the bread and wine used in the communion services. By the Middle Ages, the sign of the cross was made with the hand, touching first the forehead, then the breast, left shoulder, and finally the right shoulder. Words were said during this gesture: "In the name of the Father, and of the Son, and of the Holy Spirit. Amen." In some Eastern Orthodox Christian traditions, the Sign of the Cross also included touching the abdomen and touching the earth. After the Reformation this blessing gesture fell into disuse by many Christians.

Energetically, let us look at the flow of energy with this simple gesture. This is a blessing and an opening for the upper spiritual energy centers. The brow, throat (lips) and heart energy centers are touched energetically in this gesture, opening these centers to God's blessing and healing presence. The "Sign of the Cross Blessing" technique is derived from this gesture of blessing in faith. We will call upon God's healing presence to open and balance all the energy centers in the body. In the Eastern tradition, if you want to add in touching the abdomen and the root or soles of the feet, that could be another variation.

Besides being profoundly relaxing and calming, this healing blessing may serve to reawaken the person to the joys of life. As it balances and opens the field, it will lighten and alleviate fears making it easier for the person to come to a place of surrender to the will of God in their life. Since this healing technique can be so profoundly relaxing, it can assist in pain reduction. Allow the person

"I offered my fears up to the Beloved,
   and Love heard my cry;
I sought the One who ever listens;
   Once again, I knew Love's Presence.
Yes, You, O beloved, bring
   my fears to the fore,
   exposing them to the Light;
I abandon myself into your hands,
Into your Heart I commend my soul,
   in You will I trust."
Psalm 55

Nan Merrill, *Psalms for Praying*, pp. 107-108.

to rest without disturbing them after you complete this blessing. It may be helpful once they start to move around, to ground them by holding their feet.

There can be many variations of this Sign of the Cross Blessing. Allow the Spirit to guide you in your prayer as you gently bless the person before you.

If essential oils are desired for this healing technique, first assess for the appropriate oil. Some suggestions include:

Spikenard, sandalwood, cedarwood, myrrh, or Peace & Calming can be used for deep calmness.

Scripture
"I pray that according to the riches of his glory,
he may grant that you may be strengthened
in your inner being with power through his Spirit,
and that Christ may dwell in your hearts through faith,
as you are being rooted and grounded in love."
Eph 3:16-17

Angelica or hyssop for protection from evil spirits.

Frankincense, or Mystical Rose to increase spiritual awareness of one's path in life.

Lemon or bergamot can be used to lighten and calm the field, lifting sadness and enabling a sense of letting go.

Pine to relieve melancholy and pessimism and reawaken the person to the joys of life.

Begin by standing on the right side of the table. Center and connect to the Holy Spirit and set your intention for the work. Starting at the crown of the head, pass your right hand slowly and gently down through the center of the body passing over all of the energy centers from the crown to beyond the root. Your hand will be approximately 4-6 inches above the body. Then, pass your hand horizontally from the recipient's right to left, passing over the crown center. This acts as a blessing as you spread the energy from the crown center across the field.

Next, pass your hand again vertically down through the center of the body, passing over all the centers. You will follow this by passing your hand horizontally from the recipient's right to left over the brow center. Repeat these two movements (vertical and horizontal) for the throat and heart centers.

Repeat this series of gestures for two more rounds. You may end this technique by placing one hand on the recipient's heart and one hand on their brow. Optional steps include the vertical and horizontal movements of your hand for the solar plexus, sacral and root centers before returning to the crown.

Try blessing the person with each passing of your hand through the field, remembering the spiritual meaning of the crown, brow, throat and heart.

The Light of Christ Blessing

As facilitators of God's healing for others, we are also bringers of the Light. The Christ Light of healing is available to us at all times if we only ask. Job declared, "Behold God is mighty and despises no one." Job 36:5. God never stops loving us and is always extending the Light of healing to us. The tradition of lighting the Paschal Candle is an ancient one that has continued to this day. The symbolism is that of welcoming the resurrected Christ into our darkened world. Since the Middle Ages, there has been the practice of tracing or cutting a cross into the paschal candle while proclaiming "Christ yesterday and today, the beginning and the end," adding the first and last letters of the Greek alphabet, "Alpha and Omega."

As Christians, we proclaim that Jesus is the way, the truth and the light, the true light that enlightens everyone. When the three disciples were taken up the mountain with Jesus, they saw for the first time, the true light of Jesus. The light emanated from within him and shown all around them. Their eyes were opened and they saw Jesus as the light of the world. What is this light, but energy. The mystics and saints tell us that God is like fire, light and overwhelming energy that floods our souls with ecstasy. St. Augustine even says that "One who has come to know the truth knows the light."[7] With the light of God within, we are able to understand truths that before that moment, were hidden.

In this healing technique we reach upwards and with intention, draw down the Light of God, holding it for a few moments in the

[7]William Johnston, *Mystical Theology, the Science of Love*, p. 63.

"Six days later, Jesus took with him Peter and James and his brother John and led them up a high mountain, by themselves. And he was transfigured before them, and his face shone like the sun, and his clothes became dazzling white." Matt. 17: 1-2

vortex of each energy center, then brush the light gently through the field. This movement is repeated several times, each time with a prayer of blessing or welcoming of the light. I have found this technique to be helpful for those who are in pain—physically, emotionally or spiritually. Psychic pain can manifest in a physical way but responds readily to this energy healing as the body relaxes and lets go. You may have come across several variations of this healing technique already. It is done with the recipient lying on their back on the healing table or on a raised bed.

Scripture
"Let your light so shine before others, that they may see your good works, and give glory to your Father in heaven." Matt. 5:16

Prayer
I call upon the Light of Christ to be with me
As I open to be a vessel for God's healing Light.
Christ with me and before me,
Christ behind me and Christ in me.
Christ beneath me and above me.
Christ on my right and on my left,
Christ as my shield, Christ as my source.

If essential oils are desired for this healing technique, first assess for the appropriate oil. Some suggestions include:

Spikenard, myrrh, lavender, Joy, or White Angelica enhance a sense of restful peacefulness.

Fir may help to resolve emotions that may be trapped in the field.

Aloes/sandalwood, juniper, lemon, or pine may assist with tranquil calming.

Frankincense will increase spiritual awareness, uplift spirits and promote meditation.

If sleep is difficult, cedarwood, chamomile, or bergamot may be helpful.

Begin by centering and connecting with the Spirit at your heart. Set your intention for the work. Then standing at the head of the table, extend your arms upwards above the recipient's head and visualize holding the Light of Christ between your hands. Your hands are about 10-12 inches apart, facing each other. You may feel warmth or the presence of energy between your hands. Slowly, bring this ball of light down to rest for a few moments in the vortex of the crown center. Then slowly separate your hands brushing this energy to the edges of the field as a blessing.

Again raise your arms upwards to the Light of Christ and bring down the light to rest in the brow center. Then slowly, brush this energy to the edges of the field as a blessing. Repeat this motion for the throat, heart, solar plexus, sacral and root centers. Each time, hold the light for a few moments in the vortex of these energy centers before brushing the energy to the edges of the field as a gesture of blessing. Repeat this whole sequence for two more rounds.

Each time you bring down the light, you can bless the person with a prayer of blessing. For example, in bringing down the Light, say "The Light of Christ." When brushing the energy to the edges of the field, say "Thanks be to God."

You may also choose to bless the person with special blessings at each energy center as you do the Light of Christ Blessing:

Crown center	Bless [name of person] with an awareness of the presence of God in his/her life.
Brow center	Bless [name of person] with clear visions, with wisdom and insight for their path in life.
Throat center	Bless [name of person] with an ability to speak out their truth.
Heart center	Bless [name of person] with an open and loving heart.
Solar plexus center	Bless [name of person] with a greater sense of self-esteem and courage as they choose the Christian path.
Sacral center	Bless [name of person] with an ability to creatively bring new things to life.
Root center	Bless [name of person] with a sense of rootedness and steadfastness in the Christian community.

Structural Balancing

This particular technique is a way of balancing the energies of the physical body as well as the etheric body. It is most helpful for those who have sustained trauma to the physical body itself, especially when there has been a sudden propelling of the physical body from the etheric body. This occurs in accidents where there may be a traumatic stopping. Whiplashes, falls, and car accidents, fit this description. Before beginning this technique, it is wise to assess the field to find the energetic edges of the field. If the field is pushed up or off the body, first bring the field back onto the body before beginning this healing technique. What this specific healing pattern does energetically is re-establish the connection between the physical body and the etheric body by balancing the energy at the major joints in the legs then in the arms in a grid work pattern. These steps are followed by balancing the energy at each of the major energy centers (chakras), beginning at the root and moving upwards to the crown. It is done with the recipient lying on their back on the healing table or on a raised bed. Even though there are many steps to this healing technique, the pattern can be easily learned.

Prayer
You are Christ's Hands
Christ has no body now on earth but yours,
   No hands but yours,
   No feet but yours,
Yours are the eyes through which is to look out
Christ's compassion to the world
Yours are the feet with which
   he is to go about
   Doing good;
Yours are the hands with which
   he is to bless men now.
St. Teresa of Avila

If essential oils are desired for this healing technique, first assess for the appropriate oil. Some suggestions include:

In using oils with this technique, you will want those that will give a maximum of relaxation to the physical body.

Lavender is considered a "rescue remedy" and helps stabilize mind and heart and decrease anxiety.

Peace and Calming, myrrh, bergamot, chamomile, clary sage are all helpful for relief of anxiety and stress.

Rose of sharon is calming to the nerves, spikenard helps settle nervous tension and anxiety and like valerian, is helpful for insomnia.

Cedarwood in particular, helps release nervous tension and stress related to survival.

Valor is helpful for resetting the electrical system within the body.

Some suggestions on how to use the oils with this technique: *Valor* in particular is useful when rubbed on the soles of the feet to begin this healing. All of the oils can be rubbed on your palms and they can be put on the soles of the client's feet or used to anoint the energy centers.

Begin by centering and setting your intention for this healing. For this healing technique you will be standing at the foot of the healing table. Begin by holding the soles of both feet until you feel a flow of energy. Next, move your hands to both ankles and wait until the energy flows at these points. Without taking your hands from the ankles, move around to the right side of the table. Then move your upper hand to the knee farthest from you and balance the energy between the knee and the ankle. Now, move your lower (right) hand to the ankle closest to you in a diagonal pattern. You will feel the energy shift and for some, it may take a few moments before the energy balances.

Next, move your upper hand to the knee closest to you and balance the energy between the knee and the ankle of this leg. You will next move your lower hand to the opposite ankle in another diagonal pattern. Now move your lower hand to the knee so that both hands are on the knees. You have now completed the structural balancing of the lower leg.

This same pattern is now repeated for the upper legs. Move your left hand to the hip farthest from you and balance the energy in the upper leg from hip to knee. Then, move your lower hand to the knee closest to you in a diagonal pattern. Following the pattern already set, move your hand at the farthest hip to the hip closest to you and balance the energy in this upper leg from hip to knee. Follow this by moving your lower hand to the opposite knee in another diagonal pattern. Then, move your lower hand to that hip so that you are now balancing both hips.

You are now ready to balance the energy between the hips and shoulders in the same pattern as in the legs. Take your left hand and place it on the shoulder farthest from you and balance that shoulder and hip. Follow this movement by placing your lower hand on the hip closest to you in a diagonal pattern across the body. Now move your hand at the shoulder to the shoulder closest to you and balance the energy between this shoulder and hip. Then, move your lower hand to the opposite hip in a diagonal pattern. Complete this structural balancing of the shoulders and hips by moving your hand at the hip to the shoulder so that you are balancing both shoulders.

Optional—You can add in the arms in the same pattern as with the legs.

You are now ready to balance the energy at each of the energy centers up through the center of the body. Move your lower hand to the root, holding it a few inches above that center. Place your upper hand at the sacral center. (You can either hold it above the body or lightly rest it on the body.)

Next, slide your lower hand underneath your upper hand and move your upper hand to the solar plexus center. Follow this movement of your hands up through all the energy centers of the body, holding the sacral and solar plexus, solar plexus and heart, heart and throat, throat and brow, brow and crown. Finally, move your lower hand to the crown center and your upper hand turned upward to the transpersonal point (approximately 12 to 18 inches above the crown). The transpersonal point represents our first connection to the divine. You can end this healing technique with a gentle sweep through the field as you complete your prayer.

Blessing of the Senses

For centuries in the Christian tradition, it was a practice to bless the physical body by anointing the senses, hands, and feet as an anointing for the sick. The early Church was quite holistic in its understanding of healing for body, mind, and spirit and expected healing for the whole person in its rituals. For them the body was seen as "good" but in later centuries was deemed sinful and held less value than the all-important soul. This was due largely to the influence of Augustine in the fourth century. Along with the anointing of the body, there were prayers offered for the forgiveness of sins com-

"They cast out many demons, and anointed with oil many who were sick and cured them." Mark 6:13

mitted by sight, hearing, touching, etc. Eventually the anointing for healing was done only on the forehead and became the last anointing or extreme unction. In this form it became a sacrament of the church and was not given to those who might recover but rather to those who were transitioning to the next life. For well over 500 years, this anointing was only for one's final moments upon this earth. It has only recently in the last forty years been changed to reflect its original purpose of anointing for healing in body, mind and spirit.

"Do you not know that you are God's temple, and that God's Spirit dwells in you?" I Cor. 3:16

This particular technique is based on the anointing of the brow, eyes, ears, throat, hands, feet and heart. It is specifically done with oil for anointing and with prayers of blessing for the physical body, mind and spirit. It is done with the recipient lying on their back on the healing table or on a raised bed.

Prayer
Lord, make me an instrument of Thy peace.
Where there is hatred, let me sow love;
Where there is injury, pardon;
Where there is doubt, faith;
Where there is despair, hope;
Where there is darkness, light;
Where there is sadness, joy.
O divine Master, grant that I May not so much seek
To be consoled as to console,
To be understood, as to understand,
To be loved as to love;
For it is in giving that we receive;
It is in pardoning that we are pardoned;
It is in dying to self that we are born to eternal life.
    St. Francis

To begin this healing technique, first center and connect with Spirit, setting your intention. Then, put a few drops of your chosen anointing oil in the palm of your hand and gently rotate both your palms together in a clock-wise fashion. Place one hand on the brow and the other hand behind the head. Bless this person with keen insights and clear thinking; with kindness and wisdom; with knowledge of who he/she is in the sight of God.

Next, place your palms over each ear and hold for several minutes. Bless this person with clear hearing and with an ability to listen to the Voice of God and act accordingly in their life.

Now, place your palms gently over the eyes with the heel of your hand on the brow and the palms cupped over the eyes. (If the oil you have chosen is a strong one, raise your hands several inches so as not to irritate the eyes.) Hold this position for several minutes or until you feel the energy equalize in your palms. Bless this person with good eyesight and inner vision to see more clearly the path that is theirs.

Now, place one palm cupped over the throat and the other palm directly behind the neck and balance the energy at the throat, front and back. Bless this person with an ability to speak their truth in love and to make their needs known. Bless them with an enthusiasm for life, with joy and an ability to laugh. Bless with an ability to breathe in the breath of God and to breathe out what needs to be let go.

Move around to the side of the table, and take the recipient's hand holding it between both of your hands, opening the palm energy center. Bless this person with hands that touch all of life with gratitude and reverence. Reach across the table and do the same for the other hand (or walk around the table if the reach is too great.)

Now, go to the feet and hold the recipient's foot with one hand above and one hand on the sole of foot. Wait until the energy balances. Bless this person's feet that walk upon the earth. May God bless them with a firm foundation, grounded and centered in life. Go to the other foot and repeat the same gesture.

Any of the Bible oils would be appropriate for this particular anointing. Ask for spiritual guidance on which oil(s) are needed in this moment of healing. Some suggestions include:

Frankincense and myrrh are two of the oldest Bible oils used by the church for holy anointings: Frankincense for spiritual awareness and to promote meditation and uplift the person's spirits. myrrh for instilling deep tranquility and inner stillness.

Spikenard for a profound sense of peace.

Aloes/sandalwood for tranquil effects on troubled souls.

Angelica or hyssop for protection of the angels against evil spirits.

Rose for spiritual attunement.

Lavender for letting go.

Lemon to lift sadness, calm and lighten their soul. Also, for detachment and alleviating fear.

To end this healing technique, go to the heart and place both hands on the heart, finishing your prayer of blessing. Bless this person with a healthy heart and a compassionate, loving heart, filled with generosity and kindness.

Final Thoughts

There are so many ways we can use our hands in a healing way to assist those who are suffering or in pain or simply out of balance with their life. We live in such a touch-deprived age that we have lost sight of appropriate healing touch. Bringing the power of anointing with essential oils together with prayer and hands on healing is a powerful tool and will enhance whatever traditional healthcare the person is receiving. As you become good at this work and able to keep your focus on God and not yourself, your spiritual vibration will be raised. The frequencies of the oil and the energetic healing will work synergistically. Remember, you are the instrument that God happens to be using in the moment. God does the healing. When we come from an intention to help, God hears your prayer and will work through both you and the recipient.

CHAPTER 6

CREATING RITUALS OF HEALING AND ANOINTING

Ritual governs even the very simple things in our daily lives. Children create rituals around going to bed; adults have rituals around getting up in the morning and going to work. Family rituals might include how we celebrate birthdays, anniversaries or graduations. We have rituals around family dinners and special events like Christmas and Thanksgiving. Many of the organizations and clubs we belong to create ritual in their gatherings and in the ways they open their meetings, pass on the baton of leadership and honor certain members with recognition. In our homes we ritualize our meals with saying grace, gathering at the dinner table, and even in turning off the TV; we honor our times of prayer with lighting candles, playing inspirational music or burning incense; and we may even ritualize our days off with sleeping in, dressing down, cleaning house or going to a movie. Ritual provides patterns of behavior we can rely upon. Ritual relieves the stress of the unknown. Ritual connects us to one another and to our spiritual source.

Rituals can have a deeper meaning for our souls. Creating rituals are our way of communing with the divine forces in our life—of making sacred our rites of passage, of communicating and celebrating important occasions. Ritual makes concrete our spiritual quest for meaning in life. Ritual brings the sacred and the mysterious into our walking and waking life. We honor the very core of our existence through our ritual making. Ritual is the visible expression of our common bonding with one another; it gives meaning, richness and structure to our lives.

Whether we are consciously aware of it or not, we create rituals of healing and anointing in our various healing practices. How we pray with our clients, assess their needs and go about helping them with their healing process falls within ritual making. Our goal in working with others is a holistic healing of body, mind and spirit. Doing our work within a ministry context, we invite the Divine Mystery to make sacred this healing time and place. The Christian Church has had a long history in creating rituals in its worship and community gatherings and has much to teach us in regard to healing rituals. There are lessons to be learned as we enter into the sacred and mysterious "place, time and meaning" of healing.

Learning from the Christian Church's Experience with Ritual Making

Rituals in our Christian worship are most evident in how we do sacraments within our various churches. James White, a leading Protestant historian calls them "sign-acts." They are ways that make visible God's actions in our lives. The sacraments, White says, call us to "O taste and see" (Ps. 34:8), to touch, to hear, even to smell "that the Lord is good."[1] They make visible, the deeper spiritual realities. Paul Tillich, an earlier twentieth century Protestant theologian writes that "any object or event is sacramental in which the transcendent is perceived to be present. Sacramental objects are holy objects, laden with divine power."[2] His words are reminiscent of Augustine in the fifth century who believed that any sacred symbol or ceremony could

[1] James F. White, *Introduction to Christian Worship,* p. 176.

[2] Joseph Martos, *Doors to the Sacred, A Historical Introduction to Sacraments in the Catholic Church,* p. 3.

"any object or event is sacramental in which the transcendent is perceived to be present. Sacramental objects are holy objects, laden with divine power."
Paul Tillich

"While Peter was still speaking, the Holy Spirit fell upon all who heard the word. The circumcised believers who had come with Peter were astounded that the gift of the Holy Spirit had been poured out even on the Gentiles, for they heard them speaking in tongues and extolling God. Then Peter said, 'Can anyone withhold the water for baptizing these people who have received the Holy Spirit just as we have? So he ordered them to be baptized in the name of Jesus Christ." Acts 10:44-48

be called a *sacramentum.* He noted that anything in the world could be considered a sacrament since all of creation was a sign of God. In this broader view, sacrament is a sign or symbol of something that is sacred and mysterious. Christian usage of the term sacrament however, became quite restrictive after Augustine and by the sixteenth century was extremely narrow in scope.

We read in the Gospels that Jesus submitted to baptism, he forgave sins, and he kept the Jewish feasts. From the Acts of the Apostles we know that his disciples faithfully followed suit and carried on his sacramental mission. They baptized new followers, they laid on hands and prayed for healing and they broke bread together. We see words of healing, sealing, and forgiving in the descriptions of their practices. What we don't see are clearly defined rituals or even how many "signs" actually exhibit the sacred and mysterious. But taken as a whole, there is a richness in their communal life and practice of faith. Thankfully they gave us a foundation for a sacramental life, one in which God is continually disclosed to us. And so we assemble in our churches, we sing, praise, preach, honor the scriptures, and Christians of all denominations make pilgrimages to their "holy" or honored sites. These actions point us to something beyond themselves—something mysterious, something sacred. And in this regard, Augustine would call them *sacramentum,* sacred and holy.

The number of sacraments is not really the issue, neither is it the various rituals that we use in these various "sign-acts." If we understand the true meaning of sacrament, we have to acknowledge that what makes them significant in our lives is God's actions in the "sign-act." They are designed, as Calvin put it so rightly, to lead us to God. They are God's actions upon our souls as a true act of the gift of love made visible in the community.

Many of our healing techniques can be "sign-acts" in that they can open the possibility of God's actions upon the person we lay-on our hands and anoint. Through our healing actions, the gift of love is made visible.

"Doors to the Sacred"

One way of looking at the sacraments is to see them through the eyes of a hurting individual in need of healing in body, mind and spirit. Baptism cleanses us, confirmation strengthens us, Eucharist nourishes us, reconciliation raises us when we have fallen, and anointing of the sick heals us physically and spiritually. Our sacramental ceremonies are symbolic expressions of sacred realities through which we are restored, strengthened, fed and healed through faith. Joseph Martos quoting twentieth century religion scholar Mircea Eliade, calls the sacraments of all religions "doors to the sacred," or invitations to religious experiences. He says that having such a sacred experience is like entering into another dimension of space and time and discovering a whole new world of meaning. Space becomes sacred, as does time and meaning.[3] The potential is there for a transformation of consciousness and an opening to the transcendent dimension. Is this not what we desire in our healing experiences?

Creating Sacred Space

We do our healing work within "sacred space" which is different from ordinary space. We have all had experiences of going to places where we immediately sense the presence of the holy and know with certainty that we have entered sacred space. For some it may be entering a grand cathedral such as St. Peter's in Rome or St. John Divine in New York; for still others it may be entering the Crystal Cathedral in California or their own local sanctuary. Some may find sacred space experienced under the canopy of trees in nature or in visiting the home of a relative or friend who is dearly loved and admired. At times, these are just ordinary spaces but at other times they are charged with significance for us. Sometimes in our healing classes, there is the awareness of sacred space as well. You can feel it in the air and it is almost palpable—a sense of the holy being pres-

Baptism cleanses us, confirmation strengthens us, Eucharist nourishes us, reconciliation raises us when we have fallen, and anointing of the sick heals us physically and spiritually.

[3]Joseph Martos, *Doors to the Sacred, A Historical Introduction to Sacraments in the Catholic Church*, p. 7.

"You brought them in and planted them on the mountain of your own possessiion, the place, O Lord, that you made your abode, the sanctuary, O Lord, that your hands have established." Exodus 15:17

ent. The classroom space has somehow changed and become imbued with significance.

Creating sacred space is not something we do necessarily by formula but there are some practical steps we can take that may help us to experience ordinary space as sacred. We first create sacred space within our own hearts, making room for the divine spirit. We ask for spiritual guidance and we declare silently or aloud, the intention for this holy work of anointing and hands-on healing. Prayers of blessing and protection of this space call upon God to be actively present.

We first create sacred space within our own hearts, making room for the divine spirit.

Sacred space is enhanced by those elements around us that like the cathedral draw us into the transcendent experience of healing. The colors, fragrances, sounds and beauty that we choose in our healing space all assist in amplifying and focusing intention. Prior to the client arriving, try clearing and protecting the space by diffusing a fragrance such as *Peace and Calming*™, *Purification*™, lavender, fennel, cedarwood, rosemary or juniper. Some like to bless water and sprinkle it throughout the room to clear the space. You can add an essential oil like lavender, sandalwood, pine, cedarwood or sage to the water and use an evergreen branch to sprinkle this "holy water." Or you can use a spray bottle with 4 oz of purified water mixed with 10-20 drops of an essential oil to mist the area. Native Americans might prefer to smudge the room with sage or sweetgrass to clear the energy.

You can also anoint the linens with a fragrant oil. Lavender, *Joy*™, rose, lemon, orange, neroli, and bergamot are wonderful fragrances that will help create a healing space by filling it with positive energy.

Some find lighting candles or subdued lighting helpful. Light symbolizes the divine illumination in our lives. Simply acknowledging the Light and saying a blessing brings awareness to our purpose in the healing work. Sound can also be used. The tone of a clear bell or chime can clear the space. Special music played during the healing session may help bring you into that conscious awareness of the angels and the divine presence. The Christian Church has used sound in voices and instruments to honor the divine presence and align us with the Divine will. There are so many fine choices of music appropriate for healing available today. Allow your spiritual guidance to assist you in the appropriate selection of sounds.

Try to create beauty in your healing space. Colors, artwork, and simplicity of the furnishings all contribute to creating sacred space and aiding the healing experience. I try to simplify the furnishings and decorations in my healing room as much as possible so there are few distractions to take me from the sacred space in which I do my work. I have a sacred shelf where I place objects that are significant to my work. Some may call this a "sacred altar." Just be sure that clutter does not accumulate. If an object or picture no longer connects you to spirit, it is time to let go of it and move it on.

Once you have created and cleared your sacred space, fill it with your intentions for this healing work. Fill it with your heart's unconditional love and compassion. And like the incense spoken of in the Bible, let your prayers rise before the altar of God.

How do you create sacred space within your home or office? Have you ever considered doing this and seeing if there is a difference in your awareness or in your feelings?

Creating Sacred Time

Sacred time is different from ordinary time as sacred space is different from ordinary space. Most of us keep pretty busy and time has a way of slipping by quickly on us. But on some occasions our consciousness of time is altered and we enter a sacred moment. This may be a moment we have dreamed of or waited for like a birth or a significant milestone in our life. It could be a moment we have

"It was the duty of the trumpeters and singers to make themselves heard in unison in praise and thanksgiving to the Lord, and when the song was raised, with trumpets and cymbals and other musical instruments, in praise to the Lord, For he is good, For his steadfast love endures forever. 2 Chronicles 5:13

"Let my prayer be counted as incense before you, and the lifting up of my hands as an evening sacrifice." Psalm141:2

Our healing time with a client takes place within sacred time. We cannot force a sacred moment of healing; we can only be open and inviting to it happening.

dreaded like a death of a loved one or death of another kind in being fired or laid off from our job. What is different about the moment is that time seems to stand still; it is out of the ordinary passing of time. It lingers rather than rushes by. In prayer and meditation, sacred time may be a precious experience. Breath even slows in recognition of the sacred moment. Time has become special, charged with importance. Something meaningful is happening.

The special intent you bring to this healing time will take you and the client out of ordinary time into sacred time. We cannot force a sacred moment of healing; we can only be open and inviting to it happening. The words we speak, the sounds, fragrances, colors, and movements of our hands are all part of the experience of sacred time. As you and the client become receptive to the movements of the Spirit, the wind will blow where it will in the present moment. It is difficult, perhaps even impossible, to invite the sacred presence when our minds are filled with clutter and the many things we have to do. Both practitioner and client need to take a deep breath and let go of all other things to make room for a sacred time experience.

Pause for a moment and allow this to be a sacred moment in your day. Take a deep breath, and r e l a x.

Creating Sacred Meaning

Sacred meaning is when we experience something significant and it has meaning out of the ordinary for us. It may be an idea, thought, belief, judgment or an opinion or we may have significant meanings to feeling love and being accepted by others or needed by them. We may have value-laden meanings to honesty, courage, friendship, freedom and loyalty. These become important because we want them or because they give us direction in life.

Meaning adds richness to our lives. Creating sacred meaning to our healing work takes quite simply, an awareness of the awesomeness of the connection between human and divine.

We may attach some symbolic meaning to an object such as a cross or Bible or another object that for us holds sacred dimensions. Some symbols are comforting, reminding us of deeper realities. Other objects because of events draw us into an experience of the holy. Since September 11th the American flag has taken on sacred, if not religious meaning for many because of the events that changed the world on that day. The flag is revered by more people now than at any other time in our history. Objects can take on an importance in our lives, drawing us into a world of sacred meaning. In this regard, some objects can be a "sacramental" experience, meaning they are a source of encounter with the divine.

Meaning adds richness to our lives. Creating sacred meaning to our healing work takes quite simply, an awareness of the awesomeness of the connection between human and divine. It is being in the present moment, in this present space, and experiencing God as total gift and total grace. Our healing rituals are ultimately aimed at the regeneration and the maintenance of health and wholeness. They embody our values of hope and health. Whether we pray, lay-on hands, anoint or all three, we are conveying sacred meaning to the healing process.

Again, pause and remember those things that give meaning to your life. In our healing work, we become the midwives of sacred space, sacred time and sacred meaning for others.

Entering the Healing Mystery in our Rituals

Disease, illness and death are all viewed as mystery. We don't understand them and for many, they appear to be aberrations of what ought to be normal or at least, ought to be the status quo. Just as we find disease, illness and death mysterious, so is the healing process a mystery. We really don't understand how it occurs. Yes, our scientific investigations examine the biology, chemistry, and psychology of healing but have not come near offering sufficient understanding

For more information on sickness and healing in the Old Testament, see *Called into Healing, Reclaiming our Judeo-Christian Legacy of Healing Touch* by Linda Smith.

Anointing needs to be done with reverence for the sacred wholeness of life. Each act of anointing opens us to the possibility of receiving God's favor—God's healing grace.

of how healing actually occurs. It simply does in some circumstances and not in others. And so we look for the meaning in life's sufferings. Our spiritual beliefs at least offer hope in an otherwise confusing mystery. Part of the healing process is looking for meaning in the suffering we all experience in life. When we are able to make some sense out of suffering, it gives a strength that is sustaining.

In the Old Testament, the Genesis accounts tie physical and spiritual reality together. Health and sickness in this ancient writing described both physical and spiritual reality. In the sacred order of things, physical sickness was a result of spiritual disobedience. Healing was therefore a restoration of both the physical and spiritual as well. In treating physical illnesses, natural medicines of the earth like the aromatic herbs and oils could be used. Wounds could be washed with wine and oil. But all treatments were used in conjunction with prayers so they could set the sacred order of things right. All healing was in the hands of God as shown in many of the Psalms. In this regard, our forebears expressed a holistic understanding of our body/mind/spirit being that we today are only beginning to glean insights about.

From our earlier discussion on the laying-on of hands and anointing in our Christian history, we can enter into the mystery of the healing process through the healing techniques and the healing oils that we choose in our present-day work with others. Healing is a mystery and we gladly enter that mystery as participants both in our own healing and in that of others. Prayer, hands-on healing and anointing become three cornerstones for our healing rituals.

Take a few minutes and enter into sacred space and time. Ask God in your prayers for a restoration of physical and spiritual health. Pick an essential oil and anoint yourself as a sign of God's great love for you.

Modern Day Spiritual Anointing Rituals

When we anoint either ourselves or another person, it must be done with reverence for the sacred wholeness of life. Our act of anointing the human body is an act of blessing, honoring, revering, and respecting the sacredness of the body. Among the various spiritual paths of the world anointing is a spiritual practice that has the purpose of connecting us to the Divine in all life—to our Source. Each act of anointing opens us to the possibility of receiving God's favor—God's healing grace. Anointing then provides opportunities for God's many blessings to shower us. Whether we are anointing our bath water with an aroma that enhances our release of negativity and openness to unconditional love or diffusing an essential oil into the room to create a sacred healing environment, we are honoring the gift of God present in our daily lives. God has truly blessed the earth with all kinds of plants for our use. When we take the very essence of the plants, the essential oils, and breathe them, rub them on our bodies or take them within, we accept the gift of blessing from God. We are reminded that through anointing, God has set his seal upon our hearts. We are claimed as God's own.

There are many ways we can anoint ourselves and others. Put a drop or two in one palm and then rub both palms together several times. Or, place a few drops in one palm and use the index finger of your other hand to dip into the oil you intend to use for anointing.

I like to begin my healing work with my clients by placing a drop of oil in my palm. After rubbing them together, I gently brush my hands through the field. I begin above the head and brush down and off the feet. This has a way of gently clearing any congestion in the field.

Where on the body is it appropriate to anoint directly with oil? Here are some suggestions.

- Crown of the head, inviting Divine guidance.
- Brow, asking for wisdom, intuition, and knowledge.
- Throat, asking for clarity of speech and ability to speak one's truth.
- Heart, calling upon God's compassion and unconditional loving heart to fill this person.
- Solar Plexus, asking for self-esteem, and firmness of direction.
- Sacral, asking for an openness to creativity.
- Root, grounding and connecting this person to heaven and earth.
- Spine, inviting God's support and assistance for this person to carry-on life's journey.
- The whole back, balancing the physical and emotional self, releasing those emotions that hold this person back.
- Shoulders, asking for support for this person to carry life's burdens and challenges.
- Hands, to bless whatever this person touches.
- Hips, asking for support to walk forward in life.
- Knees, asking for flexibility in life.
- Feet, that this person's path will always be a sacred one.
- Senses—ears, eyes, nose, mouth-to open hearing, seeing, smelling and tasting to higher knowledge. *(Be careful not to put oil directly in the ears, eyes, nose or mouth.)*

Take a few moments and reflect on the scents that have been spiritually uplifting for you. Is it a memory of church incense from your childhood or the smell of lavender or cinnamon in potpourri? Perhaps it's the smell of clean sheets drying in the wind or your mother's favorite perfume. All aromas have the potential of taking us to a greater spiritual awareness. Blessings abound all around us.

CHAPTER 7

the oils
of ancient
scriptures

There are many healing oils referred to by name in the Bible. We are not sure if some of our modern-day plants that go by the ancient names are actually the same plants. However, researchers believe that they are relatively close and belong to the same species. Some of the aromas of these oils are very uplifting, calming, and refreshing. Others have an earthier, more pungent fragrance. Through investigation, we know a lot about the oils spoken of in the scriptures. We know their chemistry, how they were used in ancient times and how they can be used today. We know how to produce therapeutic grades of these oils. And, we know how to best use them for healing. There are over a 1,000 references in the Bible to essential oils and aromatic oil-producing plants with at least 33 different species named. Thirty-six of the thirty-nine books of the Old Testament and ten of the twenty-seven books of the New Testament contain references to essential oils and the plants that produced them. They were the perfumes, medicines, anointing oils, and incenses used on a daily basis. These are the oils that were part of our Judeo-Christian heritage. They are the oils of our ancient scriptures. The following is a description of eighteen of the oils used by the Israelites as well as the early Christian church.

Aloes/Sandalwood *(Santalum album)*
The Oil of Inner Stillness and Unity

Sandalwood is one of the oldest known essential oils with at least 4,000 years of use. It has been used as incense, in cosmetics, perfume and embalming material all over the East. Its wood was used in temples and furniture making because of its resilience and its resistance to insects. It has a rich history both as a fragrance and as a therapeutic healing oil. aloes/sandalwood is one of the oldest oils known for its spiritual qualities.

Scriptures: Referred to in the Bible as Aloes, it is mentioned 5 times: Numbers 24:6; Psalms 45:8; Proverbs 7:17; Song of Solomon 4:14

"Nicodemus came bringing a mixture of myrrh and aloes, weighing about a hundred pounds." John 19:39

Aroma: Aloes/sandalwood has a woody, sweet and slightly musky, earthy, yet tranquil odor. It blends well with other oils particularly cypress, frankincense, ginger, lemon, myrrh, patchouly, ylang ylang, spruce, chamomile, geranium.

Source: Primarily grown in Indonesia and India, this oil comes from a parasitic evergreen tree that can grow up to 30 feet high. It is considered parasitic because it sinks its roots into a host tree and draws mineral nutrients. The tree must be at least 30 years old before it is ready for production of sandalwood oil. The oil is produced through distillation of the roots, and heartwood of the tree.[1]

[1]Susan Curtis, *Essential Oils,* pp. 116-117.

Predominant
Chemistry: Sesquiterpenes; sesquiterpenols: α and β—santalols 67% sesquiterpenals; carbonic acid.

Ancient Uses: Traditionally this oil was used for assistance in meditation to come closer to God, for skin revitalization, and for embalming—it was used in a mixture to anoint the body of Jesus for his burial. aloes/sandalwood being a spiritual oil, was used to help carry the soul into the next life.

Modern Uses: For the Body: aloes/sandalwood is particularly helpful for cystitis and urinary tract infections and good for skin care especially for acne, dry and cracked skin. It is considered the classic choice for dry and chapped skin. It makes an excellent after shave with a carrier oil. It may be beneficial for menstrual problems, sleep, respiratory infections, and nervous tension. In Ayurvedic medicine (traditional Indian) sandalwood is valued for its anti-inflammatory, antifebrile and anti-infectious properties. It is mainly used for urinary and respiratory infections and for acute and chronic diarrhea.[2]

For the Mind and Spirit: Sandalwood can be clarifying and stilling for the mind creating space for inner unity of body, mind and spirit. It is known for its tranquil and calming effects on troubled souls.[3] Perhaps this is why sandalwood has been used for thousands of years to aid meditation. aloes/sandalwood can bring you into higher states of consciousness not through out of body experiences but through its "earthy" awareness of self. It is at once, a "grounding oil" and an oil that can bring a sense of inner stillness and unity within one's own being.

This oil is particularly helpful when you are trapped in fear, allowing you to come to a place of surrender to the divine will. Use it to encourage positive emotions of comfort, serenity, trust, harmony, peace,

[2] For more extensive information on the uses of Sandalwood oil in Ayurvedic medicine, see Gabriel Mojay, *Aromatherapy for Healing the Spirit,* pp. 116-117.

[3] Denise Whichello Brown, *Aromatherapy,* p. 75.

self-esteem, openness and unity; and to counteract negative emotions of anxiety, possessiveness, unforgiving heart, insecurity, selfishness, irritability, and dwelling on the past.[4]

Applications for Healing Work:

This will be one of your most frequently used oils from the Bible. It can be diffused in the room, applied topically to various parts of the body, ingested orally or burned as incense. When taken as a dietary supplement, dilute with soy or rice milk since it has a bitter taste. For skin conditions, it can be used with warm compresses. This oil can be blended with many other oils for specific conditions: cystitis—blend with lavender, tea tree and geranium; for respiratory conditions, blend with eucalyptus and geranium. When used in healing work with the laying-on of hands, it can be diffused in the room, applied to the healer's hands and run through the field for general support and comfort, and can be applied to any of the energy centers.

Safety Data:

Aloes/sandalwood is non-toxic, non-irritating, non-sensitizing. It will be a frequently called upon oil which has many uses in healing work.

[4]Valerie Ann Worwood, *The Fragrant Mind, Aromatherapy for Personality, Mind, Mood, and Emotion,* p. 360, and Light Miller and Bryan Miller, *Ayurveda and Aromatherapy, The Earth Essential Guide to Ancient Wisdom and Modern Healing,* pp. 290-291.

Calamus *(Acorus calamus)*
Oil of spiritual and mental clarity

Calamus is not a frequently used oil today and is difficult to even obtain. In fact, few recommend its use except externally. Traditionally it was esteemed as an aromatic stimulant and tonic. It is still used in Turkey and India where it is a valued traditional medicine. There it is sold as a candied rhizome for dyspepsia, bronchitis and coughs.

"Your channel is an orchard of pomegranates with all choicest fruits, henna with nard, nard and saffron, calamus and cinnamon, with all trees of frankincense, myrrh and aloes, with all chief spices-a garden fountain, a well of living water, and flowing streams from Lebanon." Song of Solomon 4:13-15.

[5]Julia Lawless, *The Illustrated Encyclopedia of Essential Oils,* p. 214.

[6]Light Miller and Bryan Miller, *Ayurveda and Aromatherapy, The Earth Essential Guide to Ancient Wisdom and Modern Healing,* p. 230.

Scriptures: Mentioned three times in the Bible
Exodus 30:23, Ezekiel 27:19

Aroma: Calamus has a woody-spice fragrance that is not very pleasant. It blends well with cinnamon, frankincense, patchouly, and cedarwood.

Source: Calamus is a reed-like water plant about 3 feet high with sword-shaped leaves, small greenish-yellow flowers and it puts down long-branched rhizomes in the mud. The whole plant is aromatic.[5]

Predominant Chemistry: Phenylpropanoids, Beta-asarone

Ancient Uses: Calamus was used as a holy anointing oil and in perfumes and incense. Calamus was traditionally used to help improve mental focus, wisdom and sexuality.

Modern Uses: For the Body: Calamus is antispasmodic, anti-inflammatory, and soothes inflammation of the gastrointestinal tract. It is helpful for asthmatic bronchitis, kidney congestion after alcohol intoxication, cystitis, gout and low blood pressure. In India, it is used to strengthen the adrenals making it helpful in periods of weakness.[6]

For the Mind and Spirit: Calamus is spiritually uplifting as part of a holy anointing oil. It is clarifying for one's path and enables listening to the experiences of others.

Applications for Healing Work: This oil can be used topically over the abdomen for its soothing affect on the GI tract. When applied to the soles of the feet, it may help with foot odor. It can be applied to the temples, brow and throat for spiritual connection and clarity of thought. Calamus can also be used as in incense. This oil may not be one of your first choices in healing work; however, don't overlook its potential when blended with frankincense, or one of the other holy anointing oils. It is an oil for spiritual and mental clarity.

Safety Data: Not recommended to be taken internally.

Cassia *(Cinnamomum cassia)*
One of God's holy anointing oils

Cassia is toxic to the skin and not recommended for internal use. It is used as a local domestic spice in Ceylon for digestive complaints and in China for vascular problems.

Scriptures: Mentioned 3 times in the Bible
Exodus 30:24; Ezekiel 27:19

"Your robes are all fragrant with myrrh and aloes and cassia." Psalm 45:8

Aroma: Cassia has a strong pungent, less sweet fragrance than cinnamon.

Source: Cassia is a slender evergreen tree with leathery leaves and small white flowers. It is usually cut to grow as bushes to increase its oil production. It is produced through steam distillation of the leaves and water distillation from the tree bark, leaves, twigs and stalks. This plant is grown in China.[7]

[7]Julia Lawless, *The Illustrated Encyclopedia of Essential Oils*, p. 214.

Predominant
Chemistry: Mainly aldehydes 75-90% esters with some phenols. While its aroma is similar to cinnamon, cassia is chemically and physically quite different.

Ancient Uses: It was used as an ingredient in the holy anointing oil given to Moses.

Modern Uses: For the Body: Antibacterial, antiviral, anti-fungal, immune system builder.

Applications
for Healing
Work: Because of its toxicity to the skin, cassia will not be a frequently used oil in healing work. It can however be blended with frankincense, myrrh or aloes/sandalwood and diluted in a carrier oil to create a holy oil for anointing. Cassia can also be diffused or used in incense.

Safety Data: Cassia may cause irritation if applied to the skin without diluting with a carrier oil. Not recommended for pregnant women.

Cedarwood *(Cedrus atlantica)*
The oil of strength in times of crises

Cedarwood or the Lebanon Cedar, was a very popular tree in ancient times and came from the species—*cedrus libani.* The Egyptians used its oil for embalming, cosmetics and perfumes. They found that the wood from the trees repelled ants, moths and harmful insects that made it highly prized as building material. It was the Lebanon cedars that grew in large forests all over Lebanon and were the trees cut down for Solomon's great temple in Jerusalem. Today only a few hundred survive in that part of the world. The aromatic wood was distilled for its oil and used mostly for bronchial and urinary tract infections, and as a preservative. *Cedrus atlantica* is a close relative of the biblical cedar of Lebanon and comes from Morocco.[8] This is the oil that is available to us today.

[8]Gabriel Mojay, *Aromatherapy for Healing the Spirit,* pp. 58-59.

Scriptures:	Mentioned 6-7 times in the Bible Leviticus 14: 6, 49, 51, 52; Numbers 19:6 and Song of Solomon 5:15

"The priest shall command that two living clean birds and cedarwood and crimson yarn and hyssop be brought for the one who is to be cleansed." Lev. 14:4

Aroma:	Cedarwood has a woody, balsamic yet sweet odor. Many will recognize it as the smell of cedar chests. It blends well with frankincense, fir, lavender, juniper, pine, bergamot, cypress, calamus, orange blossom, clary sage, and rosemary.
Source:	Cedarwood trees are majestic evergreens that can grow up to 130 feet high. The wood is hard and strongly aromatic. The oil is obtained through steam distillation of the bark as well as the stumps and sawdust. It is grown in Morocco and Algeria although the oil is produced mainly in Morocco.
Predominant Chemistry:	Sesquiterpenes—the highest of any oils; sesquiterpenols; sesquiterpenones.
Ancient Uses:	Cedarwood was used in ritual purification after touching anything "unclean." It was used to cleanse lepers and evil spirits; it was used in cosmetics and for various skin problems. The Egyptians used it for embalming; and it was used in various medicines for its calming effects. Cedarwood was used in very similar ways to Sandalwood. Both helped with skin, urinary tract and bronchial problems. Like sandalwood, cedarwood has a sedative effect and was used for anxiety and nervous tension. For biblical people, this oil symbolized abundance, fertility, and spiritual strength.[9]

[9]Robert Tisserand, *The Art of Aromatherapy*, pp. 208-210.

Modern Uses:	For the Body: Cedarwood can be used as an insect repellent, for hair loss, acne, dandruff, eczema,

fungal infections, and other skin disorders. Cedarwood is particularly helpful for oily skin. It can be used for improving circulation and joint mobility in arthritis and rheumatism. Cedarwood is helpful as a decongestant for the respiratory system—bronchitis, congestion, coughs. It is also found to be helpful for cystitis. This oil has a mildly diuretic action and therefore is helpful for edema and fluid retention. For fluid retention, blend with eucalyptus, thyme and lavender. Cedarwood has a similar action to red cedar which is grown in the U.S. Although similar, they are in different conifer families.

For the Mind and Spirit: As the highest oil in sesquiterpenes, it can help in deprogramming misinformation in the brain. It can also enhance deep sleep, emotional releases, and clear the mind and brain. It helps relieve nervous tension and stress-related conditions. Use cedarwood to enhance positive emotions of strength, support, confidence, balance, stability, comfort, and fortitude; and to counteract negative emotions of thoughtlessness, fixation on the past, anxiety, obsessions, irrationality, touchiness, gloomy thoughts, worry, fear, paranoia, and selfishness.[10]

[10]Valerie Ann Worwood, *The Fragrant Mind, Aromatherapy for Personality, Mind, Mood, and Emotion,* p. 290.

Applications for Healing Work:

Cedarwood can be diffused in the room, applied topically to various parts of the body or used as a dietary supplement in capsules. Cedarwood is wonderful for cleansing the atmosphere in a room. When used in conjunction with the laying-on of hands or Healing Touch, it can be applied to the healer's hands and run through the field for general support, strength and endurance. It can also be applied topically as an anointing oil to the energy centers, brow, temples, and the soles of the feet. This is an excellent oil to use in times of spiritual crises since it both grounds and gives strength enabling the person to weather the storm of emotions. Excellent in times of spiritual confusion that often accompanies a crisis.

Safety Data: Cedarwood is non-toxic and non-irritating making it a wonderful oil to use in healing work either as a single oil or blended with many other oils. Best avoided during pregnancy.

Cinnamon *(Cinnamomum verum)*
An oil of warmth and happiness

Cinnamon is a spice that has been around for thousands of years and used in a variety of ways. Most would think of it as a flavoring agent for foods but its primary use in ancient times was medicinal for a variety of physical complaints. It was considered important enough to be included in God's holy anointing oil.

Scriptures: Mentioned 4 times in the Bible
Exodus 30:23; Song of Solomon 4:14;
Revelation 18:13

"I have perfumed my bed with myrrh, aloes and cinnamon." Proverbs 7:17

Aroma: A sweet spicy somewhat harsh fragrance. It blends well with frankincense, lemon, orange, mandarin, benzoin, rosemary, lavender and all other spice oils.

Source: The cinnamon tree is an evergreen that can grow as high as 50 feet. It has very thick bark and shiny green leathery leaves. The leaves have a spicy fragrance when bruised. The oil is produced by steam distillation of the leaves and twigs, and from the dried inner bark. This was one of the spices brought by trade caravans from Indian and Persian Gulf ports. It was obtained from a tree native to Ceylon but also cultivated in India and East Indies islands.[11] Today it comes from Sri Lanka where it has been produced for over 2,000 years.

[11] *New World Dictionary Concordance to the New American Bible*, p. 90.

Predominant Chemistry: Esters, phenols, aldehydes and coumarins.

Ancient Uses: Cinnamon was used in holy anointing oils, perfume and it had many culinary uses. Used for a variety of physical complaints including colds, flues, digestive problems, menstrual problems, rheumatism, kidney troubles. In the Middle Ages, healers like Hildegard of Bingen recommended boiling cinnamon in wine and drinking it often for such things as gout, stuffy head and fevers.[12]

[12] *Hildegard von Bingen's Physica,* translated from the Latin by Priscilla Throop, pp.20-21.

Modern Uses: For the Body: The Coumarins in cinnamon are antibacterial and antiviral. This makes cinnamon one of the most powerful antibacterial, antiviral oils of all-even stronger than most antibiotics. Cinnamon bark is a powerful antioxidant. It is used as a sexual stimulant, for tropical infections, typhoid, and vaginitis. It may also be beneficial for circulation, infections, coughs, exhaustion, respiratory infections, digestion, rheumatism, and warts. This oil also fights viral and infectious diseases.[13] Cinnamon is also used for parasites especially lice and scabies. For scabies, combine it with oils of eucalyptus, pine, rosemary and thyme and comb through the hair; for lice, combine it with bergamot and cedarwood and apply to the skin.[14]

[13] *Essential Oils Desk Reference*, p. 40.

[14] Susan Curtis, *Essential Oils*, pp. 50-51.

For the Mind and Spirit: This is a warming oil for the spirit as well as for the body. It restores wakefulness in the presence of fatigue. It is vitalizing, refreshing as well as warming. Use it to encourage positive emotions of benevolence, strength, practicality, realism, directness and to counteract negative emotions of instability, spitefulness, coldness, fear, nervous exhaustion, debility, introversion and superficiality.[15]

[15]Valerie Ann Worwood, *The Fragrant Mind, Aromatherapy for Personality, Mind, Mood, and Emotion*, p. 290.

Applications for Healing Work: Cinnamon can be diffused, used topically, orally, or as incense but <u>with caution.</u> Never put cinnamon bark on or near one's face. It can be blended in a massage oil as long as it is well diluted.

Safety Data: Leaf oil is relatively non-toxic but oil from the bark may be hot due to its higher aldehyde ingredient. Always recommended to <u>dilute with a carrier such as a good vegetable or massage oil</u> before applying to the skin. Caution is also recommended in diffusing this oil. Do not inhale directly from the diffuser since it may irritate the nasal membranes.

Cypress *(Cupressus sempervirens)*
An oil for transition and transformation

Cypress is another ancient oil made from trees. The Egyptians found it to be an exceptional wood and used it to carve their sarcophagi. The oil from the cypress tree was used for many medicinal purposes and for incense. In medieval times, Hildegard of Bingen wrote that cypress signifies "secret of God." She recommended boiling some of the wood in wine and even bathing in water in which branches have been soaked. Doing this would help someone regain their strength from illness. She also believed that the heartwood of the cypress was particularly sacred and could ward off evil spirits.[16]

[16]*Hildegard von Bingen's Physica*, translated from the Latin by Priscilla Throop, p. 119.

"The glory of Lebanon shall come to you, the cypress, the plane, and the pine, to beautify the place of my sanctuary; and I will glorify where my feet rest." Isaiah 60:13

Scriptures: Mentioned twice in the Bible
Isaiah 41:19, Isaiah 60:13

Aroma: Like the other conifers, it has a woody but almost a smoky sweet fragrance. Its odor is lighter than many of the other evergreens and astringent almost like turpentine. Cypress blends well with the oils of other trees like juniper, cedarwood, pine, and sandalwood, also with the citrus oils of lemon, bergamot, orange and mandarin. It can be blended with lavender and clary sage as well.

Source: The cypress tree is an evergreen conifer that can grow to a height nearly of a 150 feet. Oil is obtained through steam distillation of the tree branches and the dark green leaves. Cypress trees are native to the eastern Mediterranean area and now grow in France and Spain, Italy, North Africa and England. Most of the oil is produced in France, Spain and Morocco.

Predominant Chemistry: Monoterpenes: α-pinene; sesquiterpenes; sesquiterpenols; diterpenols.

Ancient Uses: The ancient Assyrians used cypress leaves for their astringent properties to cure hemorrhoids. The Greek physician Galen (165 A.D.) recommended cypress for internal bleeding and diarrhea. It was famed for its ability to alleviate menstrual cramps. Cypress was also used for arthritis and for healing scar tissue. The Greeks also believed the cypress tree to have spiritual properties and associated it with death and eternity. They planted cypress trees in their graveyards as a symbol of grief and as a source of comfort to the grieving.[17]

[17]Gabriel Mojay, *Aromatherapy for Healing the Spirit*, pp. 66-67.

Modern Uses: For the Body: Can be used for a wide range of problems: arthritis, bronchitis, insomnia, intestinal parasites, pulmonary infections, rheumatism, spasms, throat problems and fluid retention. It is a powerful antispasmodic making it useful for asthma, whooping cough and all spasmodic coughs. Its astringent properties make it beneficial for increasing circulation, strengthening blood capillaries, controlling hemorrhages and nosebleeds, and relieving angina pain and reducing varicose veins. It relieves menstrual pains and menopausal symptoms. It is also anti-infectious, antibacterial, and anti-microbial. In addition, it acts as an insect repellent.[18]

[18]Robert Tisserand, *The Art of Aromatherapy,* pp. 215-217.

For the Mind and Spirit: Cypress has distinct psychological effects conveying a feeling of cohesion and stability. This makes it useful in relieving anger, irritability and stress related conditions.[19] Cypress is a spiritual oil particularly helpful in times of inner turmoil and transition. Life is filled with lessons and change. Cypress can assist in giving courage for surrendering to God's will that is called for in spiritual transformation. Use cypress to encourage positive emotions of strength, comfort, change, control, understanding, balance, sensitivity, generosity, contentment, stillness, confidence, inner peace, purity of heart, stability, patience and trust; and to counteract negative emotions of grief, sorrow, jealousy, lethargy, fear, timidity, emotional turmoil, isolation, frustration, distraction, regret, lack of concentration, and overwhelming loss.[20]

[19]Denise Whichello Brown, *Aromatherapy,* p. 50.

[20]Valerie Ann Worwood, *The Fragrant Mind, Aromatherapy for Personality, Mind, Mood, and Emotion,* p. 302.

Applications
for Healing
Work: Massage along the spine, on the feet, heart or chest. It can be applied to the healer's hands and run through the field to support and strengthen the person in times of spiritual change, grief and loss.

Safety Data: This is a safe and non-toxic oil that is generally not sensitive to the skin.

Fir *(Abies alba)*

An oil for balancing emotions

Fir is the traditional Christmas tree today. In biblical times, it had many medicinal uses but was used especially for respiratory problems and rheumatism.

(Depending on Bible translation, this may be referred to as cypress)

"So Hiram supplied Solomon's every need for timber of cedar and cypress [fir]."
I Kings 5:10

Scriptures: Mentioned 18 times in the Bible
1 Kings 5:8, 6:15, 34, 9:11; 2 Kings 19:23; 2 Chronicles 2:8, 3:5; Psalms 104:17; Song of Solomon 1:17, Isaiah 14:8, 37:24, 41:19, 60:13; Ezekiel 27:5, 31:8; Hosea 14:8; Nahum 2:3; Zechariah 11:2

Aroma: Fir has a fresh pleasing aroma that generally reminds one of Christmas. It blends well with frankincense, cedarwood, myrtle, rosewood, galbanum, lavender, rosemary, lemon, pine and marjoram.[21]

[21]Julia Lawless, *The Illustrated Encyclopedia of Essential Oils,* p. 71.

Source: The fir tree is a small conifer with silvery white bark. Oil is produced through steam distillation of the needles of the tree. Fir oil is primarily produced now in the Balkans.

Predominant
Chemistry: Monoterpenes 90-95%: alpina-Pinenes, camphene,
                 limonene.

Ancient Uses: Respiratory conditions and muscular and rheumatic
                 pain.

Modern Uses: For the Body: Just as in ancient times, fir is used for
                 respiratory infections, fighting airborne bacteria,
                 arthritis, asthma, bronchial obstructions, coughs,
                 rheumatism, sinusitis, and urinary tract infections.
                 Many massage therapists add fir to their massage oil
                 to relax muscle spasms. It can be a substitute for pine
                 and is milder on the skin.[22]

                 For the Mind and Spirit: When negative emotions
                 move through us they can be a source of growth and
                 change. But when they become stagnant, they can
                 manifest as blocks in our energy centers. Fir can
                 help to resolve emotions trapped in our energy
                 centers.[23] Use fir to encourage protection, steadiness,
                 grounding, harmony, compassion, clarity,
                 achievement, strength and inner unity.

Applications
for Healing
Work: Fir can be diffused or used topically on the brow,
                 energy centers, or the soles of the feet. It can also
                 be applied to the healer's hands and run through the
                 field to clear emotions.

Safety Data: Fir is a non-toxic, non-sensitizing oil so it is safe to use
                 on the skin.

[22]Light Miller and Bryan Miller, *Ayurveda and Aromatherapy, The Earth Essential Guide to Ancient Wisdom and Modern Healing*, p. 254.

[23]Joni Keim Loughran and Ruah Bull, *Aromatherapy Anointing Oils*, pp. 42-43.

Frankincense *(Olibanum* [oil of Lebanon]-*Boswellia carteri)*
An oil of spiritual freedom and quiet contemplation

Of all the oils, frankincense probably played the most significant religious role not only for the Israelites but also for Ancient Egypt, Babylonia, Persia, Greek and Roman civilizations. Along with myrrh, it has been used for spiritual awareness and connection to the Divine for over 5,000 years. Its name—*olibanum* means the oil of Lebanon. We get the word frankincense from an English translation of the Medieval French word *franc,* meaning "pure" or "luxuriant" and the Latin word *incensium* "to smoke." Hildegard of Bingen wrote about Frankincense in her book on healing. She recommended smelling it often for strength, clearing the eyes and filling the brain.[24]

[24]*Hildegard von Bingen's Physica,* translated from the Latin by Priscilla Throop, p. 82.

[25]*Essential Oils Desk Reference,* p. 49.

"Moses said to Aaron ,'Take your censer, put fire on it from the altar and lay incense (Frankincense) on it, and carry it quickly to the congregation and make atonement for them. For wrath has gone out from the Lord; the plague has begun.' So Aaron took it as Moses had ordered, and ran into the middle of the assembly, where the plague had already begun among the people. He put on the incense, and made atonement for the people. He stood between the dead and the living; and the plague was stopped." Numbers 16: 46-49

"A multitude of camels shall cover you, the young camels of Midian and Ephah; all those from Sheba shall come. They shall bring gold and frankincense, and shall proclaim the praise of the Lord." Isaiah 60:6

"On entering the house, they saw the child with Mary his mother; and they knelt down and paid him homage. Then opening their treasure chests, they offered him gifts of gold, frankincense, and myrrh." Matt. 2:11

Scriptures: There are over 52 references in the Bible to Frankincense since the word "incense" is translated from the Hebrew/Greek as "frankincense" and is referring to the same oil.[25]
Exodus 30:34; Leviticus 2:1, 15-16; 5:11; 6:15; 24:7; Numbers 5:15; 1 Chronicles 9:29; Nehemiah 13:5,9; Song of Solomon 3:6; 4:6, 14; Isaiah 59:20; 60:3,6 Matt. 2:11; Revelations 18:13

Aroma: Frankincense has a warm, rich balsamic yet fresh aroma. For many people, it immediately reminds them of "church" since it is a commonly used incense in Christian rituals. It blends well with most other essences.

Source: Both the oil and the incense comes from the resin produced by making incisions in the trunk of the tree. A milky-white resin will exude and harden into an orange-brown gum which is then steam distilled to produce the oil. The frankincense tree is a small one reaching heights of 9 to 22 feet. It grows on the slopes in Somalia, Ethiopia, Southern Arabia and in China. Frankincense and myrrh were the first oils produced from resins.[26]

[26]Gabriel Mojay, *Aromatherapy for Healing the Spirit*, pp. 74-75.

Predominant
Chemistry: Monoterpenes—α pinene, limonese, sesquiterpenes; terpene alcohols: Borneol.

Ancient Uses: Frankincense was extremely valuable during ancient times. The Egyptians used it to fumigate their homes, especially the sick room, for ritual incense and for cosmetics. When the frankincense resin is charred, it produces a black powder called *kohl* used by Egyptian women to paint their eyes. It was considered a holy anointing oil and was used as a general cure-all for diseases. Frankincense has traditionally been used to enhance meditation and elevate spiritual consciousness. In addition, frankincense was used to anoint the newborn sons of kings and priests. As an incense, the resin from the tree was beaten into a fine powder and burned before the altar of God. There were particular directions given for the composition of incense for worship-stacte, onycha, galbanum, sweet spices and pure frankincense were blended together in equal parts to make a "salted, pure, holy" incense. It was forbidden to use this mixture for profane use under pain of being outlawed from the people (Ex. 30:34-37).[27] Frankincense formed an important part of the Sabbath day offering and it was one of the three gifts given by the Magi to the Christ child.

[27]*New World Dictionary Concordance to the New American Bible*, p. 267.

Modern Uses: For the Body: Since frankincense is fairly high in sesquiterpenes, it goes beyond the blood brain barrier and helps stimulate the limbic system of the brain (the center of the emotions) as well as the hypothalamus, pineal and pituitary glands. The hypothalamus is the master gland of the human body, controlling the release of many hormones including thyroid and growth hormone. Frankincense is being studied in some European hospitals for its ability to improve human growth hormone production. The monoterpenes in frankincense reprogram cellular memory thus promoting permanent healing; it is used for cancer, depression, allergies, headaches, bronchitis, herpes, tonsillitis, typhoid, warts, brain damage, and it stimulates the body's production of white blood cells. Frankincense is one of the few oils that is anti-tumoral. It is a strong antiviral, antioxidant, antifungal, antibacterial, antiseptic and expectorant oil.[28]

For the Mind and Spirit: Frankincense oil has the ability to relax and revitalize at the same time. It makes an excellent treatment for nervous tension and nervous exhaustion. Its fragrance increases spiritual awareness and promotes meditation. It may also help improve attitude and uplift spirits, which may help to strengthen the immune system and decrease depression. Like sandalwood, it is ideal for contemplation and prayer, ceasing mental chatter and stilling the mind. Frankincense in this regard is spiritually liberating, tranquilizing, yet clarifying. It aids the mind to focus and eliminate distractions. Frankincense is a sacred oil that helps heal one's spirit and comforts one's heart. Use frankincense to encourage positive states of stability, protection, introspection, courage, fortitude, acceptance and inspiration; and to counteract negative emotions of fear, grief, over-attachments, burnout, exhaustion, insincerity, panic, anxiety,

[28]Rev. Marcy Foley DC, ND, *Embraced by the Essence! Your Journey into Wellness Using Pure Quality Essential Oils,* p. 73.

repression, resistance, self-destruction, apprehension and despair.[29]

[29]Valerie Ann Worwood, *The Fragrant Mind, Aromatherapy for Personality, Mind, Mood, and Emotion*, p. 310.

Applications for Healing Work: Frankincense will be one of your most frequently used oils with the laying-on of hands and Healing Touch. In this regard, it can be considered a general purpose healing oil affecting the energy field and centers. It can be diffused, used topically, orally, or as incense. It can be applied to the healer's hands and run through the field for general support, balance and focusing. It can be used to anoint the brow, energy centers, hands and soles of the feet.

Safety Data: Frankincense is non-toxic and non-irritating to the skin. It can be applied directly or blended with other oils.

Galbanum *(Ferula gummosa)*
An oil for letting go of old ideas

In ancient civilizations, galbanum was burned as incense. In Egypt it was used for embalming and for cosmetics. It was also known for its medicinal properties.

Scriptures: Mentioned only once in the Bible.

Aroma: Galbanum has a very distinctive earthy, pungent odor. It blends well with flower essences like violet, narcissus, lavender, geranium and tree oils like pine and fir.

Source: Galbanum is a large perennial herb with shiny leaflets and small flowers. When slits are made in its stems, it exudes a milky substance that hardens into a resin.

"The Lord said to Moses: Take sweet spices, stacte, and onycha, and galbanum, sweet spices with pure frankincense and make an incense blended as by the perfumer, seasoned with salt, pure and holy; and you shall beat some of it into powder, and put part of it before the covenant in the tent of meeting where I shall meet with you; it shall be for you most holy. When you make incense according to this composition, you shall not make it for yourselves; it shall be regarded by you as holy to the Lord."
Exodus 30:34-36

The oil is produced through steam distillation of the resin. Grown in Iran, Turkey and Lebanon and usually distilled in Europe or the U.S.

Predominant Chemistry: Monoterpenes, α pinene, camphene, limonene, and sesquiterpenols.

Ancient Uses: Used in holy anointing oils; also used in various medicines, perfume, spiritually uplifting yet very grounding, used for treating wounds, inflammations and skin disorders, pain relief, spasms and cramps, and as a diuretic.

Modern Uses: For the Body: Can be helpful for abscesses, acne, asthma, chronic coughs, cramps, indigestion, muscular aches and pains, scar tissue, wrinkles, wounds. The monoterpenes reprogram cellular memory, the coumarins are antibacterial/antiviral. Although galbanum has a low vibrational frequency, when combined with other oils like frankincense or sandalwood, the frequency rises dramatically.[30]

[30]*Essential Oils Desk Reference,* p. 50.

For the Mind and Spirit: Helpful for emotional balancing and nervous tension. Galbanum is called a sacrificial fragrance that allows for the shedding of old ideas and attitudes. Its odor helps in seeing the path ahead. It is grounding, yet leads to a surrendering to God.[31] Use galbanum to encourage calm, stability, direction, concentration, fortitude and focus.

[31]Valerie Ann Worwood, *The Fragrant Heavens, the Spiritual Dimension of Fragrance and Aromatherapy,* p. 231.

Applications for Healing Work: Galbanum will not be one of your frequently used oils in healing work unless blended with other oils. This is because of its pungent odor. It can be used topically or taken internally. When taken as a supplement, it should be added to food or soy/rice milk.

Safety Data: Galbanum is generally non-toxic and non-irritating to the skin.

Hyssop *(Hyssopus officianalis)*
An oil for purification and protection

Hyssop is another ancient oil with a lot of history. It was highly prized by the Hebrews and is one of the bitter herbs mentioned in the Old Testament used to purify the temple. It has a rich history in ritual, culinary, and medicinal uses.

Scriptures: Mentioned 12 times in the Bible
Leviticus 14:4,6,49,51-52; Numbers 19:6, 18; 1 Kings 4:33; John 19:29; Hebrews 9:19

"Purge me with hyssop and I shall be clean." Psalm 51:7

"Take a bunch of hyssop, dip it in the blood that is in the basin, and touch the lintel and the two doorposts with the blood in the basin. None of you shall go outside the door of your house until morning." Exodus 12:22

Aroma: Hyssop has a sweet, kind of spicy aroma that is very pleasing. It blends well with lavender, rosemary, myrtle, sage, fennel, clary sage, geranium and the citrus oils.

Source: Hyssop is a small shrub about 1-2 feet in height that likes to grow on walls. It has small linear leaves and whorls of purple-blue, pink or white flowers that are strongly aromatic and attract bees and butterflies. The oil is produced by steam distillation of the leaves and flowering tops. Hyssop is native to the Mediterranean region but now grows wild throughout America, Russia and Europe. It is cultivated mainly in France and Hungary.

Predominant

Chemistry: Monoterpenes; β pinenes; sesquiterpenes; sesquiterpenols; phenols.

Ancient Uses: The Romans used hyssop to protect against plague and to disinfect their homes. For the Israelites, it was traditionally used to drive away evil spirits; it was considered to be spiritually uplifting and used in meditation and for spiritual purification. Hyssop was part of the ritual in creating purifying waters used in many of the ancient Hebrew ceremonies.[32] It became a symbol of spiritual cleansing and associated with baptism and the forgiveness of sins in the early Christian Church. It was used in various medicines for respiratory relief, as a decongestant, and expectorant. Jesus was offered hyssop on the cross. This may have been offered in crucifixions as an act of mercy. Death was by slow suffocation as one's lungs filled up. The hyssop may have eased their congestion and given them some relief both physically and emotionally. In the Middle Ages, Hildegard recommended Hyssop for lung and liver problems. She directed the sufferer to eat it often in cooked food and to chew Hyssop that had been soaked in wine.[33]

Modern Uses: For the Body: Hyssop has been used to relieve anxiety, arthritis, asthma, respiratory infections, parasites, sore throats, cuts and wounds. It can strengthen the lungs and help prevent the recurrence of colds and flu and ward off infection. It can be used with eucalyptus, tea tree and thyme for bronchitis and sinusitis. Hyssop strengthens the spleen-pancreas and stimulates and warms digestion. It may be used for appetite loss, slow digestion, and abdominal bloating. It also has a mild diuretic action

[32]Raymond Brown, J. Fitzmyer, and R. Murphy, *The New Jerome Biblical Commentary*, p.1274

[33]*Hildegard von Bingen's Physica*, translated from the Latin by Priscilla Throop, p.39.

making it useful for fluid retention. Robert Tisserand, who is one of early pioneers in essential oils, reports that hyssop has an unusual regulating effect on the blood pressure, tending to lower it if it is high, and raise it if it is low.[34]

[34]Robert Tisserand, *The Art of Aromatherapy,* p. 236.

For the Mind and Spirit: Hyssop is distinctly invigorating for the mind. It is used for poor concentration, short-term mental fatigue and chronic nervous conditions. This makes it helpful for melancholy and pessimism. Traditionally it was considered an oil of protection of one's space (home) from evil spirits. In this regard, it certainly can strengthen one's field and protect personal boundaries.[35] Use hyssop to encourage acceptance, fulfillment, encouragement, direction, clarity, balance and harmony.

[35]Gabriel Mojay, *Aromatherapy for Healing the Spirit,* pp. 74-75.

Applications for Healing Work:

Since hyssop is known for its purifying and protecting qualities, it will be a helpful oil with hands-on healing like the laying-on of hands and Healing Touch. Use it to clear and protect the healing space before beginning your healing work with the person. It can also be applied to the healer's hands and run through the field for general protection and support of the energy field boundaries.

Safety Data: Hyssop is generally non-toxic and non-irritating to the skin. Do not use during pregnancy or by those with epilepsy.

Myrrh *(Commiphora myrrha)*
An oil of tranquility and peace

Myrrh is another ancient oil with a rich history. Along with frankincense, it is one of the oldest spiritual oils known to man. Its name is derived from the Arabic *murr,* meaning "bitter." The gum resin has been used in the Near East and Mediterranean area for thousands of years. This was an extremely important oil among the ancient civilizations for its medicinal qualities, its preservative qualities in embalming, and in spiritual and ritual enhancement of life.

"The Lord spoke to Moses, Take the finest spices of liquid myrrh five hundred shekels, and of sweet-smelling cinnamon half as much, that is, two hundred fifty, and two hundred fifty of aromatic cane, and five hundred of cassia-measured by the sanctuary shekel-and a hin of olive oil; and you shall make of these a sacred anointing oil blended as by the perfumer; it shall be a holy anointing oil." Exodus 30:22-25

"I have perfumed my bed with myrrh, aloes, and cinnamon." Proverbs 7:17

"I arose to open to my beloved, and my hands dripped with myrrh, my fingers with liquid myrrh, upon the handles of the bolt." Song of Solomon 5:5

(Also referred to as Stacte in the Bible)

Scriptures: Mentioned between 13-16 times in the Bible. Several references could be referring to Cistus or Rose of Sharon
Genesis 37:25; 43:11; Esther 2:12; Psalm 45:8; Exodus 30:34 as "Stacte"; Song of Solomon 1:13; 3:6; 4:6, 14; 5:1, 5, 13; Matt. 2:11; Mark 15:23; John 19:39

Aroma: Myrrh has a rich musty balsamic incense-like smell that is not sweet. It blends well with frankincense, sandalwood, benzoin, cypress, juniper, geranium, mandarin, thyme, mints, lavender, pine and spices.

Source: There are many species that the myrrh of the Bible could be. They are shrubs that grow in arid desert areas and can reach as high as 9 feet. Myrrh has knotted branches and scanty leaves with small white flowers. Through small fissures in its bark, this plant exudes a pale yellow resin that will harden into reddish-brown "tears" when exposed to the air. The oil is steam distilled from the gum resin tears. These species are native to the Red Sea region-Somalia, Yemen and Ethiopia.

Predominant
Chemistry: Hydrocarbons; sesquiterpenes; ketones; aldehydes.

Ancient Uses: Myrrh was used by midwives in childbirth to prevent
               infection and was massaged on the perineum to aid
               in stretching to allow for an easier birth delivery.
               It was used on the umbilical cord to prevent infection
               as well. Myrrh was used for skin conditions, oral
               hygiene and embalming. Women believed it
               preserved a youthful look and so it was used in
               cosmetics. In the Book of Esther, the writer relates
               that six of the twelve months devoted to the
               purification of women was done with the oil of
               myrrh. Myrrh was also a good insect repellant.
               Wine mixed with myrrh was drank in Hebrew
               tradition to prepare oneself for religious ceremonies.
               It was a way of raising their consciousness.[36]
               Interestingly, it was also given to the condemned on
               the cross to ease the pain of crucifixion.[37] Myrrh
               was one of the gifts along with frankincense that
               was brought to the Christ child. Biblical scholars
               believe myrrh symbolized Christ's redemptive
               suffering.[38] In the Middle Ages, myrrh was still
               considered an important healing substance.
               Hildegard felt that myrrh held closely to the body
               would ward off evil of all kinds and that you would
               be less likely to suffer from magic spells and bad
               words with myrrh streaked on the chest or stomach.
               Myrrh drunk in warm wine was also a remedy for
               great fevers and was reported to help curb lust.[39]

Modern Uses: For the Body: Myrrh has a lot of healing properties.
               It is anti-infectious, antiviral, anti-parasitic, anti-
               inflammatory, hormone-like, anti-hyperthyroid, and
               supports the immune system. It is a very good
               expectorant and therefore is good for bronchitis,

[36]Gabriel Mojay, *Aromatherapy for Healing the Spirit,* pp. 98-99.

[37]*New World Dictionary Concordance to the New American Bible,* p.467.

[38]Raymond Brown, J. Fitzmyer, and R. Murphy, *The New Jerome Biblical Commentary,* p. 636.

[39]*Hildegard von Bingen's Physica,* translated from the Latin by Priscilla Throop, p.39.

coughs, colds and conditions that produce excess thick mucus. For respiratory and throat conditions, blend it with eucalyptus, tea tree and pine. It is good for diarrhea, thrush in babies, vaginal thrush, athletes foot, ringworm, viral hepatitis, chapped skin, and wrinkles. It has a pronounced effect on the mouth. It is good for mouth ulcers, and for the gums. Its astringent qualities make it excellent for reducing hemorrhoids and for healing ulcers of all kinds.[40]

[40]Robert Tisserand, *The Art of Aromatherapy*, pp. 257-260.

For the Mind and Spirit: Myrrh can be used for emotional releasing. Like frankincense, myrrh affects the nervous system in a gentle calming way. It can be used to instill deep tranquility, inner stillness and peace. When used in grief, it tends to ease sorrow. Use myrrh to encourage fortitude, peace, calm, sympathy, acceptance and courage.

Applications for Healing Work:

Myrrh can be used topically and orally. It can be applied to the healer's hands and run through the energy field to bring about a sense of peacefulness and tranquility. It can be used to anoint the brow, energy centers, hands and the soles of the feet. Myrrh has been known to help bring about a spiritual connection between "heaven" and "earth" when anointing the crown and root centers. A link is formed strengthening the entire energy system, enhancing inner peace.

Safety Data:

Myrrh is generally non-toxic and non-irritating to the skin. Because of its strong astringent properties, it is not recommended during pregnancy.

Myrtle *(Myrtus communis)*
An oil of freshness and new beginnings

The myrtle plant was a sign of immortality to the ancient peoples in the Near East. Perhaps this is because myrtle will stay fresh for weeks after it is cut. As one of the fragrant plants of Israel it was included among the spices used for Sabbath evening.

Scriptures: Mentioned 3 times in the Bible
Nehemiah 8:15; Isaiah 41:19

Aroma: Myrtle has clean, fresh, camphor-like, sweet, odor similar to eucalyptus. Its fragrance is elevating and for some, it is euphoric. It blends well with bergamot, lavender, rosemary, clary sage, hyssop, lime, laurel, ginger, clove and other spice oils.

Source: Myrtle grows as a large bush or small tree with lots of tough slender branches. It has small sharp-pointed leaves and white flowers and puts out small black berries. Both the leaves and the flowers are fragrant. The oil is obtained through steam distillation of the leaves and twigs. Myrtle is native to North Africa but grows all over the Mediterranean region. Its oil is produced in Tunisia, Morocco, Corsica, Spain, Italy, the Balkan area and France.

Predominant Chemistry: Monoterpenes: α pinene, β—pinene; sesquiterpenes; alcohols; esters; oxides; aldehydes.

Ancient Uses: Traditionally, myrtle was used in religious ceremony. However, there is not much history passed down on how the ancient peoples actually used myrtle. By the 16th century we know that it was a major ingredient of "angel's water," a skin care lotion of that day.[41]

"For you shall go out in joy, and be led back in peace; the mountains and the hills before you shall burst into song, and all the trees of the field shall clap their hands. Instead of the thorn shall come up the cypress; instead of the brier shall come up the myrtle; and it shall be to the Lord for a memorial, for an everlasting sign that shall not be cut off." Isaiah 55:12-13.

[41]Julia Lawless, *The Illustrated Encyclopedia of Essential Oils*, p. 182.

Modern Uses: For the body: This is a fairly mild oil and therefore can be used for children's coughs and chest complaints. It is soothing to the respiratory system acting as a decongestant. It is good for sinus infections, tuberculosis, colds, flu, coughs, bronchitis, and asthma. For skin conditions, its astringent properties make it useful for acne, psoriasis, blemishes, bruises, oily skin and hemorrhoids. Myrtle is also useful for decongesting the prostate.

For the mind and spirit: Use myrtle to encourage uplifting feelings of comfort, forgiveness, acceptance, empowerment and harmony.[42] It can be rubbed on the throat area near the thyroid to encourage feelings of balance. It is elevating, clarifying and cleansing.

[42]Valerie Ann Worwood, *The Fragrant Heavens, the Spiritual Dimension of Fragrance and Aromatherapy,* p. 231.

Applications for Healing Work: Myrtle oil can be used by inhalation, diffusion or used in a humidifier. It is very safe for children. The oil can also be rubbed on the chest or feet for respiratory and immune disorders or on the prostate area for prostate congestion.

Safety Data: Myrtle is non-toxic and non-irritating to the skin.

Onycha *(Styrax benzoin)*

This is one of those ancient oils that has gone by several names. It was called onycha in the Bible but it was more commonly referred to as benzoin or styrax. For thousands of years in the East it was considered a medicine and an incense. In the Middle Ages, it was referred to as "Friars Balsam" and was used for respiratory complaints and as an antiseptic for skin conditions.

Scriptures: Mentioned only once in the Bible
Exodus 30:34-36 (See Galbanum for this quote.)

Aroma: Onycha has that characteristic "benzoin" odor that used to be associated with hospitals a few decades ago. Depending on where it comes from, it could have a sweet vanilla-like aroma that is quite pleasing. It blends well with sandalwood, rose, jasmine, frankincense, myrrh, cypress, juniper, lemon, and the spice oils.

Source: Styrax benzoin comes from a large tropical tree that can grow up to 65 feet in height. It has pale green citrus-like leaves that are white underneath. The oil comes from the tree's resin that is dissolved by solvents which are later removed. Benzoin trees are native to tropical Asia primarily Sumatra, Java and Malaysia. The oil known as "onycha" is very thick and does not pour.

Predominant
Chemistry: Phenolic aldehydes—Benzoic aldehyde and vanillin which gives onycha its characteristic aroma.

Ancient Uses: Onycha/benzoin was used both as medicine and as incense. It was also in perfume, and blended in holy anointing oils. The ancient peoples found it comforting, soothing, uplifting, and they used it as an ointment to heal skin wounds. Since the 16th century it has been used as a tincture for respiratory complaints and for cuts and skin conditions.

Modern Uses: Onycha/benzoin can be inhaled for sinusitis, bronchitis, colds, coughs and sore throats. Its anti-inflammatory and antiseptic properties are useful for dermatitis and skin wounds. It has been known to relieve stress when used in massage oil.

Applications
for Healing
Work: Can be inhaled, used in massage, applied topically in
wound dressings. Normally not used with the laying-
on of hands or Healing Touch.

Safety Data: Non-toxic, non-irritating but some may be sensitive.

Pine *(Pinus sylvestris)*
An oil for invigoration and rejuvenation

Pine is mentioned a number of times in the Bible depending
on your translation. It has wonderful medicinal properties especially
for the lungs but is not an oil that had a wide audience in ancient
times. It was the pine that provided valuable timber for building and
for ship masts through the centuries. The ancient Egyptians used to
eat the kernels added to their bread. Native Americans used to add
pine branches to their smudge sticks for ceremonial cleansing. Both
Native Americans and some Europeans used the needles in their
bedding to repel lice and fleas.

"The glory of Lebanon shall come to you,
the cypress [fir], the plane, and the pine, to
beautify the place of my sanctuary; and I
will glorify where my feet rest." Isaiah 60:13

Scriptures: There are 3 references in the Bible
Nehemiah 8:15; Isaiah 41:19

Aroma: Pine has a strong, dry, turpentine-like odor. It blends
well with cedarwood, rosemary, tea tree, sage,
lavender, juniper, lemon, eucalyptus and marjoram.

Source: There are many species of pine. *Pinus sylvestris,*
the Scotch pine is the safest and most therapeutic
in its oil. These trees grow to a height of 130 feet and
have a flat crown. The bark is reddish-brown with
deep fissures and the needles are stiff and grow in
pairs. The cones are pointed and brown. The best oil
is obtained from steam distillation of the needles

only. The Scotch pine is native to Europe and Asia especially Russia and Finland, it is cultivated in Eastern U.S. and Canada.

Predominant
Chemistry: Monoterpenes: α and β—pinenes, limonene; sesquiterpenes; terpenols; sesquiterpenols; esters.

Ancient Uses: Pine oil was used for breathing disorders. The kernels were eaten by the Egyptians and native peoples used the needles for bedding. The Greeks recommended boiling the cones with horehound and honey for "old coughs." Only later it became a tradition to beat the young shoots and add to bath water to relieve rheumatic pain and nervous exhaustion.[43]

[43]Gabriel Mojay, *Aromatherapy for Healing the Spirit,* pp. 110-111.

Modern Uses: For the Body: Its primary use is for the respiratory system: asthma, pulmonary infections, bronchitis, and sinusitis. Pine is reported to be an excellent restorative for consumption.[44] It may also help as a good first aid for cuts, cysts, fatigue, gout, lice, nervous exhaustion, scabies, skin parasites, sores, stress. With its antiseptic and anti-inflammatory properties it may be used for urinary tract infections. Pine is considered a tonic for the lungs, kidneys and nerves and ranks along with thyme and rosemary as one of the most effective oils for fatigue and nervous debility. Pine is used in massage for stressed muscles and joints. It works well with *Eucalyptus globulus* and the action of both oils is enhanced when blended. Pine is a great rejuvenator physically and mentally when added to bath water. Pine has also been found helpful with a number of other physical problems. Interestingly, it is hormone-like in action and could be helpful for diabetes. Pine oil may

[44]Julia Lawless, *The Illustrated Encyclopedia of Essential Oils,* p. 200.

help increase blood pressure and stimulate the adrenal glands and the circulatory system.[45]

[45]*Essential Oils Desk Reference,* p. 67-68.

For the Mind and Spirit: Pine oil is psychologically fortifying. It invigorates the body/mind/spirit, opening the chest, instilling a positive attitude and restoring self-confidence. Its fresh pungent fragrance disperses melancholy and pessimism and helps to reawaken the person to the joys of life.[46] Use pine to encourage positive emotions of humility, simplicity, assurance, perseverance, mindfulness, and trust; and to counteract negative emotions of regrets, guilt, self-blame, self-criticalness, self-reproach, unworthiness, exhaustion, and feeling inadequate.[47]

[46]Gabriel Mojay, *Aromatherapy for Healing the Spirit,* pp. 110-111.

[47]Valerie Ann Worwood, *The Fragrant Mind, Aromatherapy for Personality, Mind, Mood, and Emotion,* p. 352.

Other Uses: Pine oil is also used in cleaning products, cosmetics, and toiletries.

Applications for Healing Work: Pine may be used for inhalation, diffusion or may be applied topically with care.

Safety Data: It may be sensitive to skin and in that case, will need to be diluted with either a good vegetable oil or massage oil.

Rose of Sharon/Cistus *(Cistus ladanifer)*
An oil for elevating the emotions

This is one of the early aromatic oils of the ancient world. The gum was used for many medicinal problems including diarrhea and dysentery. Women used it to promote menstruation. This is another oil that goes by several names. It is called *Cistus ladanifer, labdanum* and rock rose.[48]

[48]David Stewart, *Healing Oils of the Bible,* p. 298.

Scriptures: Mentioned 2-4 times in the Bible depending on translations. Some references are to cistus, another name for rose of Sharon. Genesis 37:25 and 43:11 refer to Myrrh in English but the Hebrew word in these passages is ladanum, which is actually Rock Rose.

"I am a rose of Sharon, a lily of the valleys." Song of Solomon 2:I

Aroma: Rose of Sharon/cistus has a rich, sweet, musky, balsamic odor. It blends well with clary sage, pine, juniper, calamus, lavender, bergamot, cypress, sandalwood, frankincense and chamomile.

Source: Rose of Sharon/cistus is a small sticky shrub that likes to grow in rocky areas. It can reach a height of 10 feet. It has beautiful fragrant white flowers with deep red in each petal that resemble a wild rose. The resin is obtained either by steam distillation of the branches or by boiling the plant material in water. Native to the Mediterranean mountainous areas, it is now found throughout the whole region and into France, Spain, Portugal, Greece, Morocco, cyprus and the Balkan areas.

Predominant
Chemistry: Monoterpenes—α pinene, camphene; aldehydes, ketones.

Ancient Uses: It is really unclear as to the ways the ancient peoples used Rose of Sharon/cistus. More than likely it was used for some medicinal qualities and for perfume.

Modern Uses: For the Body: Rose of Sharon/cistus has been studied for its effects on the regeneration of cells. It is helpful for respiratory conditions such as bronchitis, lung infections, coughs, and rhinitis. It has been found to be an anti-hemorrhaging agent, anti-

[49] *Essential Oils Desk Reference*, p. 41.

inflammatory, anti-infectious, and neurotonic. For skin care, it helps with wrinkles and can be used on wounds.[49]

For the Mind and Spirit: Rose of Sharon/cistus has been found to be calming to the nerves and elevating for the emotions.

Applications for Healing Work:	This oil can be diffused or used topically with massage oil.
Safety Data:	Generally non-toxic and non-irritating. Avoid during pregnancy.

Spikenard *(Nardostychys jatamansi)*
An oil of faith and surrender

Spikenard was one of the early aromatics used by many of the ancient peoples—Egyptians, Hebrews, and Hindu. It was used both in ceremonial rituals and for healing. Record shows that it was one of the most precious oils used by priests, kings, or high initiates. It was the oil that Mary of Bethany used to anoint the feet and head of Jesus, filling the room with its aroma. It was preparation for his death and burial.

"Mary took a pound of costly perfume made of pure nard [spikenard], anointed Jesus' feet, and wiped them with her hair. The house was filled with the fragrance of the perfume." John 12:3

"While he was at Bethany in the house of Simon the leper, as he sat at the table, a woman came with an alabaster jar of very costly ointment of nard, and she broke open the jar and poured the ointment on his head." Mark 14:3

	(Also called Nard in the Scriptures)
Scriptures:	Mentioned 5 times in the Scriptures Song of Solomon 1:12; 4:13-14
Aroma:	Spikenard is a very sweet-woody, spicy fragrance similar to valerian oil. It blends well with Rose of Sharon, lavender, pine and spice oils.

Source: Spikenard is a tender aromatic herb that can grow as
                 high as three feet. It has large lance-like leaves with
                 small greenish flowers. The oil actually comes from
                 the fragrant rhizome-root. A member of the valerian
                 family, this herb is similar in its aroma and action to
                 Indian valerian. The oil is obtained by steam
                 distillation of the plant roots. Spikenard is native to
                 the mountainous region of northern India but the oil
                 is distilled mainly in Europe or the U.S.

Predominant
Chemistry: Sesquiterpenes—the third highest in sesquiterpenes
                 of all known oils (only cedarwood and vetiver have
                 more; esters, phenols.

Ancient Uses: There is a rich history in the use of spikenard by the
                 ancient peoples. They used it for perfumes,
                 medicines, skin tonic, incense, and as a mood
                 enhancer. It was considered one of the sacred chrisms
                 for anointing monarchs and high initiates.
                 The Greek and Roman perfumers used it in the
                 preparation of *nardinum,* one of their most celebrated
                 scented oils of the first century. Spikenard was the last
                 oil Jesus received before being arrested and going to
                 the cross.[50]

[50]*Essential Oils Desk Reference,* p73.

Modern Uses: For the Body: Modern use is mainly for regulating
                 the nervous system and the heart. It is helpful for
                 rapid and irregular heartbeat. Its antispasmodic
                 properties aids digestive action and therefore helps
                 nausea, constipation and intestinal colic. It is
                 recommended for hemorrhoids, varicose veins and
                 migraine headaches. The oil is known for is ability
                 to help allergic skin reactions and it is used for
                 wounds that will not heal.

For the Mind and Spirit: Spikenard oil calms the heart, stabilized the mind and settles the emotions. It can be used for nervous tension, anxiety, and insomnia. It acts like valerian in its antidepressant properties. It has a decidedly calming effect instilling a profound sense of peace.[51] Use spikenard to encourage positive emotions of forgiveness, fearlessness, calm, centering, balance and resolution.

[51]Gabriel Mojay, *Aromatherapy for Healing the Spirit*, pp. 118-119.

Applications for Healing Work:

Spikenard may be applied to the healer's hands and run through the field. It may be applied to the abdomen, the feet, and the head or distilled in the room. Its fragrance as one of the holy oils will fill the room and like myrrh, will assist the person to a place of calm surrender, yet one of strong faith. Spikenard soothes the deepest anxieties and replaces negative emotions with acceptance and compassion. Like Jesus, we are moved to a place of great faith and connection to the Divine.

Safety Data: Non-toxic, non-irritating and non-sensitizing.

Chapter 8

OILS USED BY CHRISTIAN MEDIEVAL HEALERS

As Christians began to disperse throughout the world, many continued the practice of anointing with oils for healing. Sometimes the oils in the Holy Scriptures were not available or simply too expensive to acquire. By the Middle Ages, some began to experiment with producing oils from plants native to their particular region like lavender, sage and rosemary. They tried other culinary herbs like basil, chamomile, thyme, oregano, parsley, marjoram, mint, fennel, and yarrow, distilling, brewing or pressing them to see if they would produce oils for healing. (Many of these herbs produced essential oils available during the Biblical times but not specifically mentioned in the scriptures.) Likewise, they worked with angelica, juniper, clary sage, melissa, jasmine, neroli (orange blossom), and pennyroyal. The European explorers brought back bergamot, lemon, orange, mandarin, bay, cardamom, coriander, eucalyptus, geranium, ginger, rose, and ylang-ylang. Most likely, the efficacy of these oils was determined through experimentation for various physical, mental and spiritual problems to see what worked and what did not. Often the "experts" were the master herbalists who resided in the monasteries and abbeys of Europe and the pharmacists in the local apothecaries. Only much later did the chemists begin to take a leading role in the understanding of the healing properties of these aromatic oils.

Listed in this section are additional essential oils not specifically mentioned in the scriptures that were probably used by Christian healers over the past two millenniums. Many of the writings of the saints like Hildegard of Bingen testify to the use of healing herbs and aromatic oils for healing on all levels. Hildegard's writings in particular have been used as a point of reference for healers for the last nine hundred years. Since I have a great love and admiration for this phenomenal woman, I will reference her healing recipes and advise that have stood the test of time.

Angelica *(Angelica archangelica)*
An oil of angelic protection

For many centuries, Europeans have called Angelica the "oil of angels" or the "Holy Spirit" root. There are over 30 different varieties of Angelica worldwide.

Aroma: It has a strong aromatic scent that was considered of "divine origin." It blends well with patchouly, clary sage, vetiver, and most of the citrus oils.[1]

[1]Julia Lawless, *The Illustrated Encyclopedia of Essential Oils,* p. 84.

Source: Oil is produced by steam distillation of the roots and rhizomes, and secondly from the fruit or seed. It is native to Europe and cultivated mainly in Belgium, Hungary and Germany.

Predominant
Chemistry: Monoterpenes; esters, terpene alkaloids; rich in coumarins.

Traditional
Use: From the time of Paracelsus in the Middle Ages, Angelica was used to protect against the plague. The stems were chewed during the plague of 1660 to prevent the infection. When the plant was burned, the seeds and roots were thought to purify the air.[2] In Europe it was also used for bronchial ailments, colds, coughs, indigestion, wind and to stimulate the appetite.

[2]*Essential Oils Desk Reference,* p. 33-34

Modern Uses: For the Body: Angelica is just as useful today as it was in centuries past for respiratory ailments such as coughs, colds and infections. It is also helpful for indigestion and colic. Other uses include menopause, premenstrual tension, rheumatic conditions and as a urinary antiseptic for cystitis. It may also help with irritated skin conditions, such as psoriasis.

For the Mind and Spirit: Just as the people in the Middle Ages used this beautiful oil for angelic connection, we can use Angelica to open to the inspiration and the protection of the angels. This is an oil to guard against evil spirits and thus it strengthens the boundaries of the energy field. Use Angelica to promote peace and self-awareness.

Other Uses: This highly prized fragrance is a component in soaps, lotions, and perfumes. It is also used as a flavoring agent in foods, beverages, especially liqueurs.

Applications for Healing Work: Angelica may be a difficult essential oil to find since it is an expensive one. However you may find it in many different blends. Angelica can be applied topically or diffused. It can be applied to the healer's hands and run through the field as a general blessing and protection. Angelica assists in maintaining the meditative state and therefore can be a favorite oil for healing work.

Safety Data: When applying to the skin, caution should be taken when there is exposure to the sun or ultra-violet light. Angelica contains bergopten that may cause photo-sensitivity.

Basil *(Ocimum basilicum)*
An uplifting and strengthening oil

Basil has a long tradition both in the East as a medicinal herb and in the West where it is primarily used as a culinary herb.

Aroma: Basil oil has a sweet odor with a camphor-tinge. It blends well with bergamot, wintergreen, cypress, geranium, hyssop, lavender, lemongrass, and marjoram.

Source: Basil oil is produced by steam distillation from the herb leaves and flowering tops. The oil is produced in Egypt, Morocco, South Africa, Brazil, U.S., and France.

Predominant
Chemistry: Mainly Methyl chavicol, with small amounts of linalol; terpene alcohols; terpene esters; phenols.

Traditional
Use: In the 16th century, the powdered leaves were inhaled to treat migraines and chest infections.[3] In the Ayurvedic tradition, it is used for respiratory problems such as bronchitis, coughs, colds, asthma, flu and emphysema and as an antidote for poisonous insect or snake bites.[4] Basil was considered sacred to the Hindus and was an herb men placed on their chest when resting. It was thought to deter demons and thus was considered a protective plant. In Greece, basil is also venerated because it is said that it sprung up at the place where St. Helen found the true cross of Jesus.[5] Hildegard of Bingen used basil as a treatment for someone with palsy of the tongue (can not speak) and for strong fevers.[6]

[3]*Essential Oils Desk Reference,* p. 34-35.

[4]Julia Lawless, *The Illustrated Encyclopedia of Essential Oils,* p. 185.

[5]Valerie Ann Worwood, *The Fragrant Heavens,* pp. 200-201.

[6]*Hildegard von Bingen's Physica,* translated from the Latin by Priscilla Throop, p. 97.

Modern Uses: For the Body: Basil is excellent for the relief of migraines and mental fatigue. It is also helpful in relaxing muscles and soothing insect bites. It can be used for respiratory conditions, skin disorders like itching or ringworm. Since it is considered a "hot" oil, it is good for fainting. When used in a bath, basil can be uplifting and refreshing yet tingling, similar to peppermint. Basil can be used in a tea, in cooking, inhalation, or directly on the body (diluted for sensitive skin).

For the Mind and Spirit: Basil can be used to encourage a positive outlook, sense of purpose in one's life, to improve concentration, decisiveness, trust, enthusiasm, clarity, cheerfulness and strength. Basil can counteract indecision, negativity, fear, confusion, apathy, resentment, doubts, shame, melancholy and sadness.[7] Basil opens the heart and brings harmony to the mind. It has strong effects on the emotions, and can be very strengthening especially in times of fear or sadness. Dr. Valnet considers basil oil a good aromatic nerve tonic. It clears the head, relieves fatigue and gives the mind strength and clarity.[8]

[7]Valerie Ann Worwood, *The Fragrant Mind*, p. 279.

[8]Jean Valnet, *The Practice of Aroma-therapy*, p. 97.

Applications for Healing Work: Basil can be applied to the spine, the energy centers, soles of the feet or the back of the neck.

Safety Data: May be sensitizing to the skin, use with caution or dilute with a carrier oil. Best to avoid this oil during pregnancy.

Bergamot *(Citrus bergamia)*
An oil for releasing and relaxing

Bergamot was named after the city of Bergamo, Italy where the oil was first produced by expression. The fruit was first brought from the Canary Islands to Europe in the 15th century by Christopher Columbus. Bergamot is used in the production of Earl Grey tea and gives the tea its distinctive flavor.

Aroma:	The scent of this oil is sweet and citrusy with a floral quality about it. It blends well with most other essences particularly jasmine, cypress, lavender, geranium, lemon, chamomile, juniper, coriander, violet and neroli. Along with neroli and lavender, bergamot is one of the principal ingredients of the classic Eau-de-Cologne.[9]
Source:	This oil is produced by cold expression of the peel of the nearly ripe fruit. Bergamot is a citrus tree with smooth oval leaves bearing small round fruit that ripens from green to yellow and looks like miniature oranges. Bergamot trees grow throughout the Mediterranean area but particularly in Italy. They are native to tropical Asia.
Predominant Chemistry:	Known to have over 300 compounds. Monoterpenes, α–pinene, aldehydes.
Traditional Use:	Bergamot has been used in Italian home remedies for centuries primarily for fever and for worms. It was also used for skin conditions associated with oily complexion.

[9]Robert Tisserand, *The Art of Aroma-therapy*, p. 43.

Modern Uses: For the Body: Bergamot is both a tonic as well as a calming oil and may be helpful for a number of conditions. For the skin, it can help acne, boils, cold sores, eczema, insect bites, oily complexion, psoriasis, scabies, and varicose ulcers. For the respiratory system, it may help with bad breath, mouth infections, sore throat, and tonsillitis. For the digestive system, it can help with flatulence and loss of appetite, and for the genital-urinary system, it is reported helpful with cystitis, itching and thrush.

For the Mind and Spirit: Bergamot is helpful in times of anxiety and stress-related conditions. It is particularly good in cases of grief. There are some reports that bergamot has antidepressant qualities by helping the person feel refreshed and uplifted.[10] If the depression is a result of unexpressed anger, bergamot will help free the flow of energy. Bergamot oil helps us to relax and "let go." It is an oil for releasing and relaxing, and therefore an oil to encourage positive emotions of confidence, balance, strength and joy. Use Bergamot to dispel feelings of depression, anxiety, helplessness, apathy, burnout, despondency, emptiness, hopelessness, sadness, and loneliness.[11]

[10]Light Miller and Bryan Miller, *Ayurveda and Aromatherapy*, p. 225.

[11]Valerie Ann Worwood, *The Fragrant Mind*, p. 281.

Applications for Healing Work: Bergamot can be diffused, used as an anointing oil for the brow or temples and it can be used on location for stings and bites. Bergamot also makes a nice deodorant. Bergamot oil is wonderful to use on the bed sheets or pillow especially for someone who is either distressed or depressed.

Safety Data: May cause sensitivity to sunlight for the skin.

Chamomile *(Matricaria recutita*—German variety, *Chamaemelum nobile*—Roman variety)
An oil of calmness

There are two varieties of chamomile commonly distilled for their oils. The German chamomile is referred to as blue chamomile and has a deep blue, almost black color to the oil. The Roman variety is pale yellow with a slight blue tinge to it. It has a milder, sweeter smell. Roman chamomile shares all the therapeutic properties of blue chamomile but is milder in effect and is particularly suitable for treating infants or people in a weaken condition.[12] Hildegard referred to the German chamomile and used it in a gentle ointment for intestinal pain. She instructed that chamomile be mixed with water and lard or oil. As it cooked, flour would be added to make a porridge that would then heal the intestines.[13]

[12]Susan Curtis, *Essential Oils,* pp. 88-89.

[13]*Hildegard von Bingen's Physica,* translated from the Latin by Priscilla Throop, p. 62.

Aroma: Chamomile has a sweet, fruity-herbal scent. It blends well with bergamot, clary sage, jasmine, orange blossom, rose, geranium and lavender.

Source: Chamomile is a perennial herb about 10-12 in high with a much-branched hairy stem, half spreading or creeping. It has feathery leaves and daisy-like white flowers. The Roman variety is smaller than the German. It is cultivated extensively in Europe and the U.S. The oil is produced by steam distillation in Europe.

Predominant
Chemistry: (German chamomile) Sesquiterpenes, sesquiterpenols; sesquiterpene oxides; coumarins, ethers. (Roman chamomile) Mainly esters. Alcohols, terpenes, acetates, ketones and sesquiterpenes.

Traditional
Use:

This herb has a traditional use that dates back thousands of years. The Egyptians, Moors and Saxons all counted it as an important if not sacred herb. It was used for nausea, anorexia, vomiting in pregnancy, flatulence, nervous bowel, tension headaches and sleeplessness.[14]

[14]Julia Lawless, *The Illustrated Encyclopedia of Essential Oils,* pp. 109, 168.

Modern Uses:

For the Body: Chamomile is excellent for skin care and is used in many cosmetics, soaps, and perfumes. It is widely used in massage blends, skin care creams and bath oils. The main effects however, are on the digestive and nervous systems. As a digestive aid it is good for anything that arises from a nervous origin including colic, indigestion, nausea and nervous stomach. Since chamomile is so mild, it is suitable for treating children's digestive upsets. The pain relieving qualities make it excellent for treating teething pains in infants. Its antispasmodic properties make it good for treating menstrual cramp, and relieving menopausal problems. Chamomile has a very calming and sedative effect on the nervous system making it good for headache, insomnia, nervous tension, migraine and stress related complaints.

For the Mind and Spirit: Chamomile is a profoundly soothing and calming oil. Use chamomile to encourage stillness, calmness, softness, gentleness, relaxation, serenity, spiritual awareness, emotional stability, inner peace, understanding and cooperation.[15] Chamomile can counteract nervousness, irritability, temper, anger, depression, fear, anxiety, exhaustion, worry, grief, emotional imbalance, broken heart, grumpiness, discontent, impatience, melancholy, spiritual disconnectedness.[16]

[15]Valerie Ann Worwood, *The Fragrant Heavens,* p. 215.

[16]Valerie Ann Worwood, *The Fragrant Mind,* p. 293.

Applications for Healing Work:	Chamomile can be diffused, added to food or water as a dietary supplement, or applied topically on location. It is among the gentlest oils and is appropriate for use with children. Chamomile is particularly helpful for the solar plexus, helping to ease tension in this energy area.
Safety Data:	Chamomile is non-toxic, non-irritating and non-sensitizing.

Clary Sage *(Salvia sclarea)*
A revitalizing and clarifying oil

This herb was highly esteemed in the Middle Ages and is beginning to make a come-back into use today. Its name is derived from the Latin word clarus meaning "clear" which reflected its role in treating eye complaints. The name salvia comes from the Latin salvere meaning "to save, or heal." It was even referred to as *herba sacra* or "sacred herb" by the Romans.[17] In Germany hundreds of years ago, they added clary sage to their beer making which added to the beer's euphoric qualities.

[17]Gabriel Mojay, *Aromatherapy for Healing the Spirit*, p. 62.

Aroma:	Clary sage has a warm, bittersweet, musky kind of odor. It blends well with juniper, lavender, coriander, cardomon, geranium, sandalwood, cedarwood, pine, jasmine, frankincense, bergamot and other citrus oils.
Source:	The oil is produced from steam distillation of the flowering tops and leaves. Clary sage is cultivated all over the world. The clary sage grown in the Mediterranean area and in England is considered of superior quality.

Predominant
Chemistry: Monoterpenes: α and β–pinenes; sesquiterpenes; monoterpenols; sesquiterpenols; diterpenols; terpene esters; ethers; oxides; ketones; aldehydes; coumarins. Constituents vary according to geographical origin.

Traditional
Use: Clary sage was traditionally used for eye ailments. Hildegard of Bingen was familiar with it in the 12th century and recommended its use for digestive problems.[18] In her book on medicine, she declares that clary sage is effective against poison unless it is so potent that the person dies. For someone with a weak stomach, easily upset by food, clary sage should be mixed with pennyroyal and fennel and cooked in wine with a bit of honey.[19]

Modern Uses: For the Body: Some refer to this oil as "a gift to the female."[20] It helps to get rid of monthly bloat, depression, and anxiety. It regulates menses and cools down hot flashes. It is known to be euphoric, giving a sense of clarity and empowerment. Clary sage also has a rejuvenating effect on the endocrine system. It balances the pituitary and the pancreas making it helpful for diabetics. Clary sage also helps reduce high cholesterol, supports hormones, is anti-infectious, antifungal, antispasmodic, relaxing, antibacterial and may help with epilepsy.

For the Mind and Spirit: Clary sage oil is effective for calming the mind and easing tension. It is strengthening yet relaxing. It can produce a mental-emotional uplift and euphoria. This does not result in ungrounding but the contrary. This oil is therefore helpful for depression and nervous anxiety characterized by mood changes, indecision and

[18]Wighard Strehlow and Gottfried Hertzka, *Hildegard of Bingen's Medicine*, p. 55.

[19]*Hildegard von Bingen's Physica*, translated from the Latin by Priscilla Throop, p.76.

[20]Light Miller and Bryan Miller, *Ayurveda and Aromatherapy*, p. 242.

emotional confusion.[21] Clary sage may be used to encourage positive feelings of calmness, confidence, grounding, tranquility, revitalization, balance and restoration. It can help dispel worry, anxiousness, compulsive feelings, depression, hostility, lethargy, panic, melancholy, burnout, absentmindedness, and weepiness.[22]

[21]Gabriel Mojay, *Aromatherapy for Healing the Spirit*, p. 63.

[22]Valerie Ann Worwood, *The Fragrant Mind*, p. 298.

Applications for Healing Work: Clary sage can be diffused or applied topically to the soles of the feet, ankles, and wrists. It may be taken internally, added to food or soy/rice milk as a dietary supplement.

Safety Data: Non-toxic, non-irritating and non-sensitizing. Avoid during pregnancy and do not use when drinking alcohol since it will exaggerate drunkenness.

Clove *(Syzygium aromaticum)*
An oil of inner warmth and cheerfulness

Clove is another one of the ancient spices that traveled the caravan routes. It has been used as a medicinal and culinary herb for thousands of years.

Aroma: Clove has a rich, warm spicy aroma. It blends well with lemon, geranium lavender, chamomile, ginger, ylang ylang, sandalwood, mandarin, jasmine, and clary sage.

Source: Clove oil comes from steam distillation of the buds. (Stem and leaf oil is too caustic for therapeutic use.) The clove tree originally comes from Indonesia but is now cultivated throughout the world.

Predominant
Chemistry: Eugenol Acetate.

Traditional
Use: Clove has long been recognized as an aid for
                digestive upsets, for intestinal parasites, and
                for toothaches. In the 16th century after the Dutch
                conquerors destroyed the clove trees on the island
                of Ternate, the native peoples all succumbed to
                western epidemics. Their natural immunity had been
                destroyed when they no longer had their clove spice
                trees.[23] Cloves was one of the ingredients of the "Four
                Thieves Vinegar" a mixture that warded off the
                plague in the Middle Ages. Hildegard recommended
                it for sick intestines and for gout.[24]

Modern Uses: For the Body: Clove oil has been studied for its
                antimicrobial ability against contagious diseases.
                Dr. Jean Valnet describes clove oil as a powerful
                antiseptic and feels it should be used more in
                medicine.[25] It is good for intestinal disorders such as
                spasms, flatulence, diarrhea and intestinal parasites.
                It is helpful for respiratory infections and
                tuberculosis. It's an aid for preparation for childbirth
                and for healing the umbilical cord; its anti-neuralgic
                properties soothe the pain of toothaches and
                abscesses; its analgesic properties are beneficial for
                rheumatism, arthritis and muscular sprains. Clove
                is also a useful treatment for repelling insects and
                parasites. It is particularly helpful against scabies.

                For the Mind and Spirit: Use clove oil to encourage
                trust, inner warmth and regeneration and to promote
                a feeling of protection and courage. Clove is an oil
                for contentment, creativity, focus, happiness and self-
                awareness.

[23]René Gattefossé, *Gattefossé's Aromatherapy*, p. 48.

[24]Bruce Hozeski, *Hildegard's Healing Plants*, pp. 28-29.

[25]Jean Valnet, *The Practice of Aromatherapy*, pp. 114-11.

Applications for Healing Work:	Clove oil may be diffused or used in dilution on the body.
Safety Data:	Clove oil is non-toxic but should only be used in dilution.

Eucalyptus *(Eucalyptus globulus* and *Eucalyptus radiata)*
An oil of openness and freedom

Eucalyptus has over 700 varieties, all of which are in the myrtle family. Eucalyptus globulus and eucalyptus radiata have the most frequently called upon healing qualities. Eucalyptus is included in this list because of its tremendous healing properties although it was only introduced to Europe and the Christian world in the 19th century.

Aroma:	Eucalyptus has a somewhat harsh camphor-like odor that is also woody in scent. It blends well with thyme, rosemary, lavender, marjoram, pine, cedarwood, tea tree, and lemon.
Source:	Eucalyptus is native to Australia and was brought to North Africa, Europe, and to the Americas by the explorers. The trees grow to great heights, over 300 feet and have fragrant leaves. Oil is produced through steam distillation of the leaves and twigs.
Predominant Chemistry:	Monoterpenes: α and β–pinenes; sesquiterpenes, terpene oxides.
Traditional Use:	The aboriginal people in Australia used to burn the leaves as a form of fumigation for the relief of

fever. They used it for respiratory ailments, and the leaves were even smoked for asthma. It was used on wounds, aching joints, for dysentery, and ringworm.

Modern Uses: For the Body: Eucalyptus is used today much as it was in the past. Its healing abilities spread to Europe, Africa, and the Americas by botanists looking for new healing plants. It is good for burns, blisters, cuts, insect bites, herpes, lice, wounds, and as an insect repellent. *Eucalyptus globulus* can be used for muscle and joint aches, arthritis, and sprains. It is especially good for aches due to the cold. For the respiratory system, both *eucalyptus globulu*s and *radiata* maintain healthy lung function. Eucalyptus is a major expectorant essential oil. Its antibacterial, antiviral action makes eucalyptus useful for the common cold, laryngitis, bronchitis, coughs, sinusitis, and throat infections. It is also good for cystitis. It may be combined with other oils like tea tree or thyme to strengthen and prevent infection from recurring.[26]

For the Mind and Spirit: Eucalyptus is used to encourage emotional balance, concentration, and centering and to counteract exhaustion, mood swings, lack of concentration, and cluttered thoughts. Its action on the mind and spirit are closely related to the actions on the respiratory system. As breathing improves and the chest opens, its pungent, yet soothing fragrance dispels melancholy and revives the spirit, thus restoring vitality and positive outlook. It is especially good for someone who feels constricted by his/her surroundings. This fragrance dispels negative feelings and gives the person "room to breathe."[27]

[26]Julia Lawless, *The Illustrated Encyclopedia of Essential Oils,* p. 185.

[27]Gabriel Mojay, *Aromatherapy for Healing the Spirit,* pp. 68-69.

Other Uses: Eucalyptus is widely used in liniments, inhalants, cough syrups, ointments, toothpaste, veterinary practice and dentistry. It is used as a fragrance in soaps, detergents and toiletries.

Applications
for Healing
Work: Eucalyptus is a warming oil with excellent antiseptic properties. It may be used in massage blends and bath oils and is very good as an inhalation or it can be diffused in the room. It can be used directly on the skin with care. It can be rubbed on the soles of the feet or on location. It makes an excellent antiseptic room spray to fumigate a sickroom or use it in a humidifier.

Safety Data: Eucalyptus is non-toxic, non-irritating and non-sensitizing externally. Not to be taken internally.

Fennel *(Foeniculum vulgare)*
An oil for longevity, courage and strength

This is a plant that has been used for thousands of years. In the Middle Ages, it was one of Hildegard's favorite herbs and she used it for many ailments. Fennel in any form she said, "makes us happy, gives a healthy skin color, produces a pleasant body odor and supports a good digestion. Fennel seeds are 100 percent good for your health." [28]

[28]Wighard Strehlow and Gottfried Hertzka, *Hildegard of Bingen's Medicine,* p. 45.

Aroma: Fennel has a very sweet, anise-like scent. It blends well with geranium, lavender, rose and sandalwood.

Source: Fennel oil comes from steam distilling the crushed seeds of this perennial herb. It can grow as high as 6 feet, has feathery leaves and golden yellow flowers and is cultivated worldwide. The main oil producers are in Europe.

Predominant
Chemistry: Monoterpenes; α pinene; limonene; monoterpenols; phenols; methyl chavicol; aldehydes; ketones; coumarins.

Traditional
Use: Fennel was believed to convey longevity, courage and strength. In the Middle Ages, they used it to ward off evil spirits, to strengthen eyesight and to neutralize poisons. Hildegard found it particularly helpful for blue-eyed people and recommended it for clear sight.[29]

[29] *Hildegard von Bingen's Physica,* translated from the Latin by Priscilla Throop, p.40.

Modern Uses: For the Body: Fennel's primary use is with the digestive system as it works on the lower bowel. It is used to relieve flatulence, digestive spasms and constipation. The oil can be rubbed on the abdomen to encourage proper digestion of food and to relieve bloating after a large meal. Fennel oil is also important for the lungs. It is a mild expectorant and helps to relieve phlegm. Fennel is well known for its ability to increase milk production in nursing mothers. It may also help to relieve engorged or painful breasts. This oil is antiseptic, antispasmodic and analgesic.

For the Mind and Spirit: The actions on the mind and spirit will be reflected in how it calms and clears the bowel. For those who find self-expression difficult, feelings may be bound up, affecting the bowels as nervous spasm and gas. Fennel oil helps free feelings that have become stagnated, clearing away a congested mind.[30] Use fennel oil to encourage feelings of balance, motivation, clarity, perseverance, courage, confidence and assertiveness and to counteract mental and emotional blockages, fear of failure, and lack of creativity.

[30]Gabriel Mojay, *Aromatherapy for Healing the Spirit,* pp. 72-73.

Applications for Healing Work:

Fennel oil may be used in massage blends and rubbed on the feet or abdomen. It can be diffused or inhaled.

Safety Data:

Non-irritant, relatively non-toxic, should not be used by epileptics or during pregnancy and should be used with caution by nursing mothers.

Geranium *(Pelargonium graveolens)*
An oil for reconnecting to our feelings

Geranium is a plant native to South Africa and was exported to Europe probably in the seventeenth century. From there it was hybridized and re-exported to the various French and British colonies around the world. Today geranium is an important oil for blending in the perfume industry, often used as a substitute in the place of rose oil.

Aroma:

Geranium has a rosy-sweet, minty smell that blends well with lavender, patchouli, clove, rose, orange blossom, sandalwood, jasmine, juniper, bergamot and other citrus oils.

Source:

The geranium plant is a small shrub with hairy, serrated heart-shaped leaves and rosy pink flowers. Geranium oil is produced by distilling the leaves, stalks and flowers of the plant. Today, the oil is mainly produced in Morocco although it is believed that the best oil comes from the Reunion Islands.

Predominant
Chemistry: Monoterpenes; sesquiterpenes; monoterpene alcohols; terpene esters; oxides; ketones.

Traditional
Use: Geranium has been used since the days of antiquity for skin care, dysentery, hemorrhoids, inflammations and excessive menstrual bleeding. It was also used for diarrhea and peptic ulcers.

Modern Uses: For the Body: Geranium oil has a calming, uplifting and strengthening effect particularly on the nervous system. It is a helpful oil for treating menopausal symptoms including hot flashes and vaginal dryness. It is an effective treatment for dysentery or gastroenteritis. The oil can be diluted with a carrier oil and rubbed on the abdomen for GI disturbances. Geranium helps promote blood circulation and it promotes normal liver function. The analgesic properties of this oil can help relieve the pain of neuralgia and shingles. Geranium oil is most famous for its skin care properties. It is helpful in the treatment of acne, eczema, psoriasis, and dermatitis and is particularly helpful in clearing up oily skin.[31]

For the Mind and Spirit: Geranium is particularly helpful if you feel "stuck" and are afraid to move on to the next stage in life. The fragrance relaxes the nerves and makes this oil helpful in anxiety states. Mojay believes this oil will help to "reconnect us to our feeling-life, to our emotional sensitivity and relaxed spontaneity." With this comes a healthy openness for pleasure and enjoyment.[32] Use Geranium oil to encourage feelings of hope,

[31]Susan Curtis, *Essential Oils*, pp. 100-101.

[32]Gabriel Mojay, *Aromatherapy for Healing the Spirit*, p. 77.

consolation, solace, regeneration, friendliness, balance, stability, tranquility and steadiness. It will help eliminate feelings of anxiousness, depression, fear, moodiness, insecurity, over-sensitivity, apprehension, discontent, worry and heartache.[33]

[33]Valerie Ann Worwood, *The Fragrant Mind*, p. 312.

Applications
for Healing
Work: Geranium oil may be diffused, used in steam inhalation or applied topically either directly on the body or diluted with a carrier oil or lotion and rubbed on the body. Use it in a massage blend or bath oil or as a warm compress for painful areas. Blend it with melissa or chamomile for skin conditions. Geranium oil is wonderful in bath oils and lotions for the skin. May also be added to food as a supplement.

Safety Data: Non-toxic, non-irritating and generally non-sensitizing.

Ginger *(Zingiber officinale)*
An oil of valor and courage

Ginger has been used for thousands of years both in the East and the West. It was one of the first spices to travel the spice route from Asia to Europe. Both the Greeks and the Romans used ginger for medicinal and culinary uses. In the 16th century, the European explorers introduced ginger to the West Indies where it quickly adapted.

Aroma: Ginger has a fresh, woody-spicy scent that is pungent and sweet. It blends well with sandalwood, patchouli, frankincense, cedarwood, rose, orange blossom, and other citrus oils.

Source:	Ginger oil is produced by steam distillation from the unpeeled, dried, ground root of a perennial herb. It grows as a reed-like plant that has thick tuberous rhizomes from which both the spice and the oil are produced. It is native to Asia but is now cultivated all over the tropics, particularly in the West Indies. Most oil is distilled in Britain, China and India. The Jamaican ginger is said to be the best.
Predominant Chemistry:	Monoterpenes; α and β-pinene; sesquiterpenes; monoterpene alcohols; aldehydes; ketones.
Traditional Use:	Traditionally, ginger has been used for both medicinal and culinary purposes. In China it was used for colds and chills to promote sweating and to expel mucus. The Greeks used it as a digestive stimulant. Hildegard used Ginger for multiple ailments including eyesight, digestive problems and acne.[34]
Modern Uses:	For the Body: Just as in earlier times, Ginger is useful as a digestive aid. It is considered invigorating and decongesting. Ginger oil is helpful for poor appetite, indigestion, abdominal distention and flatulence. It relieves nausea, vomiting and dizziness associated with motion making it excellent for travel and morning sickness. For the circulatory system, Ginger oil helps warm cold hands and feet, and decrease fatigue and angina pectoris and for the lungs, it has an expectorant action helpful for bronchitis. When combined with other oils like eucalyptus or tea tree, it can help counteract colds and flu characterized by chills, fatigue and aching. Also

[34] *Hildegard von Bingen's Physica,* translated from the Latin by Priscilla Throop, pp.17-19.

combining it with cypress in a footbath will help alleviate cold and flu. For the muscular system, Ginger helps rheumatic pain, especially from the cold. It is also a help in relieving low back pain associated with muscular fatigue. Combine it with peppermint and juniper in a massage oil for joints. The stimulating properties of Ginger make it helpful for strengthening the immune system by stimulating the adrenals.

For the Mind and Spirit: Ginger has a fragrance that brings strength to the weak, giving a sense of courage. Use Ginger to encourage warmth, empathy, courage, optimism, and assurance and to discourage a sense of purposelessness, apathy, burnout, fatigue, loneliness, and sadness.[35]

[35]Valerie Ann Worwood, *The Fragrant Heavens*, p.233.

Application for Healing Work: Ginger can be diffused or applied topically to the body. It may be added to food as a dietary supplement or flavoring. Ginger makes a great warming oil when blended with any number of other essential oils in a base oil.

Safety Data: Ginger oil is non-toxic, non-sensitizing and non-irritating in dilution.

Juniper *(Juniperus communis)*
An oil to fortify and empower

Juniper has a long history in humanity. Juniper berries have been found in archeological digs of prehistoric man. Throughout history, people have burned these aromatic branches to fumigate and to ritually cleanse. Tibetans and Native Americans burn juniper as part of their ritual cleansing. In the Middle Ages, juniper was used to ward off witches. Hildegard, writing in the 12th century, recommended its use for respiratory conditions, advising its use in saunas and warm baths.[36] In the 19th century the berries were burnt in French hospitals to prevent the spread of smallpox. Oil from only the berries is used to flavor gin.

[36] *Hildegard von Bingen's Physica,* translated from the Latin by Priscilla Throop, pp.128-129.

Aroma:	Juniper oil has a sweet, fresh, woody, balsamic fragrance that blends well with vetiver, sandalwood, cedarwood, galbanum, cypress, clary sage, pine, lavender, fir, rosemary, benzoin, geranium and the citrus oils.
Source:	Juniper is an evergreen tree that can reach heights of 40 feet. It has bluish-green stiff needles and produces small flowers and berries that change over the years from green to blue to black. The therapeutic oil is produced from steam distillation of the mature berries. Distillation of the wood is of less therapeutic use. The oil is mainly produced in Europe—France, Italy and Yugoslavia being the main producers.
Predominant Chemistry:	Monoterpenes: α–pinene; sesquiterpenes; terpene alcohols; aldehydes; ketones.
Traditional Use:	Includes fumigation to ward off contagious diseases, respiratory infections, and for urinary tract infections. Juniper sprigs were place in homes to protect against evil spirits and the witches in the Middle Ages, and were burned along with the berries for purification, especially in the hospitals.
Modern Uses:	For the Body: Juniper is a powerful aromatic

decongestant. Its astringent qualities makes it helpful for hemorrhoids, acne, and skin conditions like dermatitis and eczema; its blood cleansing and diuretic qualities make it particularly helpful for rheumatism and arthritis, especially in cold weather; as a digestive stimulant, it's a remedy for colic and flatulence; its invigorating effects aid tired muscles, cold hands and feet and low backache. Juniper also helps cleanse oily skin and acts as an antiseptic. The primary use of juniper however is for the urinary tract where it is one of the classic diuretics and remedies for urinary tract infections.[37]

For the Mind and Spirit: Juniper is refreshing and helpful in states of anxiety and stress. Its sedative actions will help those who find it difficult to sleep due to worries and tensions and its pungent aroma will help to break through psychological stagnation. It is particularly helpful for those who are self-absorbed in worry that is rooted in the fear of failure. Juniper evokes feelings of health, love and peace and encourages a warmer, friendlier state of being. It can dispel feelings of nervous or emotional exhaustion, guilt, lack of self-worth, listlessness, emptiness, conflict and defensiveness.[38]

[37]Robert Tisserand, *The Art of Aromatherapy*, p. 242.

[38]Valerie Ann Worwood, *The Fragrant Mind*, p. 312.

Applications for Healing Work: Juniper can be diffused or applied topically. It can be used in body lotions and bath oils or used with warm compresses.

Safety Data: Juniper is non-toxic, non-irritating and non-sensitizing making it a very good universal oil.

Lavender *(Lavandula angustifolia, L. officinalis)*
An oil of calmness

The name Lavender comes from the Latin lavare, meaning "to wash." The Romans used to scent their bath water with the fragrant flowers of this plant. Lavender has a long history as a healing agent for both body and mind. Hildegard spoke highly of its use and recommended it for many ailments. The English lavender or "true lavender," has the most medicinal properties among the various varieties. Today lavender is a popular oil in the perfume industry and is used in a host of products including skin care. Lavender will be one of your most used healing oils.

Aroma: Lavender has a sweet floral-herbal scent that is very characteristic. It blends well with most other oils, especially the citrus and florals. It also blends well with cedarwood, clove, clary sage, pine, geranium, vetiver, patchouly, and frankincense.

Source: Although the whole plant is aromatic, the oil is produced by steam distillation from the fresh flowers only. The plant has long spikey leaves with bluish white flowers and grows to a height of about three feet. Lavender is grown all over the world with France being the major producer of the oil.

Predominant
Chemistry: Lavender has over 100 constituents. Monoterpenes: α and β–pinenes; sesquiterpenes; nonterpene alcohols; esters; oxides; ketones; sesquiterpenones; aldehydes; coumarins.

Traditional
Use: Lavender is a well-established traditional or folk remedy. It was used by the Romans for scenting the bath, by healers like Hildegard of Bingen for

everything from eliminating lice to warding off evil spirits.[39]

[39]Bruce Hozeski, *Hildegard's Healing Plants,* p. 34.

Modern Uses: For the Body: The most celebrated use of lavender is for burns. René Gattafossé, the father of aromatherapy suffered sever burns over most of his body and was healed using lavender oil. To his shock, the second and third degree burns healed without scarring. Lavender oil is also good for abscesses, acne, allergies, athletes foot, boils, bruises, dandruff, dermatitis, eczema, psoriasis, ringworm, sores of all kinds, sunburn, insect bites and stings. It is also good for repelling lice. Because of its antispasmodic and analgesic qualities, lavender can help problems like colic, irritable bowel, menstrual pain, and muscular stiffness and aching. Its antiseptic properties make it an effective treatment for flu, bronchitis and pneumonia and its anti-bacterial properties help with genital-urinary infections when added to bath water. Lavender has been called a "universal healing oil."

For the Mind and Spirit: Lavender oil calms and stabilizes the mind and heart bringing about a sense of equilibrium. It can ease nervous tension and decrease feelings of panic and hysteria. In this regard, it is a wonderful "rescue remedy" calming strong emotions that threaten to overwhelm the person. Lavender is good for headaches, depression, hypertension, insomnia, migraines and stress-related illnesses. Use lavender to encourage feelings of security, gentleness, compassion, vitality, calmness, comfort, acceptance, inner peace, and emotional balance. Lavender will help to counter anxiety, irritability, mental exhaustion, hysteria, panic, apprehension, insecurity, restlessness, moodiness,

[40]Valerie Ann Worwood, *The Fragrant Mind,* p. 326.

psychosomatic illnesses, worry, agitation, and burnout.[40]

Other Uses: Lavender is an excellent deodorant and room spray. It can be used to repel mosquitoes and other flying insects. It makes an excellent ingredient in massage oils to calm and restore.

Applications for Healing Work: Lavender can be diffused, inhaled with steam, used with warm compresses, and applied neat on the body at places of discomfort. It can be used as an anointing oil for the brow, hands, feet and energy centers. It can be applied to the healer's hands and run through the field to clear stagnant energy and to calm fears.

Safety Data: Lavender is non-toxic, non-irritating and non-sensitizing.

Lemon *(Citrus lemonum)*
An oil of refreshment

The lemon tree has its origin in Asia and first appeared in the Mediterranean area about 200 A.D. By the Middle Ages, it was being cultivated in Spain and Sicily. As a medicinal, it became popular when it was discovered that it warded off scurvy during long sea voyages.

Aroma: Lemon has a fresh citric fragrance that is both clean and tart. It blends well with lavender, orange blossom, ylang ylang, rose, sandalwood, frankincense, chamomile, benzoin, fennel, geranium, eucalyptus, juniper, and other citrus oils.

Source: Lemon oil comes from cold expression of the outer peel of the fruit. The lemon tree grows in warm climates like the Mediterranean area and California and Florida.

Predominant
Chemistry: Monoterpenes; limonene 70%; sesquiterpenes; aldehydes; coumarins.

Traditional
Use: Traditionally, lemon has been one of Europe's cure-alls especially for infectious illnesses. It was used for fevers, for scurvy, for digestive disorders, for arthritis and rheumatism, and for skin care.[41]

[41]Julia Lawless, *The Illustrated Encyclopedia of Essential Oils*, p. 120.

Modern Uses: For the Body: Lemon oil is a powerful antioxidant and supports the immune system. It has antiseptic qualities that make it helpful for colds, flu, bronchitis and asthma. It makes an excellent aerosol spray to kill bacteria and viruses and has been used for many years in hospitals for this purpose. Lemon oil is a tonic for the circulatory system, improving circulation. It is an excellent oil for treating high blood pressure. It can be used for obesity and also weakness and loss of appetite. It is cleansing and detoxifying for the liver and can benefit problems like cellulite. Lemon's astringent properties are helpful for skin wrinkles. It is also effective against scabies and other parasites.

For the Mind and Spirit: Lemon oil is beneficial for anxiety. Its bright scent helps to sharpen focus. It is clarifying and uplifting for one's mind and spirit. It calms, lightens and refreshes the heart, alleviating fears and encouraging trust. Its freshness will help dispel depression, bitterness, touchiness, lethargy, distrust, mental fatigue and fear.

Other Uses:	Lemon oil is used extensively as a flavoring agent in foods and in drugs. It is used as a fragrance in soaps, detergents, cosmetics, toilet waters and perfumes. It has insect repelling properties and can be used in a spray to rid your environment of fleas and ants.
Applications for Healing Work:	Lemon oil can be diffused, steam inhaled, used in a humidifier or vaporizer, and applied directly to the body. It can be used on the soles of the feet, or on the energy centers. It can be applied to the healer's hands and run through the energy field. Lemon oil will be a frequently used oil in healing work.
Safety Data:	Caution must be taken when skin is exposed to sunlight after using this oil. It may cause blotching or brown discoloration.

Marjoram *(Origanum majorana)*
An oil of comfort and contentment

Marjoram was a traditional culinary herb and folk remedy and was used by the ancient Greeks and Egyptians. The name of the plant is derived from the Greek and means "joy of the mountain."

Aroma:	Marjoram has a fresh herb smell that is warm, sweet and slightly woody. It blends well with lavender, geranium, orange, rosemary, bergamot, chamomile, cypress, cedarwood, tea tree and eucalyptus.
Source:	The oil is produced by steam distillation of the dried flowering herb. It is native to southern Europe and the Near East, however, marjoram can be grown in

most gardens in North America. The largest
producers of the oil are France and Egypt.

Predominant Chemistry: Monoterpenes; α and β–pinenes; sesquiterpenes; monoterpenols; terpene esters.

Traditional Use: The Greeks used Marjoram in cosmetics and medicines. It was also for the Greeks, a funeral herb to be planted on the graves of the departed. They thought that it would help their loved ones to sleep in peace and happiness. It was also associated with Aphrodite, the goddess of love and beauty. The flowers were used to crown young married couples. The Egyptians used sweet marjoram for healing and for overcoming grief since it has such calming and comforting effects on the mind.

Modern Uses: For the Body: Marjoram is a versatile oil that has a soothing, fortifying and warming effect. It aids digestive problems such as colic, constipation and gas. For the muscular system, it is helpful for arthritis, muscular aches and stiffness, rheumatism, sprains, strains and stiff joints. For skin care it helps bruises, and ticks. Marjoram has also been known to help with menstrual problems like PMS. It is reported that Marjoram can also reduce the sex drive. For the nervous system, it is good for headaches, hypertension, insomnia, migraines, nervous tension, exhaustion and stress-related conditions. Its analgesic and warming properties suggest it may be useful for the treatment of sinus pains and head colds. Susan Curtis suggests combining it with eucalyptus or rosemary and use it in a bath or a compress for the sinuses.[42]

[42]Susan Curtis, *Essential Oils,* pp. 98-99.

For the Mind and Spirit: Marjoram is especially helpful for conditions in which tiredness alternates with tension or is characterized by anxiety or insomnia. It is also helpful for someone who feels helpless and alone or who has the feeling of "no one cares." It helps to calm obsessive thinking, ease emotional craving and promote a sense of self-care. Mojay recommends Marjoram along with cypress and rose in cases of deep loss and grief.[43] Use Marjoram to encourage feelings of calmness, balance, integrity, perseverance and sincerity.

[43]Gabriel Mojay, *Aromatherapy for Healing the Spirit,* p.95.

Application for Healing Work:

Marjoram can be used in massage lotions, baths, compresses, or used neat on the body for local action.

Safety Data:

Marjoram is non-toxic, non-irritating, non-sensitizing. Not to be used during pregnancy.

Melissa *(Melissa officinalis)*
An oil of strength and serenity

Melissa, also called "balm" and "lemon balm" has been used as a medicinal herb for thousands of years. It was first used by the Greeks, then the Romans and the Arabs, and later by Christian monks and healers throughout Europe. It was a main ingredient in the healing "Carmelite Water" distilled in the 1600s.[44]

[44]*Essential Oils Desk Reference,* pp. 60-61.

Aroma:

Melissa has a pleasant lemony, fresh and sweet herbal smell. It blends well with citrus oils, chamomile, geranium, lavender, marjoram and rose.

Source:

The oil is produced through steam distillation of the leaves and flowering tops of the herb. The plant has bright bushy green leaves and small pink flowers. Distillation produces only a small quantity of oil making Melissa one of the most expensive oils to produce. Melissa is native to the Mediterranean region and southern Europe. It is now grown all over the world; however, France and Ireland are the major producers of the oil.

Predominant
Chemistry: Monoterpenols; sesquiterpenols; terpene esters and oxides; monoterpenals and coumains.

Traditional
Use: The early Greeks noticed melissa's analgesic and antispasmodic properties and used it for toothaches, asthma and for wounds. Avicenna, the famous Arabian physician of the 11th century, wrote about its use in his *Canon of Medicine*. He said it "teacheth that balm maketh the heart merry and joyful, and strengtheneth the vital spirits."[45] The physician and alchemist Paracelsus called it "the Elixir of Life" in the 1500s. It was used primarily for nervous disorders, the heart and the emotions.

[45]Gabriel Mojay, *Aromatherapy for Healing the Spirit*, p. 96.

Modern Uses: For the Body: Melissa's analgesic qualities make it useful like lavender for relieving stress headaches, migraine and menstrual pain. Its calming action on the heart and nerves helps with restlessness, insomnia and agitation. It decreases panic attacks and palpitations and decreases high blood pressure related to stress. It is also helpful for the digestive system, relieving flatulence, colic and nausea.

For the Mind and Spirit: Melissa oil is helpful in depression especially for those individuals who do not respond well to pressure. It can help restore both clarity and security for a confused, dependent person. It is the most effective oil for anxious depression and helps to counteract feelings of foreboding. Melissa may help to remove emotional blocks and instill a positive outlook in life. Use Melissa oil to encourage strength, revitalization, gentleness, peace and cheerfulness.

Other Uses: Melissa oil is used extensively as a fragrance in toiletries, cosmetics and perfumes.

Applications
for Healing
Work: Melissa oil can be diffused or applied topically. It can also be added to massage blends or bath oils.

Safety Data: Melissa is non-toxic but some may be sensitive to it. Check for sensitivity and dilute if necessary.

Orange Blossom *(Neroli)* *(Citrus aurantium)*
An oil of joy and renewal

Neroli oil is named for a famous Italian princess from the town of Neroli (near Rome) who lived in the 1600s. It was considered her signature fragrance.[46] Later, it was one of the classic perfume ingredients used in the French *eau de cologne*.

[46]Light Miller and Bryan Miller, *Ayurveda and Aromatherapy*, p. 274.

Aroma: Neroli has a fresh delicate sweet-floral fragrance. It blends well with jasmine, benzoin, myrrh and all citrus oils.

Source: Neroli oil is water-distilled from the orange blossoms of the bitter orange tree also known as the Seville orange and not from the sweet oranges we are familiar with eating. Originally from China, these trees have been grown for hundreds of years in the

Mediterranean area. The oil is primarily produced in Morocco and Tunisia.

Predominant Chemistry: Monoterpenes; α and β–pinenes; esters; aldehydes; ketones.

Traditional Use: Neroli dates back to the Egyptian times where it was used for healing body, mind and spirit. It was first cultivated in the Mediterranean area in the 10th or the 11th century by the Arabs. The European explorers carried the plant to the West Indies and then to the Americas. Not until the later 1500s do we find the Italians distilling the oil and eventually using it for healing particularly, as a gentle tonic for the nervous system.

Modern Uses: For the Body: According to Mojay, Neroli along with rose, lavender, and Melissa, is one of the best essential oils to calm and stabilize the heart and mind.[47] It is used for high blood pressure, palpitations, restlessness, and insomnia. Neroli is also an antispasmodic making it helpful for digestive disorders like colic and abdominal spasms especially for those problems arising from nervousness.

For the Mind and Spirit: Neroli helps to ease mental and emotional tension, nervous depression and chronic and acute anxiety. It encourages lightness, the lifting of sorrow and grief, joy, understanding, calmness, peace and a sense of being spiritually guided. Neroli is helpful for those who are emotionally intense who are easily agitated.

[47]Gabriel Mojay, *Aromatherapy for Healing the Spirit,* pp.100-101.

Applications
for Healing
Work: Neroli can be diffused or applied topically. It can be used as an anointing oil for the brow, the soles of the feet or applied to any of the energy centers. It can be applied to the healer's hands and run through the energy field to clear stagnant and depressed energy.

Safety Data: Neroli is non-toxic, non-irritating and non-sensitizing.

Oregano *(origanum compactum, O. vulgare, O. floribundum, O. glandulosum)*
An oil of security

There are a number of species of oregano, some dating back as much as a 1,000 years. Hildegard used oregano and recommended its use for serious problems like leprosy. After putting a mixture with oregano on the leprous sores, the person will either be cured, or die according to this great healer.[48] Oregano is in the same family with wild marjoram, also called the joy of the mountain.

[48]Bruce Hozeski, *Hildegard's Healing Plants,* pp.105-106.

Aroma: Oregano has a strong herbal aroma that blends well with basil, fennel, geranium, myrtle, pine, lavender, rosemary, thyme, and cedarwood.

Source: Oregano oil is produced from steam distillation of the dried herb. It is a common garden herb and is grown all over the world. The oil is produced primarily in the U.S., Turkey and France.

Predominant
Chemistry: Monoterpenes; α and β–pinenes; sesquiterpenes; monoterpenols; monoterpene phenols and ketones. Constituents are highly variable depending on the

area where it is grown. Thymol and/or carvacrol are the major components.

Traditional Use:
Traditionally, oregano has been used for digestive upsets, respiratory problems like asthma, bronchitis and coughs, colds, flu and inflammations of the mouth and throat. It has also been used for headaches, rheumatism and general aches and pains.

Modern Uses:
For the Body: According to Jean Valnet, MD, modern uses of oregano are the same as the traditional folk remedies. It is helpful in infectious conditions and in fact is a powerful anti-infectious agent.[49] D. Gary Young, ND reports that oregano has a large-spectrum action against bacteria, mycobacteria, fungus, virus, and parasites.[50] Oregano is also a powerful antioxidant and it supports the immune system.

[49]Jean Valnet, *The Practice of Aromatherapy*, pp.170-171.

[50]*Essential Oils Desk Reference*, p.65.

Applications for Healing Work:
Oregano may not be a frequently used oil in our healing work but is presented here because of its ability to help as an anti-infectious agent.

Safety Data:
Oregano is a caustic oil because of its high per cent of phenols (60-72%). Therefore caution must be taken when using on the skin. Best to dilute with a carrier oil. If the skin should become reddened, dilute again. It may be used neat on the soles of the feet where the skin is not as sensitive. Be extra careful not to have this oil come into contact with mucous membranes. Best to test for skin sensitivity. Not recommended to be used with pregnant women.

Peppermint *(Mentha piperita)*
An oil of emotional tolerance

Peppermint has been found in the tombs of the Ancient Egyptians. In Greece and Rome, it was an everyday part of life. The Medieval healer, Hildegard referred to several varieties of the mint family and Jesus referred to mint when he was addressing the Pharisees: "Woe to you Pharisees! For you tithe mint and rue and herbs of all kinds, and neglect justice and the love of God." Luke 11:42

Aroma:	Peppermint has a fresh, cool, sweet and minty aroma. It blends well with benzoin, fennel, orange, rosemary, lavender, marjoram, lemon, eucalyptus and other mints.
Source:	The oil is steam-distilled from the flowering herb. It is cultivated worldwide.
Predominant Chemistry:	Menthol (up to 50%). Monoterpenes: α and β–pinenes; monoterpenones; terpene oxides; terpene esters; coumarins, sulfurs.
Traditional Use:	Traditionally peppermint has been used for upset stomachs, nausea, sore throats, diarrhea, headaches, toothaches and cramps. Hildegard used another variety of mint—spearmint for the gout and for flavoring food. She found all forms of mint helped the digestive system especially after over-eating.[51]
Modern Uses:	For the Body: The effect of the oil is essentially cooling to the body whether used internally or externally. Peppermint is one of the most effective oils to soothe an upset digestive system. It relieves nausea, pain, distention and flatulence. Its

[51]Bruce Hozeski, *Hildegard's Healing Plants,* pp.73-75.

antispasmodic and anti-inflammatory actions
benefit intestinal colic, colitis and hepatitis as well
as arthritis, and other inflammatory joint problems.
One drop of peppermint oil is equal to 28 cups
of peppermint tea! For the respiratory system,
peppermint is supportive making it useful for
colds and flu characterized by fever, sore throats and
headache. Peppermint also soothes muscles spasms
and relieves headaches. The oil should be applied
to the back of the neck and not near the face. It
is best if the peppermint is diluted in a carrier oil
and applied to the shoulders, neck and temples—not
to the face where it may burn the sensitive skin. It
can be placed in the palms and inhaled.
Peppermint is a wonderful pick-me-upper for the
nervous system. It stimulates and awakens both
the nerves and the brain, enhancing concentration
and study. Combined with lavender, peppermint
makes a wonderful footbath for tired and aching feet.
It is also a natural insect repellent and can be used
to eliminate fleas, scabies and ringworm. It makes an
excellent mouthwash for bad breath.

For the Mind and Spirit: Peppermint oil enhances
concentration making it helpful for study and
learning. As we learn to "stomach" other ideas, we
learn emotional tolerance. Use peppermint to
encourage feelings of self-acceptance, concentration,
attentiveness, vitality and vibrancy. It will help to
dispel feelings of mental fatigue, helplessness,
sluggishness, and apathy.[52]

[52]Valerie Ann Worwood, *The Fragrant Mind*, p. 326.

Applications
for Healing
Work:

Peppermint can be diffused, steam inhaled or used
topically on the body. It can be applied to the soles

of the feet, massaged on the stomach, or rubbed on the back of the neck for a headache. It can be added to water or tea to support digestion.

Safety Data: Non-toxic. Avoid contact with the face, mucus membranes and especially the eyes. If peppermint is accidentally introduced into the eye, do not irrigate with water, but rather, use a carrier oil or a good vegetable oil. Do not apply directly to a wound.

Rose *(Rosa centifolia, R. damascena)*
An oil of love and trust

There are over 250 varieties of rose and 10,000 hybrids. However, only three roses are commonly distilled. The damask rose *(Rosa damascena)* is the one that has been distilled since the 16th century for its finest oil. Hildegard gives a revealing description of how rose works when she states that "rose strengthens any potion or ointment or any other medication when it is added to it."[53] We know that rose oil carries the highest frequency or vibration and when added to any other blend of oils, raises the total healing vibration of that oil. Hildegard intuited and observed this fact 900 years ago. The Arab physician, Avicenna studied the healing power of rose at length and produced a whole book on it. Most likely, he was the first one to actually distill rose oil. Prior to that, rose water was produced by enfleurage, a process of pressing the petals along with a vegetable oil to extract the essence.

[53]Bruce Hozeski, *Hildegard's Healing Plants*, p. 25.

Aroma: Rose oil has a deep, sweet-floral scent. It blends well with other oils and is useful in raising the frequency of most blends.

Source: Producing rose oil is a costly process requiring as much as 5,000 lbs of rose petals to produce one pound of oil. Most oil today is obtained by using solvents which then need to be extracted from the

oil. Today, rose oil is produced in Bulgaria and
Turkey. Since it ranks among the most expensive oils
to produce, it is often adulterated for profit.

Predominant
Chemistry: Hydrocarbons; monterpenols; sesquiterpene
alcohols; terpene esters; phenols; oxides.

Traditional
Use: Traditionally, rose oil has been used for thousands
of years for skin care. Evidence can be found for
its use in ancient Egypt, Persia, India, Greece and
Rome. Rose enhanced other treatments for the body
and soul. Rose through the ages has been used
especially for women with the Greeks referring to it
as the "Queen of flowers." The Virgin Mary has been
referred to in the mystical tradition as the "Rose,"
the "Mystic Rose," the "Queen of the Most Holy Rose
Garden," and the "Holy Rose." All of these are images
of Mary as the Queen of all Heaven and Earth.

Modern Uses: For the Body: Rose oil is excellent treatment for skin
conditions including scarring and wrinkles. Rose
is often added to skin care products. It has a
cleansing and toning effect on the uterus and is
helpful for menopausal symptoms. It is also used in
the treatment of infertility and frigidity in women and
to increase sperm count in men.

For the Mind and Spirit: Rose oil gives a sense of
security and spiritual attunement, balancing and
elevating the mind. It is an oil first of all, for the
heart, keeping this emotional center open. It reduces
depression and anger and eases sorrow, bringing
harmony and comfort. It has been called a special
gift to women both physically and emotionally.

Rose oil heals emotional wounds and helps to restore one's capacity for self-love and nurturing. Use rose oil to encourage contentment, devotion, inner vision, happiness, inner freedom, acceptance, love, sensuality, and purity. It will help counter feelings of depression, sadness, grief, anger, anxiety, emptiness, fear of not being loved, broken heartedness, guilt, shyness, jealousy, touchiness, hopelessness, and despair.[54]

[54]Valerie Ann Worwood, *The Fragrant Mind,* p. 326.

Other Uses: Rose water and rose absolute are used extensively in soaps, cosmetics, toiletries and perfumes of all types.

Applications for Healing Work: Rose oil may be diffused or used topically on the body. It can be used to anoint any of the energy centers or used on the healer's hands and run through the energy field to balance and clear the energy.

Safety Data: Rose oil is non-toxic, non-irritating and non-sensitizing.

Rosemary *(Rosmarinus officinalis)*
An oil of remembrance

Rosemary is an herb that has been around for thousands of years. In ancient Egypt, the sprigs were burnt as incense and placed in the tombs of the pharaohs to help them remember their former life. It was considered a sacred plant for the Greeks and Romans. Whenever there was a solemn occasion, rosemary would be used as garlands. They would weave headbands and wear them as symbols of trust and constancy. At funerals, rosemary was burnt as incense in remembrance of the dead. This custom lasted for centuries, well into the Middle Ages. In the medieval days, rosemary was used to bring good luck to protect against witches and magic. People had sprigs of rosemary in their homes and during the plagues, would burn rosemary to protect against infection. It was first distilled as an oil in the 13th century and was one of the ingredients in the "Four Thieves Vinegar."[55]

[55]Gabriel Mojay, *Aromatherapy for Healing the Spirit,* pp.114-115.

Aroma: Rosemary has a strong, fresh, herbal scent that is easily recognizable. It blends well with frankincense, lavender, oregano, thyme, pine, basil, peppermint, clary sage, eucalyptus, cedarwood, cinnamon, bergamot, and other spice oils.

Source: Rosemary oil is steam distilled from the fresh flowering tops or the whole plant. The oil is mainly produced in Spain, France and Tunisia.

Predominant
Chemistry: Mainly Monoterpenes: α and β—pinenes; sesquiterpenes; monoterpenols; terpene esters; terpene oxides; non-terpene ketones; monoterpenoes.

Traditional
Use: Traditionally, rosemary was used as a ritual incense, to honor the dead, to scare off witches and for the plague. It was considered a warming tonic for the body. Rosemary was an herb that could be grown in the colder northern European climate and therefore was plentiful. People used rosemary to brighten their homes and to warm their bodies. It had medicinal and culinary uses.

Modern Uses: For the Body: Rosemary has been used for a wide range of complaints including respiratory and circulatory disorders, liver congestion, digestive and nervous complaints and muscular and rheumatic pain, skin and hair problems. The primary action is on the circulatory system. It stimulates a weak heart and is used for low blood pressure and cold extremities. Used in a bath or as a massage, it can increase circulation of blood through the whole system. It can also help relieve generalized lethargy and fatigue. It is very helpful in the treatment of headaches and for migraines. For the digestive system, Rosemary is a good tonic, helping to unblock an obstructed gall bladder and to relieve hepatitis and jaundice. It can be used to treat intestinal problems like painful digestion, flatulence and colic. It alleviates diarrhea and colitis. For chronic lung conditions, Rosemary can be very beneficial as well. Its antiseptic properties can help treat colds, flu and coughs. It is one of the main detoxifying oils for the lymphatic system when blended with lavender and juniper in a massage oil. Rosemary can be a very warming oil for those who suffer from arthritis and rheumatism, especially during cold weather. Many sports blends of rubbing oils contain Rosemary. For the skin and hair, Rosemary stimulates the circulation and can be used for hair loss and dandruff. It also kills lice and scabies.[56]

[56]Susan Curtis, *Essential Oils,* pp. 110-111.

For the Mind and Spirit: Rosemary can help improve memory, concentration and mental alertness making it an excellent oil to use for studying. Rosemary can help unblock your emotions, enabling you to feel your body and to form close emotional ties with others. Rosemary warms the spirit and gives courage. As an oil of "remembrance," rosemary can help us remember our loved ones and stay true to our own calling in life. Use rosemary to encourage a sense of energy, confidence, clarity, concentration, stability, and awareness. It will dispel fatigue, indecision, nervous and emotional exhaustion, strain and sluggishness.

Applications for Healing Work:	Rosemary oil can be diffused, inhaled, or applied locally on the body. It can be added to food as a supplement or as a flavoring.
Safety Data:	Rosemary oil is non-toxic, non-irritating and non-sensitizing. Epileptics should use with caution.

Sage *(Salvia lavendulifolia, S. officinalis)*
An oil for cleansing and purifying the spirit

Sage was valued as *herba sacra,* "sacred herb" by the Romans. It has a long history of culinary and medicinal uses. It was said that sage promoted a long life and cured many ailments. Hildegard recommended sage for a whole host of illnesses. She used it in ointments, tinctures, oils and as a pulverized dried herb. She recommended treating everything from bad breath to bleeding with this healing herb.[57]

[57] *Hildegard von Bingen's Physica,* translated from the Latin by Priscilla Throop, pp. 36-37.

Aroma:	Sage oil has a warm-spicy, herbal fragrance. It blends well with rosemary, rosewood, lavender, hyssop, lemon and other citrus oils.
Source:	Sage is steam distilled from the dried leaves of the herb. There are several different varieties with the *S. officinalis* or common sage having the most pronounced healing properties. Sage grows worldwide and is cultivated in Albania, Yugoslavia, Greece, Italy Turkey, France, China and the U.S.

Predominant
Chemistry: Monoterpenes: α and β–pinenes; sesquterpenes;
               hydrocarbons; esters; phenols; oxides;
               monoterpenones; aldehydes; coumarins.

Traditional
Use: Traditionally, sage was used in Europe for oral
               infections and skin conditions. Healers used it to
               strengthen and tone vital systems.

Modern Uses: For the Body: Sage is a powerful stimulant and
               toner for the nervous system. It is excellent for
               exhaustion due to stress and works particularly well
               in combination with rosemary for this purpose. Sage
               can tone the circulatory system and can be used
               to treat low blood pressure. It can help the
               respiratory system, particularly when there are
               chronic lung problems like bronchitis. It boosts the
               immune system and helps fight off colds and flu. It
               can be used to treat indigestion and improve a
               sluggish GI tract. Sage is also very helpful in
               regulating menstrual cycles. It may help to improve
               estrogen, progesterone and testosterone levels.
               It relieves hot flashes. It can stimulate uterine
               contractions and therefore should never be used
               during pregnancy. Sage can help relieve muscular
               aches and pains and is helpful in cases of rheumatism
               and arthritis. Just as in ancient days, sage makes an
               excellent mouthwash. Its astringent properties clear
               up gingivitis, bleeding gums and mouth ulcers. It can
               also be used as a gargle for sore throats.

               For the Mind and Spirit: Sage is mentally stimulating
               and may help with coping skills for a stressful life.
               Use sage to encourage strength, courage, self-
               awareness, and perseverance.

Applications
for Healing
Work: Sage can be diffused or diluted with a vegetable oil
or a massage oil and applied to the body. It can be
used as a dietary supplement as well.

Safety Data: Non-irritant when diluted with a massage or
vegetable oil. Do not use during pregnancy. Sage
should not be used by epileptics.

Thyme *(Thymus vularis)*
An oil of strength and courage

Thyme is one of the most ancient of herbs, perhaps being used
as much as 3,500 years ago. Ancient Egyptians used it in embalming
processes and burned it to fumigate the air. The Greeks used it as a
culinary herb and the Romans used to bath in thyme before entering battle. At the time of the Crusades, knights would have thyme
woven into their scarves as they left for battle. Hildegard had many
uses for thyme in potions, ointments, tinctures, oils and in steam
saunas.

Aroma: Thyme oil has a sweet herbal, yet pungent smell that
is distinctive. It blends well with bergamot, lemon,
rosemary, melissa, lavender, marjoram, pine,
cedarwood, and oregano.

Source: Thyme oil is produced by steam distillation of
the fresh or dried leaves and flowering tops. It is
native to the Mediterranean area and to Spain. The
oil is now produced in the U.S. and France.

Predominant
Chemistry: Monoterpenols: mainly thymol and carvacrol;
terpene esters.

Traditional
Use: Traditionally, thyme was used to help tone and invigorate the body. It was used for the nerves, lungs, heart and kidneys. It was also used to prevent infections. Hildegard used thyme to treat leprosy, palsy, old age infirmities, lice, and eye disorders.[58]

[58]*Hildegard von Bingen's Physica,* translated from the Latin by Priscilla Throop, pp. 95-96.

Modern Uses: For the Body: Thyme is a very hot and invigorating oil and must be used with caution on the skin. It is a powerful germicide and is effective against many kinds of bacteria, viruses and fungi. Thyme is a powerful antioxidant. The primary action of thyme is on the genital-urinary system. It has been used to treat venereal diseases with success and is effective against many types of urinary tract infections. Thyme is also effective for respiratory infections including colds, flu, coughs and bronchitis. Thyme can strengthen the immune system. It is one of the oils being used in the treatment of HIV-related diseases.[59] Thyme has an antiseptic and a warming effect on the GI system. It is helpful in the treatment of dysentery and gastro-enteritis type illnesses. Combine it with rosemary and geranium and massage over the abdomen. Since thyme is a warm oil, it can help raise low blood pressure. It can warm and stimulate stiff muscles and relieve rheumatism and arthritis. In addition, it gets rid of lice and scabies.

[59]Susan Curtis, *Essential Oils,* p. 121.

For the Mind and Spirit: Thyme is similar to rosemary in how it invigorates the mind and memory, making it an excellent tonic for exhaustion. According to Mojay, Thyme oil is a traditional remedy for melancholy. Its ability to "open the chest" and revive the Spirit benefits depressed states and helps to eliminate withdrawal, pessimism, and self-doubt.[60] Use thyme oil to encourage a positive

[60]Gabriel Mojay, *Aromatherapy for Healing the Spirit,* pp. 122-123.

mood, balance, tolerance, courage, alertness, warmth and to boost stamina.

Applications
for Healing
Work: Caution must be taken in using thyme oil on the body. Since it is a hot oil, it should always be diluted with either a massage oil or a good vegetable oil. It can also be added to food as a supplement or as a flavoring. It can be added to other strongly antiseptic oils like clove, eucalyptus, lavender, lemon and pine and used in a room spray to fumigate. Thyme can be steam inhaled as well.

Safety Data: Always dilute before using. Do not use on sensitive or damaged skin.

Yarrow *(Achillea millefolium)*
An oil of protection and healing

There is lots of folklore surrounding the use of yarrow. It was named after Achilles, the warrior of Homer's Iliad. It has been used throughout history to treat wounds, especially during wars.

Aroma: Yarrow oil has a fresh, green, sweet-herbal and slightly camphor-like odor. It blends well with cedarwood, pine, chamomile, and valerian.

Source: Yarrow is produced through steam distillation of the dried herb. It is a perennial herb that can grow up to three feet high. Yarrow has finely dissected leaves that appear lacy, and the flowers are pink-to white dense flowerheads. The oil is produced in the U.S., Germany, Hungary, France and the former Yugoslavia.

Predominant
Chemistry: Monoterpenes: α and β–pinenes; sesquiterpenes;
terpene oxides; monoterpenones; camphor;
sesquiterpene lactones.

Traditional
Use: Traditionally, yarrow was used for wounds, rashes
and sores of all kinds. It was also used for a wide
variety of ailments including fever, respiratory
infections, digestive problems, and nervous tension.
Hildegard used it for wounds, eye problems, and
fevers.[61]

[61] *Hildegard von Bingen's Physica,* translated from the Latin by Priscilla Throop, pp. 59-60.

Modern Uses: For the Body: Yarrow has antispasmodic properties
that make it a healing oil for digestive problems like
colic, irritable bowel, and indigestion. Its analgesic
properties help to break up the pain of sprains,
rheumatism and neuralgia. Yarrow is a powerful
decongestant of the prostate and helps to balance
hormones. It is helpful as a urinary antiseptic,
soothing cystitis and urethritis. Yarrow also affects
the heart and kidneys as a gentle tonic for poor
circulation and low blood pressure. Its anti-
inflammatory and antiseptic action helps to heal
wounds and prevent scarring.

For the Mind and Spirit: Yarrow helps to release
stagnant energy and blocked emotions. It helps to
balance our highs and our lows. Yarrow helps those
in depression release bitterness and hidden rage.
Use yarrow to encourage feelings of peace, harmony,
equilibrium, intuition, centering, and visions.

Applications
for Healing
Work: Yarrow can be diffused and applied topically to the
                 body.

Safety Data: Yarrow is non-toxic and non-irritating. Some people
                 may have a sensitivity to yarrow. Best to skin test
                 before using. Caution should be exercised in using
                 this oil during pregnancy.

Chapter 9

CREATING YOUR OWN ESSENTIAL OIL BLENDS—THE ART AND SCIENCE

Essential oils do have a profound effect on one's body, mind and spirit. They can affect your energy field and energy centers, your emotions and your psyche and your spiritual self. Once you become comfortable with using essential oils with your hands-on healing practice, you may find that using only one essential oil may not be enough to enhance the effectiveness of your healing work. Layering several oils may be one possibility but learning to properly blend oils synergistically may be a better solution. This calls for knowledge of both the art and the science of essential oils. We must be creative and intuitive as well as knowledgeable about the science and frequencies of these medicines of the earth. One mistake beginners make is trying to create a blend that will address multiple systems and problems at the same time. Simply combining a number of oils may create a fragrant mess. The fragrances may work against each other rather than in harmony. At that point, you need to start over. If the blend you create is repulsive, the client will have a negative reaction but if the blend is synergistically in harmony, it will be pleasing and your purpose for the blend will be enhanced.

Blending essential oils can be wonderfully creative and enjoyable at the same time. You don't have to be a master perfumer or expert in aromatherapy in order to enjoy blending oils. In this chapter we will turn our attention to defining our purpose for blending oils and examine some simple guidelines to aid us in the art of blending essential oils.

Identifying Your Purpose

This may sound simplistic but first identify why blending one or more oils will serve your client in this healing moment. All essential oils have the power to affect us emotionally and spiritually but only those that are right for the individual at this particular juncture in their healing process will possess the subtle potential to assist in transformation. Regardless if your purpose is to create a blend on the physical level for sore muscles or for a cough, you will also affect the emotions and psyche as well.

Do you need a blend to fight infection or a blend to soothe jangled nerves? Are you looking to address insomnia or do you need a stimulating blend to help someone study for exams? Is there a need for a fragrance to soothe emotional wounds or deep grief? Do you seek a blend to help with physical, emotional or spiritual healing? Or is your aim to create a blend of oils that will affect whole person healing?

Gabriel Mojay identifies three approaches to blending that will bear upon your purpose.[1] First there is aesthetic blending which relies on your "nose," on your sensory discernment and individual creativity in coming up with pleasing aromas. As you become more and more familiar with the various oils, your nose simply knows which oils combine and support one another. Clinical blending on the other hand depends upon your knowledge both of the oils and of common ailments. The more you read and study, the more you "know" the oils and how they affect the body. Knowledge of anatomy and physiology, of chemistry and vibrational frequencies will aid your ability to create clinical blends that truly work. And lastly, psychological and spiritual blending calls for a degree of "intuition" or an ability to "sense" the condition of the spirit of the client. This calls for tuning into spiritual guidance, truly listening to how Spirit leads you in creating blends that will help another. We actually use all of these abilities but at times our approach may differ depending on the particular circumstances with each client.

[1] Gabriel Mojay, *Aromatherapy for Healing the Spirit*, pp. 132-133.

Some of these essences blended together have a mutually enhancing effect upon one another.

[2]Marguerite Maury, *The Secret of Life and Youth,* p. 95.

Creating Synergies

How you add essential oils to each other can create a synergistic whole that is greater than the sum of the parts. In other words, some of these essences blended together have a mutually enhancing effect upon one another. When blended oils work harmoniously together, they create a synergy, and a balance. To create a good synergy, requires knowledge and experience with the oils as well as a healthy dose of intuition. A blend for one client may not work at all for the exact same purpose with another client. Each blend is tailored specifically for a client's symptoms and their underlying problem, as well as their emotional and psychological needs. Madame Maury who first introduced aromatherapy to England, used to write Individual Prescriptions or IPs for her patients. These were individually designed "to serve above all to normalize the rhythm of the functions" [of the whole person.][2] For her, it was important that the mixture be well orchestrated as to density, evaporation time, and tone of each essence to serve the individual's needs. Her approach was just as rigorous as that of the perfumer who needs to respect balance and order to obtain a pleasing perfume.

Some very simple rules to keep in mind when creating synergistic blends include:

1. Blend no more than three or four oils at a time in the beginning until you've gained some experience.
2. Make sure the properties of the oils you want to blend complement each other and don't have opposite effects like calming and stimulating.
3. Your blend should be pleasant to your client. In general, floral blends do not appeal to a lot of men and women generally don't like strong woodsy fragrances.

In general, oils of the same plant family will tend to harmonize well with each other. For instance, the citrus oils like lemon, grapefruit, bergamot, neroli and orange will blend well with each other and enhance the desired effect. Most floral oils will blend well together as well as the woods, balsams, and spices. Many of the herbs like rosemary, lavender, and sage will blend very easily. Some essential oils will enhance just about any blend. Rose, jasmine and lavender are three examples of oils that act as enhancers.

The whole natural world is scented and that includes man, animals, plants, and even minerals. They all give off a smell. We even recognize scents that are good and those that are not. Some scents please us and others repel us. Some heal us and some do not. Pay attention—the nose knows.

Spiritual Blending

In chapter four I discussed the vibrational properties of essential oils and mentioned that both prayer and energetic healing methods were likewise means of shifting vibrational frequencies. Well, positive prayer and affirmations can also affect the frequencies of the oils, especially when blending. We don't always know what is in the best and highest interest for another, but we can pray that they receive healing from the blended oils that may help them find a sense of peacefulness. Try holding the bottle of blended oils you have mixed in your hands as you bless it. When you then use the oil on your client's body or diffuse it in the room, you can trust that the many different molecules will connect to the proper receptors throughout the body, bringing healing balance.

Creating Fragrance Harmonies

You may have noticed in descriptions of essential oils that they are divided into "notes." Some are described as having a top note quality, others a middle note and still others have a base note quality. In the nineteenth century, a Frenchman by the name of Piesse worked very hard to classify odors according to the musical scale.[3]

Rose, jasmine and lavender will enhance just about any blend.

"Therefore God, your God, has anointed you with the oil of gladness beyond your companions. your robes are all fragrant with myrrh and aloes and cassia." Psalm 45:7

[3]Julia Lawless, *The Illustrated Encyclopedia of Essential Oils*, p. 45.

Various fragrances when combined would then form perfect harmonies. A good blend would be considered one that balanced all three.

Top notes are described as oils that have a sharp, fresh, light quality that have a very fast evaporation rate. This is the aroma that first hits your nose and will form your first impression of any blend. From a chemical point of view, these are the aldehydes and esters and are generally found in oils from flowers, leaves and fruits. Bergamot, neroli, lemon, orange (all the citrus oils), peppermint, thyme, myrtle, eucalyptus, mandarin, tea tree, verbena, and yarrow are classified as top note oils. Marcel Lavabre recommends that a good blend will have between 20 to 40 percent top note oils in it.[4]

[4]Marcel Lavabre, *Aromatherapy Workbook*, p. 107.

The middle note is the heart of the fragrance and will make up the majority of the blend. This fragrance usually emerges after the first impression and will smooth the sharp edges of the blend. The fragrances from these middle note oils are sometimes referred to as enhancers or equalizers or balancers. They are typically warm, soft, and mellow. Chemically, these are the monoterpene alcohols and are found mostly in leaves and herbs. Some middle note oils include geranium, lavender, rosewood, chamomile, hyssop, cypress, juniper, pine, fennel, melissa, peppermint, rosemary, and marjoram. Lavabre, recommends that middle note oils make up 40 to 80 percent of the blend.

The base note has a rich, heavy and pleasant scent that will emerge later and linger longer. These will affect the chakras and the energy field. Base note oils have deep effects on the mental and emotional bodies. To smell these oils from the bottle, they may not seem very strong but when placed on the body, the heat of the body will release their power and last for several hours and in some cases, even days. Sandalwood, clary sage, frankincense, benzoin, cedarwood, patchouly, rose, spikenard, tarragon, tuberose, vetiver, ylang-ylang, cinnamon, clove, ginger, and spruce are base note oils. Often these oils are thick and dark. Chemically these are the sesquiterpenes and are found mostly in woods and gums. A blend does not necessarily have to have a base note but if it is to be put on the skin, Lavabre finds it necessary. Perhaps only 5 percent of the blend needs to be a base note oil.

Lavabre identifies another category he calls fixatives that are really base notes. These draw your blend into the skin and have an even deeper base note. They are necessary for a long lasting effect. Some fixatives include myrrh, cistus, patchouly and vetiver. Fixatives are only used sparingly in a blend and come from roots and gums. They are sesquiterpenes or diterpenes.

Some single oils are said to be balanced in their own right such as angelica, jasmine, ylang-ylang, neroli and rose. These oils will have a complex chemistry carrying the full range of smells. In reading various texts on aromatherapy you may find some authors identify a particular essential oil as a top note and others identify it as a middle note. Sometimes they are both right.

A common beginner's error is in trying to create one blend to address multiple problems.

Some Guides for Blending

In your healing work there will be times when you simply know that you need to create a synergistic blend to address the client's needs. As you gather your information about the client's physical, emotional and spiritual needs, you will assess their energy field and centers, listen to their symptoms and then begin to put the information together. You will draw upon your knowledge of the body and the emotions, knowledge of common ailments and your knowledge of the oils. Your purpose for blending an oil needs to be clear. Again, don't try to address all of the problems with one blend. You may need to create several blends if there are multiple systems involved. A blend for a skin problem may not be what is needed for supporting the kidneys or the lungs.

Once you determine the purpose of your blend, then decide how you will use it—inhalation, diffusion, in a compress, in a mas-

Creating a blend is like creating a fine painting or baking a fine soufflé. It takes great care and attention.

"Yet, in my heart I know,
        Beloved, that
    Love is the healing balm
        for fear.
I will sing and make melody!
        Awaken, my soul!"
Psalm 57

Nan Merrill, *Psalms for Praying*, p. 111

"May balance and harmony
        be your aim
    as you are drawn into the
        Heart of Love."
Psalm 132

Nan Merrill, *Psalms for Praying*, p. 280.

sage lotion, neat on the body, or a combination. If you are trying to address the energy field, you may want to combine diffusion and application to the body. Emotional issues are best treated with diffusion but application to particular areas of the body may also be necessary. The more physical problems need the blend applied to the skin either locally over the problem area or as a massage lotion covering a larger area.

When you are dealing with emotional or spiritual problems, the blend needs to be pleasant. You are creating a personal blend that will fit this individual. It's like creating a painting that has just the right colors and expressions. You may find that you want to apply an emotional blend to the chakras and have the client smell the blend several times during their day. You can teach them to place a drop or two on their palm, then rub their hands together and run them through their own field, smoothing and brushing from head to toe. I recommend that you encourage the client to keep a journal and record their thoughts and feelings through the day. Teach them to look for the various nuances of changes in their own emotions.

Another guide in blending is to simply record what you do as you create a personal blend for someone. What were your aesthetic, clinical and spiritual reasons for each addition to the blend? Record your thoughts and comments. Remember, less is often more. Just two drops of an essential oil can transform a blend. If the person you are creating the blend for likes it, they are more likely to use it. If it is a pleasing blend that works, you will want to remember the recipe.

Mixing the Blend

The first thing to do is to get the right size and color glass bottle. Try using a 5 ml or a 15 ml dark brown or blue bottle. If your intention is to create a massage lotion or oil with the essential oils in it, then use a 30 ml bottle. When essential oils are exposed to the light, their chemistry is altered and many evaporate more quickly.

So to prevent loss of their potency, always use a dark bottle. You can look in health food stores or specialty shops for these. Make sure you get ones that have a removable plastic essential oil dropper in them. Take this out when you are adding the oils to the bottle and when you are finished, replace the plastic dropper. Always close the cap of the bottle tightly since these oils evaporate easily. Next, label the bottle with the client's name, the date, and the ingredients.

When actually adding the oils to the bottle, be careful that you only drop in the number of drops your recipe calls for. One drop too many will alter the outcome. There are approximately 20 drops of essential oil in 1 ml. If you are creating a synergistic blend concentrate, you will use the smaller bottle. (Remember, a little goes a long way.) Gather all the essential oils you will need for your blend that will work synergistically and not oppose each other. Make sure your blend will be well rounded, having top, middle and base notes and is pleasant smelling. Only open one oil at a time and begin with the most viscous or thick essential oil first. After you have all the ingredients added to the bottle from your recipe, place the cap on the bottle and gently roll it between your hands to thoroughly blend the molecules of the oils together. Then turn the bottle upside down then right side up.

If you intend to create a blend with a carrier oil or a blend for a massage lotion, place the essential oils in the 30ml dark bottle first. Then add the base (carrier) oil to just above the level of the bottle's "shoulder." Approximately 10-15 drops of the combined essential oils will create a 1-3% blend. Replace the cap and roll the bottle between your hands vigorously to thoroughly mix the essential oils with the carrier oil.

Making a Carrier Formula	
Essential Oil	Carrier
40-60 drops	4 ounces (120 ml)
25-30 drops	2 ounces (50 ml)
10-15 drops	1 ounce (30 ml)
5-7 drops	1/2 ounce (15 ml)
4-10 drops	2 teaspoons (10 ml)
2-5 drops	1 teaspoon (5 ml)

Favorite base oils include almond which is well suited for making massage or body oils, hazelnut oil which is absorbed more quickly and is used in cosmetic products, avocado, sunflower, canola, and grapeseed oils will also work well on the body. Jojoba oil (a wax and not a vegetable oil) is an ideal carrier for perfume oils. Since all of these oils except the jojoba oil are fatty oils, they can go rancid. Its best to buy them in small quantities and store them in a cool place.

Some Prepared Blends

Several companies such as Young Living and Utatti offer a number of blends for a wide range of indications. Some of these may be just what you need in a particular situation. They address both physical and emotional health and were formulated to maximize their synergistic effect between the various oil chemistries and harmonic frequencies. If you are not ready to do your own blending, you may want to start with one of these time-tested blends from master blenders.

[5]*Essential Oils Desk Reference*, p. 96.

Exodus II™ [5] contains the "holy anointing oils" (cassia, cinnamon bark, calamus and myrrh) plus other ancient oils known for their healing qualities—hyssop, frankincense, spikenard, and galbanum. Notice that all of these oils are highly antimicrobial meaning they create an inhospitable environment for all kinds of microbes. No wonder the people were saved from plagues in the Bible.

Harmony[TM6] is a beautiful blend of oils created to promote physical and emotional healing by bringing about a harmonic balance to the energy centers. Harmony can instill a sense of integration. This is one of those wonderful oils that help reduce stress and create a sense of well-being. It has also been known to stop allergy attacks. Just place a few drops on the sternum and breathe deeply. Harmony contains: hyssop, spruce, lavender, geranium, frankincense, ylang ylang, sandalwood, rose, orange, bergamont, sage lavender, jasmine, palmarosa, Roman chamomile and rosewood. You will notice that many of these oils have properties known to be calming, soothing, balancing, relaxing and uplifting.

[6]*Essential Oils Desk Reference,* p. 102.

Joy[TM7] is one of my favorite oil blends and one I use every day on myself. It enhances feelings of self-esteem and brings joy to the heart. I find it a great oil to use in preparation for healing work. It contains 10 essential oils: rose, bergamot, mandarin, ylang ylang, lemon, geranium, jasmine, palmarosa, Roman chamomile, and rosewood. Some of these oils balance the hormones, calm the emotions, and relieve anxiety and tension while others are refreshing and stimulating.

[7]*Essential Oils Desk Reference,* p. 108.

Peace and Calming[TM8] was created specifically for diffusing but can also be used neat on the body. It is a very helpful oil for relaxation and a deep sense of peace. Parents and pet owners have found this oil particularly helpful for calming hyper children or small pets like dogs. It contains: blue tansey, patchouly, tangerine, orange, and ylang ylang. The oils in this blend have been used to help manage depression, anxiety, stress and insomnia. For those restless nights when sleep is difficult, Peace and Calming on the soles of the feet may be just enough to calm anxieties for a restful night.

[8]*Essential Oils Desk Reference,* p. 108.

Thieves[TM9] was created from research on a group of 15th century thieves who used oils to avoid contracting the plague in order to rob the dead and dying. Weber State University found that it has potent anti-microbial properties—99.96 percent kill rate against airborne bacteria. All of the oils within Thieves are antiviral, antiseptic, anti-

[9]*Essential Oils Desk Reference,* p. 123.

bacterial, anti-infectious and help protect the body against flu, colds, sinusitis, bronchitis, pneumonia, sore throats, cuts, etc. Thieves can be used on the soles of the feet or around the throat area. Some even brush their teeth or gargle with a tincture of Thieves to ward off colds and flu. It contains clove, lemon, cinnamon bark, eucalyptus, and rosemary.

[10]*Essential Oils Desk Reference*, p. 124.

3 Wise Men™[10] was formulated to open the subconscious mind through pineal stimulation to help release deep-seated trauma. This oil contains a different blend of the Bible oils that give a feeling of reverence and spiritual awareness. It contains: frankincense, sandalwood, juniper, myrrh and spruce. The effect of this oil is grounding yet uplifting.

[11]*Essential Oils Desk Reference*, p. 126.

Valor™[11] helps to balance the electrical energies within the body, giving courage, confidence and self-esteem. There is the story that the ancient Roman soldiers used to use a blend of these oils on themselves for courage before going into battle. It contains the following oils: rosewood, blue tansy, frankincense and spruce. Some have referred to this oil as a "chiropractor" in a bottle since it has improved scoliosis for many.

[12]*Essential Oils Desk Reference*, p. 126-127.

White Angelica™[12] is a beautiful blend of oils, some from ancient times that were known to increase the aura around the body. This blend is delicately balanced to bring a sense of strength and protection to one's field. Gary Young says that its frequency neutralizes negative energy and supports a feeling of protection and security. I find it to be both calming and soothing. It helps to maintain a positive space which is why I use it on myself before doing healing work to protect and strengthen my own field. It contains 10 essential oils: ylang ylang, rose, melissa, sandalwood, geranium, spruce, myrrh, hyssop, bergamot and rosewood.

Mystical Rose™ Ron Roth, a modern-day mystic and healer had a blend created for him that is reminiscent of the fragrance many people smell when connected to the Divine in deep meditation. It is the fragrance associated with mystics and saints but is not beyond our reach. It contains 5 essential oils in a base of olive, aloe vera and castor oils. They are rose, sandalwood, amber, musk and patchouly. The fragrance of this oil blend is quite beautiful and one I would give the description of holy.

Some blends are created specifically for the energy field. Caroline Myss, author of *Anatomy of the Spirit,* has begun to offer essential oil blends through her company for use with the seven chakras.[13]

[13]For information on these blends, please consult www.myss.com.

For the root chakra, she includes several wood oils for stability as well as roots for grounding: cedarwood, vetiver, sandalwood, grapefruit, and birch. She also suggests the single oils of cypress, palmarosa, and frankincense for the root center.

For the sacral chakra, several flowers have been included. There are oils in this blend for relieving menopausal and menstrual problems, as well as oils to relieve anger and aggression. She includes clary sage, ylang ylang, spearmint, cardamon, temple orange, and fennel. Additional oils for the sacral center include neroli, spikenard, frankincense and ginger.

Sacred oils blended for the solar plexus include helichrysum, jasmine, peppermint, ginger, Roman chamomile, and juniper berries. Other single oils recommended for the solar plexus center are cypress, orange, rosemary and palmarosa.

For the fourth center, the heart, her blend includes several oils to relieve grief, trauma and emotional shock. These help open the person to feelings of joy and expansion and enhance feelings of love. On the physical level this blend includes oils to strength the heart and circulation and open the respiratory passages. It includes elemi, neroli, calendula, rose, angelica root and melissa. Additional oils that affect the heart center include spruce, myrtle, ylang ylang, jasmine, geranium and eucalyptus.

For the throat center, she blends oils to stimulate communication and release emotions. On the physical level, there are oils in the blend that reduce mucous and open breathing passages. The blend includes rose geranium, spruce, vanilla, monarda, and anise. Other oils that she recommends for this center are rosewood, neroli, lemon, frankincense, juniper and marjoram.

For the sixth center, the brow, her blend of sacred oils includes those known to heal problems of the head. It also has oils to enhance meditation, the dream state and encourage euphoria yet improve mental clarity. Her blend includes rosewood, basil, frankincense, myrrh, and St. John's wort. Other single oils recommended for this center include lavender, sandalwood, spikenard and lemon.

For the seventh center, the crown, Myss includes several oils that increase body strength, relieve fatigue, refresh the mind, relieve headache pain and balance moods. Her blend includes lavender, champaca, mugwort, galbanum, yarrow and clove bud. Other single oils for this center include myrtle, bergamot, peppermint and lemon.

Myss recommends these blends be used during meditation, applying them directly to the chakra centers or on the corresponding vita flex points on the soles of the feet, or on the palms.

You may find other companies offering quality blends for the chakras and the energy field as well. The best way to introduce yourself to them is through the Internet. Then you will need to do your homework, investigating the quality of the various company's oils.

Don't be afraid to try your hand at creating your own blends. You will truly miss the fun of experimenting with the oils if you rely only on prepared blends. The more familiar you become with the power of the oils, the more you will be comfortable in creating blends.

There are a number of authors[14] who offer guideline tables for creating blends to address various ailments and emotional and spiritual problems. You might want to consult these as you teach yourself the art of blending.

[14]Some resources for blending essential oils for common ailments:

Marcel Lavabre, *Aromatherapy Workbook,* pp. 117-126.

Susan Curtis, *Essential Oils,* pp. 133-137.

Kurt Schnaubelt, *Advanced Aromatherapy, The Science of Essential Oil Therapy,* pp. 101-118.

Valerie Ann Worwood, *The Fragrant Mind, Aromatherapy for Personality, Mind, Mood, and Emotion.* This entire book offers suggestions on blends to address emotional healing.

Valerie Ann Worwood, *The Fragrant Heavens, The Spiritual Dimension of Fragrance and Aromatherapy.* This entire book looks at the spiritual dimensions of each individual oil and their synergistic effect in blending.

CHAPTER 10

ANOINT US WITH THE OIL OF GLADNESS

Rediscovering the power of aromatic essential oils and the power of the laying-on of hands can give new life to what it means to be called to healing ministry for others. We come out of Christianity's rich tradition of healing rituals that have been long forgotten. So like a child first learning to walk, we are learning with faltering steps, how to use these healing medicines given by God along with our healing hands and our healing prayers. Healing is a spiritual event and God has given us the tools—the same ones that Jesus gave to his disciples when he called them to healing ministry. And like the early disciples, we too must learn how to heal with humility and compassion, attuned to God's healing energy.

You might ask, "isn't my prayer enough? Why do I need to touch or to use healing oils?" Sometimes prayer is enough. Sometimes the hands-on healing is sufficient and sometimes the oils alone can heal. But hopefully you have learned in these pages that combining energy healing and essential oils with our prayer is extremely powerful. When used together, each increases the power of the other and the combined ability to heal is greater than the sum of the three. Jesus taught his disciples to use all three together and the early church modeled a ministry to others that called for healing rituals of prayer, hands-on healing and anointing. And as we have seen, when we pray over our essential oils, their frequencies increase. And when we use essential oils on the palms of our hands when we do energy healing, the effects are even more profound and last longer.

"Let the earth put forth vegetation: plants yielding seed, and fruit trees of every kind on earth that bear fruit with the seed in it... And it was so. And God saw that it was good." Genesis 1:11

There is an intelligence programmed into these oils from the time of creation. God has given us all that we need to stay healthy on this earth. In Genesis, God created the plants of the earth and saw that it was good. And he gave to everything that has the breath of life, every green plant for food. The plants nourish our bodies and keep up healthy. It is to our sorrow that we have forgotten the knowledge of these healing plants and placed our belief in an ailing healthcare system that in turn, puts its faith in pharmaceuticals—man-made and not God-made substances.

Answering the call to healing ministry calls for a commitment to faithfulness on our part. Our response must be one of learning, practicing, experiencing, and praying. We have already been promised blessings for our faithfulness. God will reward you with the support and the teachers you need. Our faith in God as the healer will sustain us through the difficult times. As we know, the Old Testament peoples prayed to God for healing and later went back to their old ways. Even when God held out the gifts of healing to the whole people, they didn't stay faithful for long. When Jesus came, he taught again, how to call upon God for healing and he extended a hand of healing to those in need. He knew the healing ability of aromatic oils and he knew how to live in harmony with nature's medicines. Daily Jesus taught his disciples and expected them to pass on this knowledge of prayer, hands-on healing and anointing with healing oils. The early Christian church was a fervent one and known for its healing ways but after a few hundred years, they too began to forget the knowledge of healing hands and healing plants and oils. The choice is now yours. But we can take comfort in knowing that

"And he said to them, 'Go into all the world and proclaim the good news to the whole creation...And these signs will accompany those who believe:.. they will lay their hands on the sick, and they will recover." Mark 16: 15,17a,18b

God does not call us to ministry without giving us the knowledge and proper tools. There are many who are discovering the healing abilities of the good green plants created by God. And there are many who are awakening to the power of prayer, hands-on healing and the healing medicines of the earth.

Be a Source of Blessing For Others

"Therefore, O Creator, O Heart of Love,
   anoint us with
   the oil of gladness to share
   with all;
   your raiment is as fragrant
   blossoms,
   healing herbs of kindness.
From every direction stringed instruments
   Will gladden our hearts;
   Our friends will be filled with integrity,
   Standing beside us in times of need."
Psalm 45

Nan Merrill, *Psalms for Praying*, p. 88

"You have loved righteousness
   and hated wickedness;
therefore God, your God,
   has anointed you
   with the oil of gladness
   beyond your
   companions."
Hebrews 1:9

We are each a blessing already. Whether we are consciously aware of our connection to the Divine, the Divine is consciously aware of us. If this were not so, we would not exist. God holds us in this world to be blessings for one another. What good we can do while we are here, we should do. When we are being a blessing, our inner light shines with brilliance and God is showering all good gifts through us. We are meant to be servants of one another. I am reminded of the many selfless acts of kindness done by human beings in times of great need. There are countless acts of kindness that no one sees yet change the face of the earth. Extending the hand of healing to one another is answering the call to be a blessing—it is answering the call to be holy. Prayer, hands-on healing and anointing with essential oils are all acts of holiness. And when we practice these with a humble and compassionate heart, we honor God and we bless one another. Take comfort. When you answer the call, God will anoint you with the oil of gladness—to share with all God's people.

Take a moment now and if you have the oil of Joy(tm) or frankincense, or sandalwood, or cedarwood, place a drop in your palm and rub your hands together. Then inhale this beautiful fragrance or anoint your brow. These are oils of gladness that will lighten your heart and your soul. Then, go out and be God's blessing for others.

HEALING TOUCH SPIRITUAL MINISTRY

Program Overview

The Healing Touch Spiritual Ministry program is a multi-level educational program presenting healing based in the Judeo-Christian scriptures. There are six workshops presented in this program. These courses progress the student through the curriculum. Eventually, students who desire to complete their work in the Healing Touch Spiritual Ministry program may receive a certificate of completion after completing a practitioner program. For more information, consult www.HTSpiritualMinistry.com. For students who desire to become certified by Healing Touch International, Inc. in the work of Healing Touch™, there is a practitioner program offered by the Colorado Center for Healing Touch. For more information on this program, consult www.Healingtouch.net.

The mission of the Healing Touch Spiritual Ministry Program is to provide an educational program on the spiritual and scriptural aspects of healing ministry and the laying-on of hands, specifically, Healing Touch, to faith communities and individuals in ministry/service setting everywhere. Classes are being held in Christian churches of all denominations, retreat centers and religious hospitals across the nation and in Europe. The Healing Touch Spiritual Ministry Program promotes the art of nursing as well as the art of spiritual presence practiced by all those in ministry. It can be used in

244   Healing Oils, Healing Hands

parish ministry and health care settings of all kinds. Hands-on healing helps those who suffer physically, emotionally, mentally or spiritually. Parish nurses, hospice and hospital nurses, prayer teams, chaplains, ministers and the lay community can benefit from these workshops.

Courses include an eight hour, Introduction to Healing Ministry, a 15-20 hour Healing Touch Spiritual Ministry Level 1, a 15-20 hour Healing Touch Spiritual Ministry Level 2 (II-A), an eight hour Art of Listening to Spiritual Guidance, a 15-20 hour Healing Touch Level 3 (II-B), and a 15-20 hour Sent to Heal and Anoint course on the use of essential oils with hands-on healing. A practitioner program is being developed as well as advanced courses in the use of essential oils with hands-on healing.

Certificates of completion are granted to all those in attendance through the Healing Touch Spiritual Ministry program which is approved as a provider of continuing education in nursing by the Colorado Nurses' Association, which is accredited as a provider of continuing education for nursing by the American Nurses' Credentialing Center's Commission on Accreditation. The Healing Touch Spiritual Ministry program is also approved by the California Board of Registered Nursing, Provider number 13181.

Appendix B

RESOURCES

The following represents a partial list of resources for essential oils. The reader is advised to investigate for themselves the quality and expertise of any company before investing in the purchase of essential oils. The author is not recommending any one company in particular but is simply offering some resources.

Young Living Essential Oils
Founder: D. Gary Young, ND
www.youngliving.com
250 Main Street
Payson, UT 84651
(800) 763-9963
Producer of over 300 products and 130 essential oils

FloraMedica
Founder: Valerie Gennari Cooksley, RN
www.floramedica.com
P.O. Box 18
Issaquah, WA 98027
Phone/Fax (877) 363-3422

Uttati International Essential Oils
Founder: Raed Rady
www.Uttati.com
400 S. Beverly Drive #214
Beverly Hills, CA 90212
(800) 552-9379
Producer of over 200 essential oils and other products

Elizabeth Van Buren
Founder: Elizabeth Van Buren
www.evb-aromatherapy.com
PO Box 7542
Santa Cruz, CA 95061-7542
(800) 710-7759

Celebrating Life
Founder: Ron Roth
www.ronroth.com
141 Gooding Street
LaSalle, IL 61301
(815) 224-3377
Contact them to order Mystical Rose oil or you can get it through Uttati oils

Caroline Myss PhD
Caroline now offers sacred essential oils through her company.
www.myss.com

Educational Classes on the Biblical Use of Essential Oils

Healing Touch Spiritual Ministry Program
www.HTSpiritualMinistry.com
Classes are held throughout the United States and Italy
For information on how to bring this education to your church or community, contact our office at (303) 467-7829 or email: Staff@HTSpiritualMinistry.com.

Center for Aromatherapy Research and Education (C.A.R.E.)
www.raindroptraining.com
Classes are held throughout the United States and concentrate on anointing with essential oils for healing. Program can lead to a certification as a Certified Care Instructor. Contact the office at (572) 238-4273 for information or email: care@clas.net.

Appendix C

a healing and anointing service

Welcome To All in the Name of the Lord.

Leader: The grace of our Lord Jesus Christ and the love of God the Father and the healing light of the Holy Spirit be with you all.

Response: *And also with you.*

Leader: We gather here in the name of Jesus, the compassionate one, who went about his ministry reaching out in healing to all those suffering in body, mind and spirit. Daily, he taught his disciples how to pray, anoint and lay-on hands for healing. Then, he sent them out in twos into the villages and towns to extend the hand of God's mercy in the form of healing. He left us his legacy of a healing ministry and expected us to carry on the work of compassion. Now we stand before the Lord Jesus in the healing light of his Holy Spirit to seek total healing—body, mind and spirit—for ourselves and for our loved ones. Let us pray:

Leader: Lord Jesus, you came as a Good Shepherd seeking what was lost. Lord have mercy.

Response: *Lord have mercy.*

Leader: Lord Jesus, you healed the blind, the lame, the deaf and the lepers. Christ have mercy.

Response: Christ have mercy.

Leader: Lord Jesus, you call us to pray for healing for ourselves and for one another. Lord have mercy.

Response: Lord have mercy.

Leader: May Almighty God have mercy upon us, heal us into wholeness and bring us to everlasting life.

Response: Amen.

Scripture Readings

The Story of The Good Samaritan

"A Samaritan while traveling came near the wounded man, and when he saw him, he was moved with pity. He went to him and bandaged his wounds, having poured oil and wine on them. Then he put him on his own animal, brought him to an inn, and took care of him. The next day he took out two denarii, gave them to the innkeeper, and said, 'Take care of him; and when I come back I will repay you whatever more you spend.'" Luke 10:33-35.

Response: Psalm 103

Bless the Beloved, O my soul,
and all that is within me;
I bless your Holy Name!
Bless the Beloved, O my soul,
and remember the goodness of Love.
You forgive our iniquities,
you heal our disease,

You save us from the snares of fear,
> You crown us with steadfast
>> love and mercy,
You satisfy our every need and
> renew our spirit like the eagle's.

The Story of The Anointing of Jesus

"A woman came with an alabaster jar of very costly ointment of nard, and she broke open the jar and poured the ointment on his head. But some were there who said to one another in anger, 'Why was the ointment wasted in this way? For this ointment could have been sold for more than three hundred denarii, and the money given to the poor.' And they scolded her. But Jesus said 'Let her alone; why do you trouble her? She has performed a good service for me...she has done what she could; she has anointed my body beforehand for its burial. Truly I tell you, wherever the good news is proclaimed in the whole world, what she has done will be told in remembrance of her.'" Mark 14:3-6, 8-9.

Reflections on the Readings

Blessing of the Oil

Leader: Let us pray: God of tenderness and mercy, you sent your Son to heal humanity of its woundedness. Breathe your Holy Spirit upon this oil that it may be a blessed source of healing for all who receive it. May we experience the warmth of your healing love surrounding us with your compassionate love. Let this anointing be with an oil of gladness to lighten our hearts and minds and restore us to wholeness with you O God. We ask this in the name of Jesus Christ, the healer.

Response: Amen.

The Laying On of Hands and the Anointing with a Healing Oil

All are invited to receive the laying on of hands and anointing with a healing oil. As you come forward, the ministers of healing will place their hands on your head and pray for healing in body, mind and spirit. Then, the ministers of healing will anoint your forehead with the healing oil. If you would like to have your hands anointed as well, simply hold out your hands, palms upward.

Prayer After Anointing

Leader: Let us pray: "God, your God, has anointed you with the oil of gladness beyond your companions; your robes are all fragrant with myrrh and aloes and cassia." We give you thanks O God for this healing through the laying on of hands and anointing with your holy oil. Let it be for us a source of on-going healing in our lives as we go back to our families and friends.

Response: Amen!

Leader: May God fill us with peace and transform our hearts in Love that we may continue to be witnesses of God's healing mercy.

Response: Amen!

Leader: Let us go in the peace and healing of Jesus.

Response: Thanks be to God!

BIBLIOGRAPHY

The New World Dictionary—Concordance to the New American Bible. USA: C.D. Stampley Enterprises, Inc., 1970.

United Methodist Book of Worship. Nashville, TN: United Methodist Publishing House, Abington Press, 1992.

Dues, Greg. *Catholic Customs and Traditions, A Popular Guide.* Mystic, CT: Twenty-Third Publications, 1998.

Brown, Raymond, J. Fitzmyer, and R. Murphy, *The New Jerome Biblical Commentary.* Englewood Cliffs, NJ: Prentice Hall, 1990.

Brown, Denise. *Aromatherapy.* Lincolnwood, IL: NTC/Contemporary Publishing, 1996.

Childre, Doc Lew. *Cut-Thru, Achieve Total Security and Maximum Energy.* Boulder Creek, CA: Planetary Publications, 1995.

Cooksley, Valerie Gennari. *Aromatherapy, Soothing Remedies to Restore, Rejuvenate, and Heal.* Paramus, NJ: Prentice Hall Press, 2002.

Curtis, Susan. *Essential Oils.* London, England: Aurum Press Ltd., 1996.

Damian, Peter and Kate. *Aromatherapy Scent and Psyche, Using Essential Oils for Physical and Emotional Well-Being.* Rochester, VT: Healing Arts Press, 1995.

Ericksen, Marlene. *Healing with Aromatherapy.* Lincolnwood, IL: Keats Publishing, 2000.

Franchomme, P. "Using Eubiotic and Antibiotic Essential Oils in Resetting the Aerobic and Anaerobic Intestinal Flora: Local and Systemic Effects," in *Integrated Aromatic Medicine, Proceedings from the First International Symposium, Grasse, France, March 21-22, 1998.* Salem, Utah: Essential Science Publishing, March, 2000, pp. 43-50.

Freidmann MD, Terry Shepherd. *Freedom through Health*. Northglenn, CO: Harvest Publishing, 1998.

Foley, Rev. Marcy. *Embraced by the Essence!* Eldridge, IA: Bawden Printing, 1998.

Fournil, Gilles. "Olfactothérapie® (Olfactotherapy)," in *Integrated Aromatic Medicine, Proceedings from the First International Symposium, Grasse, France, March 21-22, 1998*. Salem, Utah: Essential Science Publishing, March, 2000, pp. 37-42.

Gattefossé, Rene-Maurice. *Aromatherapy*. Great Britain: C.S. Daniel Company Limited, 1995.

Gerber, Richard. *Vibrational Medicine, New Choices for Healing Ourselves*. Santa Fe, NM: Bear and Company, 1988.

Gerber, Richard. *Vibrational Medicine for the 21st Century, The Complete Guide to Energy Healing and Spiritual Transformation*. New York: Eagle Brook, 2000.

Guilbert, Charles Mortimer, Custodian. *Standard Book of Common Prayer, according to the use of The Episcopal Church*. New York: Oxford University Press, 1990.

Hammarskjöld, Dag. *Markings*. New York: Alfred A Knoph, 1971.

Hervieux, L. "Aromatherapy for HIV-Positive Patients," in *Integrated Aromatic Medicine, Proceedings from the First International Symposium, Grasse, France, March 21-22, 1998*. Salem, Utah: Essential Science Publishing, March, 2000, pp. 61-62.

Higley, Alan, Connie Higley. *Reference Guide for Essential Oils*. Spanish Fork, Utah: Abundant Health, 2002.

Hildegard von Bingen. *Hildegard von Bingen's Physica*. Translated by Priscilla Throop. Rochester, VT: Healing Arts Press, 1998.

Hildegard von Bingen. *Hildegard's Healing Plants*. Translated by Bruce W. Hozeski. Boston, MA: Beacon Press Books, 2001.

Hunt, Valerie. *Infinite Mind, Science of the Human Vibrations of Consciousness.* Malibu, CA: Malibu Publishing Co., 1996.

Johnston, William. *Mystical Theology, The Science of Love.* Maryknoll, New York: Orbis Books, 1995.

Krymow, Vincenzina. *Healing Plants of the Bible, History, Lore and Meditations.* Cincinnati, OH: St. Anthony Press, 2002.

Lavabre, Marcel. *Aromatherapy Workbook.* Rochester, VT: Healing Arts Press, 1990.

Lawless, Julia. *The Illustrated Encyclopedia of Essential Oils.* Shaftesbury, Dorset, England: Element Books, 1995.

Loughram, Joni Keim and Ruah Bull. *Aromatherapy and Subtle Energy Techniques.* Berkeley, CA: Frog, Ltd., 2000.

Loughram, Joni Keim and Ruah Bull. *Aromatherapy Anointing Oils.* Berkeley, CA: Frog, Ltd., 2001.

Manwaring, Brian, editor. *Essential Oils Desk Reference*, second edition. Salem, UT: Essential Science Publishing, 2001.

Martos, Joseph. *Doors to the Sacred, A Historical Introduction to Sacraments in the Catholic Church.* Liguori, MO: Liguori/Triumph, 2001.

Maury, Marguerite. *Guide to Aromatherapy, The Secret of Life and Youth: A Modern Alchelmy.* Great Britain: C.S. Daniel Company Limited, 1995.

Mein, Carolyn L. *Releasing Emotional Patterns with Essential Oils.* Rancho Santa Fe, CA: VisionWare Press, 1998.

Merrill, Nan. *Psalms for Praying.* New York: The Continuum Publishing Co., 1998.

Miller, Light and Bryan Miller. *Ayurveda and Aromatherapy.* Twin Lakes, WI: Lotus Press, 1995.

Mojay, Gabriel. *Aromatherapy for Healing the Spirit.* Rochester, VT: Healing Arts Press, 1997.

Oschman, James L. *Energy Medicine, The Scientific Basis.* Edinburgh, England: Churchill Livingstone, 2000.

Pearsall, Paul. *The Heart's Code, Tapping the Wisdom and Power of Our Heart Energy.* New York: Broadway Books, 1998.

Pénoël, Daniel, Rose-Marie Pénoël. *Natural Home Health Care Using Essential Oils.* An American English translation from the French original titled "Practique Aromatique Familiale." Hurricane, Utah: Essential Science Publishing, 1998.

Price, Shirley and Len Price. *Aromatherapy for Health Professionals,* Second Edition. Edinburgh: Churchill Livingstone, 1995.

Prince, Menkit. *The Essential Oil Cookbook, Outrageous Recipes for Weight Control and Long Life,* Second Edition. Carmichael, CA: Earth Love Enterprises, 1999.

Ryan, Barbara S., D. Lin and M. Linn. *To Heal as Jesus Healed.* Mineola, New York: Resurrection Press, 1997.

Rupp, Joyce. *Out of the Ordinary, Prayers, Poems, and Reflections for Every Season.* Notre Dame, IN: Ave Maria Press, 2000.

Schnaubelt, Kurt. *Medical Aromatherapy, Healing with Essential Oils.* Berkeley, CA: Frog, LTD., 1999.

Schnaubelt, Kurt. *Advanced Aromatherapy, The Science of Essential Oil Therapy.* Rochester, VT: Healing Arts Press, 1995.

Smith, Linda L. *Called into Healing, Reclaiming Our Judeo-Christian Legacy of Healing Touch.* Arvada, CO: HTSM Press, 2000.

Spangler, David. *Blessing, The Art and the Practice.* New York: Riverhead Books, 2001.

Stewart, David. *Healing Oils of the Bible*. Marble Hill, MO: CARE, Inc., 2002.

Strehlow, Wighard, and Gottfried Hertzka. *Hildegard of Bingen's Medicine*. Santa Fe, NM: Bear and Company, 1988.

Tisserand, Robert B. *The Art of Aromatherapy*. Rochester, VT: Healing Arts Press, 1977.

Valnet MD, Jean. *The Practice of Aromatherapy*. Rochester, VT: Healing Arts Press, 1990.

White, James F. *Introduction to Christian Worship,* 3rd Edition. Nashville, TN: Abingdon Press, 2000.

Worwood, Valerie Ann. *The Fragrant Heavens*. Novato, CA: New World Library, 1999.

Worwood, Valerie Ann. *The Complete Book of Essential Oils and Aromatherapy*. Novato, CA: New World Library, 1991.

Worwood, Valerie Ann. *The Fragrant Mind*. Novato, CA: New World Library, 1996.

Wright, Wendy M. *Sacred Heart, Gateway to God*. Maryknoll, New York: Orbis Books, 2001.

Young, D. Gary. *An Introduction to Young Living Essential Oils,* Eleventh Edition. Payson, UT: Young Living Essential Oils, 2001.

Young, D. Gary. "Cultivating and Distilling Therapeutic Quality Essential Oils in the United States," in *Integrated Aromatic Medicine, Proceedings from the First International Symposium, Grasse, France, March 21-22, 1998*. Salem, Utah: Essential Science Publishing, March, 2000, pp. 139-150.

Young, D. Gary. *Young Living Level II Training Materials,* presented in Coeur d'Alene, Idaho, September 3-7, 2002.

INDEX

G

H

I

J

K

ORAC 69,70
orange 56,57,59,67,68,91,96,129,144,146,149,153,175,182,192,194,201,203,207,211,228,229,234,236
orange blossom 10,207
ordination 35
oregano 10,209,210
Oschman, Jim 80,81,82,83,256

P

PanAway™ 97
patchouly 38,60,98,101,138,141,176,199,229,230,234,236
Peace and Calming™ 78,98,100,129,234
pennyroyal 46,175,185
Pénoël, Daniel 49,51,53,54,256
peppermint 10,13,43,46,65,67,76,77,98,100,179,196,211,212,213,216,229,236,237
Persians 17
Piesse 228
pine 21,46,56,82,100,101,116,129,144,147,149,151,152,156,161,163,167,168,169,170,171,184,188,197,199,209,
     216,220,222,229
plague 20,21,41,45,46,153,159,176,187,216,234
Pope Innocent I 28
Presbyterians 32
Purification™ 129

R

refrigerated coil 43
Roman Catholic Church 32
root center 90,115,117,163,236
rose 9,10,21,43,49,54,60,67,69,71,98,100,107,112,114,119,122,161,169,170,171,213,214,215,228,246,256
rosemary 10,40,44,45,46,47,56,58,61,63,69,96,100,101,129,144,146,147,151,158,164,167,168,175,188,197,203,204,
     209,211,215,216,217,218,219,220,221,228,229,235,236
rosewater 43
rose of sharon 9,21,60,69,169,170,171

S

sacral center 90,99,108,120,236
sacrament 28,29,30,31,33,35,121,127
Sacred Heart 8,108,109,110,111,112,257
sacred space 96,98,128,129,130,132,133
sage 10,44,47,57,58,60,61,87,88,101,119,129,144,149,158,164,167,170,175,176,182,184,185,186,197,199,216,2
     18,219,220,228,229,234,236